Question

Company Law

THIRD EDITION

Stephen Judge

2012 and 2013

OXFORD
UNIVERSITY PRESS

OXFORD
UNIVERSITY PRESS

Great Clarendon Street, Oxford ox2 6DP

Oxford University Press is a department of the University of Oxford.
It furthers the University's objective of excellence in research, scholarship, and education by publishing worldwide in

Oxford New York

Auckland Cape Town Dar es Salaam Hong Kong Karachi
Kuala Lumpur Madrid Melbourne Mexico City Nairobi
New Delhi Shanghai Taipei Toronto

With offices in

Argentina Austria Brazil Chile Czech Republic France Greece
Guatemala Hungary Italy Japan Poland Portugal Singapore
South Korea Switzerland Thailand Turkey Ukraine Vietnam

Oxford is a registered trade mark of Oxford University Press
in the UK and in certain other countries

Published in the United States
by Oxford University Press Inc., New York

Contains public sector information licensed under the Open Government Licence v1.0
(http://www.nationalarchives.gov.uk/doc/open-government-licence/open-government-licence.htm)
Crown Copyright material reproduced with the permission of the Controller,
HMSO (under the terms of the Click Use licence)
First edition 2008
Second edition 2010

British Library Cataloguing in Publication Data
Data available

Library of Congress Cataloging in Publication Data
Library of Congress Control Number:
2011938081

Typeset by Laserwords Private Ltd, Chennai, India
Printed in Great Britain
on acid-free paper by
Ashford Colour Press Ltd, Gosport, Hampshire

ISBN 978-0-19-969762-5

10 9 8 7 6 5 4 3 2 1

Contents

The Q&A series

Key features

The Q&A series provides full coverage of key subjects in a clear and logical way.

This book contains the following features:

- Questions
- Commentaries
- Bullet-pointed answer plans
- Full model answers
- Diagrams
- Further reading suggestions

 online resource centre
www.oxfordtextbooks.co.uk/orc/qanda/

Every book in the Q&A series is accompanied by an Online Resource Centre, hosted at the URL above, which is open-access and free to use.

The Online Resource Centre for this book contains revision and exam advice, a glossary of company law terms, updates in the law, and links to websites useful for the study of company law.

Preface

This third edition of Company Law in the Q&A series is updated to include new and important case law, particularly in respect of the statutory derivative claim under s. 260 CA 2006, petitions against unfair prejudice under s. 994 CA 2006, and various aspects of the statutory duties of directors. It also includes reference to the Corporate Governance Code (2010)—which replaced the Combined Code—applicable to financial years beginning on or after 29 June 2010.

The Companies Act 2006 is divided into 47 parts and it is important that you should be able to find your way around it. The general arrangement of the Act is as follows:

Parts 1 to 7	The nature of a company, how it can be formed and what it can be called
Parts 8 to 12	The members and officers of a company
Parts 13 and 14	Decision-making by companies
Parts 15 and 16	Safeguards ensuring accountability of officers to members
Parts 17 to 25	Raising share capital, capital maintenance, annual returns, and company charges
Parts 26 to 28	Company reconstructions, mergers, and takeovers
Parts 29 to 39	Regulatory framework and other provisions
Parts 40 to 42	Overseas disqualification of directors, business names, and statutory auditors
Part 43	Transparency obligations
Parts 44 to 47	Miscellaneous and general

In some areas the Act made major changes to the existing law, while in other areas the law remains largely unchanged. The most immediate change related to the formation of companies and their constitution. A company is still formed by individuals subscribing their names to the memorandum of association, but the Act made it possible for a single person to form any sort of company (not just a private company). The memorandum ceased to be a fundamental constitutional document of the company and merely evidences the intention of the subscribers to form a company and become members of it on formation. The information that was previously delivered to the Registrar of Companies by way of the memorandum is now provided in documents to be supplied on application for registration: CA 2006, s. 9.

The main constitutional document containing the key information concerning the allocation of powers between directors and members is now exclusively in the articles of association. Transition for companies incorporated prior to the coming into effect of the 2006 Act is provided by s. 28 under which provisions in the memorandums of existing companies are to be treated as provisions in the articles.

A major change from the past is that under the current law companies have unrestricted objects unless the objects are specifically restricted by the articles (s. 31) and the introduction of a statutory derivative claim for members claiming negligence or breach of duty by the company's directors: ss. 260–264 (ss. 265–269 for Scotland). The statutory derivative claim clarified the previous common law position, while largely respecting the principles established over the years.

This approach is also seen in the codification of directors' fiduciary duties now to be found in Chapter 2 of Part 10 and ss. 170–181 but which are to be interpreted and applied with regard to the previous case law: s.170(4).

Other areas of the law remain largely unchanged, despite being the subject of criticism over many years, including the law relating to the power of directors to bind the company and the safeguarding of persons dealing with the company in good faith.

Part 13 of the Companies Act 2006 has been changed by the coming into force on 3 August 2009 of the Companies (Shareholders' Rights) Regulations 2009 (SI 2009 No 1632) implementing Directive 2007/36/EC of 11 July 2007 on the exercise of certain rights of shareholders in listed companies (OJ L184/17, 14/07/2007).

The Companies (Model Articles) Regulations 2008 (SI 2008 No 3229) establish model sets of articles for registered companies as follows: Schedule 1 prescribes the model articles of association for private companies limited by shares, Schedule 2 the model articles of association for private companies limited by guarantee, and Schedule 3 the model articles of association for public companies.

On 17 June 2010, Chancellor George Osborne announced that he was abolishing the tripartite system of regulation established by Gordon Brown in which the central bank, the Financial Services Authority (FSA) and the Treasury shared responsibilities. Legislation to effect the proposed changes is due to be in place by 2012. The Government is dismantling the FSA and giving the Bank of England (BoE) control of macro-prudential regulation and oversight of micro-prudential regulation through a new Financial Policy Committee (FPC) within the BoE, chaired by the governor. Two new regulators are to be created. The first, the Prudential Regulating Authority (PRA) charged with regulating banks and other financial institutions, which will operate under the BoE. The second, the Consumer Protection and Markets Authority (CPMA), will regulate the conduct of business of retail financial services firms; wholesale financial markets (carried out by a distinct markets division) and the regulation of exchanges and other trading platforms.

A further thing to note in reading the cases and statutes relating to company law is that the Department of Trade and Industry (DTI) frequently referred to subsequently became the Department for Business, Enterprise and Regulatory Reform (BERR). This is now the Department for Business Innovation & Skills (BIS) The departmental website is www.bis.gov.uk.

The aim of the book is twofold: to enhance your understanding of the law under the Companies Act 2006, and to provide guidance on the way in which you should answer problem and essay questions. To this end, the book aims to provide a wide coverage of the law relating to various topics within the field of company law and to provide a balanced mix of questions in the areas that are generally covered in an undergraduate company law programme of studies. The answers are calculated to be roughly the length that could be expected of a student in an examination context, and do not exceed 1,500 words.

The book is intended to be used in conjunction with relevant statutory material such as *Blackstone's Statutes on Company Law* and a suitable, up-to-date textbook. Further reading relevant to each topic is suggested at the end of each chapter.

I hope that you will find the book useful in your studies and wish you every success.

Steve Judge
6 July 2011

I would like to thank Palgrave Macmillan for permission to reproduce and adapt selected questions from the following:

Stephen Judge, *Business Law*, Palgrave Macmillan, 2009, 4th edn.
Reproduced with permission of Palgrave Macmillan.

Table of Cases

Table of Statutes

Table of Statutory Instruments

1

Business organizations and the veil of incorporation

Introduction

This chapter deals with two important aspects of company law which can be the subject of essay or problem questions—

(a) comparisons between the legal organizations available as vehicles for trade or business in the UK

(b) the company as a separate legal person and exceptions to the veil of incorporation

Business organizations compared

The main points to remember are covered below.

Sole traders

Sole traders have unlimited liability for all business losses. There are no formalities unless the business is carried on under a business name when traders must comply with the provisions under **Part 41** of the **Companies Act 2006 (CA 2006), ss. 1192–1208.** These also apply to general partnerships trading under a name other than one comprising the surnames of the partners.

General partnerships

Defined as 'the relation which subsists between persons carrying on a business in common with a view of profit' (**s. 1(1)** of the **Partnership Act 1890 (PA 1890))**, there must be at least two persons, and 'business' includes any 'trade, profession or occupation': **PA 1890, s. 45.** The partnership is not a separate legal person, and partners have unlimited joint liability for the firm's debts and obligations (**PA 1890, s. 9**); and joint and several liability for torts (**PA 1890, s. 12**)—even so-called 'sleeping partners'.

Limited liability partnerships (LLPs)

LLPs are separate legal persons whose members enjoy limited liability. Created by registration under the **Limited Liability Partnership Act (LLPA)** 2000, they are regulated by the **CA 2006** as private limited companies except that the management structure is fixed by the partnership agreement. They have the benefit of being able to secure loans by floating charges.

Registered companies

Formed by one or more persons subscribing their names to a memorandum of association and complying with the registration requirements of the **CA 2006**, companies can have unlimited or limited liability, with liability limited by guarantee or by shares. Companies limited by guarantee are for charitable, educational, and scientific purposes, while unlimited liability companies are extremely rare. Most courses concentrate entirely on registered companies limited by shares, public or private: the principal trading vehicles. The distinctions between private and public companies are:

(a) Private companies cannot invite the public to subscribe for shares or debentures: **CA 2006, ss. 755–760**

(b) The Certificate of Incorporation of public companies states that it is a public company; all others are private: **CA 2006, s. 4(2)**

(c) Public companies have a minimum share capital requirement of £50,000 (or prescribed euro equivalent): **CA 2006, ss. 761–767**

(d) Private companies need only have one director as against two for public companies: **CA 2006, s. 154**

(e) Directors of public companies are to be voted on individually: **CA 2006, s. 160**

(f) Private companies have no need of a company secretary (**CA 2006, s. 270**), public companies must have a qualified company secretary: **CA 2006, ss. 271–273**

(g) Private companies are less strictly regulated with regard to loans to directors and raising and maintenance of capital

(h) Small or medium private companies or groups enjoy less onerous disclosure in the annual return (**CA 2006, s. 380**): 'small' (**ss. 382–384**) or 'medium': **CA 2006, ss. 465–467** as amended by the **Companies Act 2006 (Amendment) (Accounts and Reports) Regulations 2008, regs. 3 and 4**

(i) Small private companies are exempt from statutory audit: **CA 2006, s. 477** as amended by the **Companies Act 2006 (Amendment) (Accounts and Reports) Regulations 2008, reg. 5**

(j) Private companies benefit from deregulation and dispense with formal meetings by written and elective resolutions: **CA 2006, ss. 288–300**

Many questions will require you to understand the nature of the group of companies and you should be familiar with the concept of the parent and subsidiary company, and the wholly owned subsidiary company. A 'wholly-owned subsidiary' has no members except the parent and the parent's wholly owned subsidiaries or persons acting on their behalf: CA 2006, s. 1159(2).

Registered companies as separate legal person—the veil of incorporation

A registered company is a body corporate and legal person separate from the shareholders: **s. 16**. The consequences of this were stated in *Salomon v Salomon & Co Ltd* [1897] AC 22: 'The company is at law a different person altogether from the subscribers to the memorandum: and [...] the company is not in law the agent of the subscribers or trustee for them.' The 'veil of incorporation' separates the incorporators from the company; in a group context it operates to make each company in the group a separate legal entity with no liability for the debts or liabilities of other group companies.

The judicial and statutory exceptions to this principle are essential matters for problem and essay questions; of particular importance is the decision of the Court of Appeal in *Adams v Cape Industries plc* [1990] Ch 433. You should pay particular attention to the notion of the façade company: a company formed to avoid existing liabilities or to escape the rules of company law.

Question 1

Edna, Fred, and Gabor run a business buying and selling antiques as a partnership. They have been advised by their solicitor to form a private company to run the business. They have contacted you for a second opinion. They are particularly concerned to know:

(a) To what extent their liability for the company's debts will be limited

(b) Whether they will be able to exercise the same control over the membership as with a partnership

(c) The extent to which they will have the same right to be involved in the management of the company, and

(d) The public disclosure to which the business would be subject as a limited company

Having discussed these aspects, advise them of what choice they should make between the two alternatives, or of any other options available to them.

 Commentary

This question requires you to be able to identify ways in which the relationship between partners of a general partnership differ from those of members of a limited liability company. These differences are important in determining the vehicle to be selected for the carrying on

of a business, depending on the priorities of the entrepreneurs. While it may appear that the question crosses individual topic boundaries, it is important for you to recognize that they are all factors in the essential choice of trading vehicle.

Answer plan

- Limited liability as opposed to unlimited liability but subject to potential liability beyond their capital contribution in certain circumstances
- Restrictions on membership in a partnership as opposed to a limited company
- Right to be involved in management of a partnership as opposed to management delegated to board of directors in a limited company
- Extent to which right to involvement can be ensured or enforced in a limited company
- Public disclosure of affairs of a limited company as opposed to a partnership by annual return and audit
- Relaxation of disclosure and audit for small private companies

Suggested answer

This question raises topics for discussion under four headings: limited liability, control over membership, involvement in management, and public disclosure. These points will be dealt with separately and advice will be given in a conclusion.

In respect of the liability of the members, a limited liability company would offer distinct advantages to Edna, Fred, and Gabor in the sense that, as members of a limited liability company, their liability would be limited to the extent of their capital contribution to the company as opposed to their being exposed to unlimited personal liability up to the full extent of their private fortunes.

One problem that they would face is that, if the newly established company were to be under-capitalized, one or more of them would be required to stand as guarantor/surety for the debts of the company in order to operate with an overdraft from the company's bank or in respect of securing supplies of goods and services on credit. In effect, in respect of securing the bank loan, this might not be greatly different from the current situation, since many banks will encourage partners of firms who have accounts with them to move their personal accounts to the bank. In the event of the business account being overdrawn and the firm becoming insolvent, the bank will be able to exercise a lien on the accounts of the individual partners and offset any credit balances on these accounts against the overdraft on the business account.

Another problem could be that if, in the event of the insolvency of the newly formed company, it was discovered that the members/directors of the company had acted in breach of their duties towards the company or its creditors, they could be held liable to contribute to the assets of the company as the court determines in powers under the **CA 2006** and the **Insolvency Act 1986 (IA 1986)**.

The issue in respect of control over the future membership of the business is that, as regards a partnership, in the absence of any agreement to the contrary, new partners can only be introduced by the unanimous consent of the existing partners: **PA 1890, s. 24(7)**. In a company, membership is through the acquisition of shares which are, unless special provision is made, freely transferable. This would mean that there would appear to be no control over the membership of the company. In effect, most private companies will, in their articles, impose restrictions on the free transfer of their shares by giving first priority to existing members before they can be offered to outsiders. In addition, most private companies will insert in their articles a provision to the effect that the directors can, without giving reasons, refuse to register any transfer of shares. If these restrictions on the transferability of the company's shares were inserted into the articles, there would be no difference in effect from the current partnership.

As regards participation in management, all partners in a general partnership have a right to be involved in the management of the firm: **PA 1890, s. 24(5)**. In a company, however, management is delegated to the board of directors. It could be thought that this problem could be resolved by the appointment of all three 'partners' to the board of the new company. The problem is that, even if they are all made directors of their company initially, directors can be removed by ordinary resolution of the Annual General Meeting (AGM) with special notice under **CA 2006, s. 168**. Thus if, in the future, two of the current partners fell out with the third, that person could be voted off the board of the company by the votes of the other two.

This can be avoided, however, by drafting a clause in the new company's articles whereby, in the event of a resolution to remove a director from the board, the shares held by that director would give him or her three votes per share on a poll, so that a resolution to remove him or her could be defeated. This was established in *Bushell v Faith* [1970] AC 1099. In addition, in a small quasi-partnership company such as this, an attempt to remove a member from the board would enable that person to petition on the grounds of unfair prejudice under **CA 2006, s. 994**. This would enable the court to order that the shares of the petitioner should be purchased by the company or by the other shareholders at a valuation fixed by the court: **CA 2006, s. 996**. Should the court find that the majority were justified in removing the member from the board because of his lack of attention to company affairs etc, the minority would, in the alternative, be able to petition for the winding up of the company on just and equitable grounds under **IA 1986, s. 122(1)(g)**. Thus in *RA Noble & Sons (Clothing) Ltd* [1983] BCLC 273, although the court in respect of a petition for unfair prejudice under **CA 1985, s. 459** (now **CA 2006, s. 994**) held that the claimant's exclusion from the management was prejudicial but not unfair because of the lack of interest he had taken in the firm's affairs, he was nevertheless entitled to petition for the compulsory liquidation of the company on the grounds that his exclusion from the management of a small quasi-partnership company was not just and equitable.

As regards the need for public disclosure of the affairs of a limited liability company, as long as the company could qualify as a 'small' company under the criteria fixed by the **CA 2006** as amended, the extent of the disclosure of its affairs would be greatly reduced. The criteria are: two out of three (tested every other year) of: turnover—not more than £6.5m; balance sheet total—not more than £3.26m; number of employees—not more than 50 (**ss. 382 and 383**). The proposed company is unlikely to exceed any of these limitations. In addition, if the turnover of the company is below £6.5m per annum, the company can claim exemption from the audit requirement of the **CA 2006**, **s. 477**. To this extent, the threat of disclosure is greatly diminished and the company can enjoy almost the same degree of privacy in respect of its affairs as a partnership.

In conclusion, the manifest advantages of incorporation vastly outweigh the problems associated with it, including the cost involved in setting up the company. The partners would, therefore, be advised that—subject to having taken the right precautions in fixing the constitution of the company—they would benefit from the change. However, it should be pointed out that the formation of a registered company is not the only avenue open to them. They could instead decide to form a limited liability partnership (LLP) which, as a hybrid form between a general partnership and a limited liability company, enjoys the benefits of each. Thus it is regulated as a private company in all respects except in relation to the management structure of the partnership.

This would enable the partners to retain their current veto over new members and to decide on the operation of the firm's management as they wished. As members of an LLP, they would also still be regarded as self-employed for taxation purposes as at present.

Question 2

It is said that the two advantages for a business of forming a company are the concepts of legal personality and limited liability. In practice, however, for small companies these concepts may prove to be as much of a handicap as a blessing, and in some respects may prove irrelevant. Discuss.

 Commentary

This question requires you to look into the supposed advantages associated with trading as a limited liability company limited by shares and to consider the potential pitfalls. Problems arise through the under-capitalization of small private companies, which in effect means that the protection of limited liability is lost where the company wishes to borrow beyond the capacity of the company. Problems also arise because people forming companies as a trading vehicle are not completely aware of the legal ramifications of such a step. A final aspect to consider is the remote possibility of directors being personally liable for negligent misstatement or misrepresentation. These are aspects of company law that you should be aware of in your approach to the subject.

Answer plan

- Potential advantages of the corporate structure
- Practical realities of under-capitalization
- Ramifications of incorporation to which attention should be paid
- Personal liability for negligent misstatement or misrepresentation

Suggested answer

Most traders choose the vehicle of the company limited by shares to benefit from the protection afforded by the rule in *Salomon*: the veil of incorporation and protection of their personal fortune in the event of the company's insolvency.

Many people commencing trading may not, however, realize that the benefits of limited liability may be compromised by the scale of their operation so as to render the protection illusory. In addition, since most of these entrepreneurs will not have the benefit of expert legal advice in the creation of their corporate vehicle and its operation, they may not be aware of the full impact of the legal consequences on other aspects of their life.

As regards the scale of the operation, it should be remembered that there is no minimum capital requirement for private companies, which can often have a nominal capital. The inadequate capital structure may mean that the company cannot borrow sums of money or buy in goods and services against the security of its own assets.

Where this is the case, it is impossible for the company to secure credit lines from banks and suppliers without external support. Banks will generally require some form of security in consideration for any loans, and suppliers may also seek some form of protection through a third party guarantee if the creditworthiness of the company is weak. This means that the company's proprietors—those seeking protection in the form of limited liability—will be required to stand as surety for any corporate loans or lines of credit. In the context of a family business, credit facilities offered by the company's bank will usually be secured by a mortgage to the bank of the family home. If the company fails and collapses into insolvent liquidation, the lender will take possession of and sell the home to recover the loans. This is subject of course to the requirement for the lender to ensure that both spouses/civil partners have fully understood and consented to the mortgage. Where the trader has signed a guarantee in respect of lines of credit to the company, the trader will have ultimate liability for the company's debts. In such situations, limited liability is illusory.

As regards a failure to fully appreciate the consequences of forming a limited liability company, there are a number of situations to consider. In *Macaura v Northern Assurance Company* [1925] AC 619, M was unaware that the fact that he had transferred property previously belonging to himself to a limited liability company in which he was virtually the sole shareholder meant that he no longer had a legal or equitable title to the property. As a result, a policy taken out in his name but covering property that now belonged to his company was not covered by the insurance since he no longer had an insurable interest in the property.

A further example is in *Tunstall v Steigman* [1962] 1 QB 593. Steigman ran a business in one of a pair of shops of which she was the landlord. The other retail unit was leased to Tunstall. Tunstall applied for a new tenancy under the **Landlord and Tenant Act 1954, s. 24(1)** and Steigman gave notice under s. 30(1)(g) that she intended to occupy the premises for the purpose of a butcher's business by extending her adjoining shop. In the meantime, Steigman promoted a company to carry on her business. She held all the shares except two which were held by nominees. The court held that she had failed to establish her intention 'to occupy ... for the purposes ... of a business to be carried on by her' since the business was to be carried on by a company which was a separate legal entity, although virtually owned and controlled by her. Obviously Mrs Steigman had failed to appreciate the full impact of transferring her business to a limited liability company.

A more complex example is *Re HR Harmer Ltd* [1958] 3 All ER 689. In this case, the company was founded by Mr Harmer to take over the running of a business set up and run by him for many years as a sole trader. Under the company's constitution, Harmer was appointed governing director for life but without specific powers, and chairman of the board with a casting vote. He exercised voting control which did not entitle him to a dividend but carried the whole of the voting power. He gifted some 'B' shares and most of the 'A' shares, which carried dividend rights, but no voting rights, to his two sons who also became life directors. Mr Harmer regarded himself as the company, disregarded board resolutions, assumed powers he did not have and acted against the wishes of his sons. The sons petitioned for an order under **CA 1948, s. 210** (now **CA 2006, s. 994**). The court ordered that the father should not interfere in the affairs of the company otherwise than in accordance with the valid decision of the board of directors, and that he should be appointed president of the company for life, but that this office should not impose any duties or rights or powers.

Other cases concern shareholder/directors who fail to recognize that the company is a separate legal person and who treat their company's assets and bank accounts as mere extensions of their private assets. In *Attorney-General's Reference (No 2 of 1982)* [1984] QB 624 it was established that a sole shareholder of a company could nevertheless be guilty of stealing from the company. In such cases it is impossible for the controlling shareholder to fall back on the identification theory in their defence claiming that, as the directing mind and will of the company, the company consented to the alleged offence.

There is also the possibility of statutory removal of the protection of the veil of incorporation under **IA 1986**. Thus in *Re Purpoint Ltd* [1991] BCC 121 the proprietor of a company was ordered under **IA 1986, s. 212** to contribute towards the assets of the company, now in insolvent liquidation, in respect of money of the company used to purchase a car on hire purchase where the evidence showed that the car was for the proprietor's new business venture rather than the company's business. In addition in *Re DKG Contractors Ltd* [1990] BCC 903 the court ordered the shareholders of a small family business with a share capital of under £100 to contribute to the assets of the company, now in insolvent liquidation, the total of £400,000 which had been paid out to the husband in fees in the ten-month period prior to the commencement of the liquidation. Orders in the same sum were made under **ss. 212, 214** (wrongful trading) and **239** (voidable preference).

Directors can also be personally liable for negligent misstatements made by the company. In *Fairline Shipping Co v Adamson* [1974] **2 All ER 967**, a cold-store company failed to keep its store at the correct temperature and Fairline's meat perished. The company went into liquidation and Fairline sued Adamson, the ex-managing director, in person. All correspondence was on A's personal notepaper, and he had indicated that the business was his own. The court held that he was liable since the contract had become his personal contract.

In *Williams v Natural Life Health Food Ltd* [1998] **1 WLR 830**, however, the House of Lords stated that liability depended on an objective test as to whether: 'the director, or anybody on his behalf, conveyed directly or indirectly ... that the director assumed personal responsibility ...'. The directors had no reason to fear personal liability for negligent misstatements or advice even if personally negligent unless they did something leading to a reasonably held belief that they accepted personal responsibility.

In *Standard Chartered Bank v Pakistan National Shipping Corpn (Nos 2 and 4)* [2002] **3 WLR 1547** O Ltd agreed to sell bitumen to be paid by a letter of credit of a Vietnamese bank confirmed by SCB requiring shipment by 25 October 1993 and presentation of documents by 10 November. Loading was delayed but the MD of O Ltd and the defendants agreed to supply documents with a false date. These were accepted by SCB which authorized payment even though they were presented late. When SCB was unable to obtain payment from the bank, it sued PNSC and O Ltd's MD in person for deceit. The court held the MD was liable and rejected his claim of contributory negligence by SCB. In *Contex Drouzhba Ltd v Wiseman* [2007] **EWCA Civ 1201** the defendant, the active director of a company which he knew was unable to pay its debts, signed an agreement with the claimants undertaking that payment would be made for goods within 30 days after shipment. Rejecting his appeal for liability for damages in deceit, the Court of Appeal held that a director signing for a company might make an implied representation of the company's capacity to meet payment terms. In *Lindsay v O'Loughnane* [2010] **EWHC 529 (QB)** the managing director of a company was personally liable for fraudulent misrepresentations inducing the claimant into entering transactions causing a substantial loss.

Thus it can be seen that the principle of the separate legal personality of the company may result in unplanned and undesired outcomes and that limited liability will not always guarantee total protection from personal liability.

Question 3

In January 1999, Ben set up in business as a sole trader supplying cakes and desserts to local restaurants from leased premises. In January 2000, he formed Just Desserts Ltd and, in consideration of the transfer of the business and its assets, including the leased premises, to the company, he was issued with 10,000 £1 shares in Just Desserts Ltd. Ben was the sole shareholder and director. He signed a contract of employment with the company and drew a salary. In December 2004, Ben made a loan to the company of £25,000 to buy new equipment. The loan was secured by a floating charge over the company's assets. In July 2006, Ben was injured in a gas explosion while at work and the building was badly damaged. Ben's insurance policy on the building and contents was taken out in his name in January 1999.

In 2007, although the business was trading profitably, Ben decided that, in view of his injuries, he would retire and dissolve the company.

Advise Ben on the following:

(a) The validity of the one-man company

(b) His right to claim under his insurance policy for the fire damage to the property

(c) His claim against the company for compensation for his injuries, and

(d) His right to claim as a secured creditor in respect of his floating charge and for arrears of salary

Commentary

This problem question requires you to apply a number of post-*Salomon* decisions that follow the general principle and extend it to other aspects of the shareholder's relationship with the company controlled by them.

Answer plan

- Principle of separate legal personality
- Possibility of a one-man company post-1897
- Members' lack of legal or equitable interest in company property
- Possibility of controlling shareholder being employee of company
- Controlling shareholder's rights as creditor

Suggested answer

This problem requires the application of the consequences of *Salomon v A Salomon & Co Ltd* and subsequent decisions applying the principle of the separate legal personality of the company.

In respect of (a), one of the major aspects of importance of the *Salomon* decision was the implied recognition of the one man company. At that time, company law required a minimum of seven subscribers to the memorandum in order to incorporate a company. The subscribers in this case were Mr and Mrs Salomon and their five children who each took one share in the company. Mr Salomon later transferred his business to the company in consideration, among other things, of the issue to him of 20,000 shares in the company. The recognition of the legality of this as a legal company meant that, from then on, it was possible for a person to form a limited liability company with the other subscribers to the memorandum taking shares in the company as mere nominees of the founder. Thus the 'one-man company' was established de facto in English law long before the position was recognized in the **Companies (Single Member Private Limited Companies) Regulations 1992** which allowed the registration of the one-man private company. Under the **CA 2006**, it is also possible for a public company to be registered with one member (although there is a requirement that the company should have at least two directors).

In this case, the company was registered after the coming into effect of the 1992 Regulations and the company is perfectly legally established. The only problem would be if Ben had formed his company to escape some existing legal liability or as part of a scheme to evade the rules of company law. In this case, the company could be regarded as a façade and the veil of incorporation could be lifted: *Gilford Motor Co Ltd v Horne* **[1933] Ch 935**.

In respect of (b), in spite of the fact that Ben is the sole shareholder of the company, he has no legal or equitable title over the company's property. This was established in *Macaura v Northern Assurance Company* **[1925] AC 619** where M tried unsuccessfully to claim under an insurance policy taken out in his own name to cover the destruction of property that had previously been transferred to a company that he had incorporated and in respect of which he held all the shares except for some held by nominees. Since the policy was taken out in Ben's name prior to the incorporation of Just Desserts Ltd, any claim under the policy would fail on the grounds of lack of Ben's insurable interest. The only thing that could change the position would be if Ben had assigned the policy to the company along with the rest of the property. This does not appear to have happened.

In respect of (c), *Lee v Lee's Air Farming Ltd* **[1961] AC 12** established that a person could be the controlling shareholder, managing director and yet also be an employee under a contract of employment with their own company. However, in *Clark v Clark Construction Initiatives Ltd* **[2008] EWCA Civ 1446** the court held that an alleged contract of employment could be ignored (i) where the company itself was a sham; (ii) where it was entered into for an ulterior purpose; and (iii) where the parties did not conduct their relationship in accordance with the contract although the mere fact that an individual had a controlling shareholding did not of itself prevent a contract of employment arising but might raise doubts as to whether he was an employee. The court held that the employment tribunal had reached a reasonable decision in rejecting C's claim to be an employee. Subject to this, Ben can therefore claim as an employee for compensation under the **Employers' Liability (Compulsory Insurance) Act 1969**.

In respect of (d), Ben's rights include the right to claim as a creditor against the liquidator. The potential claims could be (i) as an employee in respect of any arrears of salary and unpaid holiday remuneration; (ii) as a secured creditor in respect of his loan to the company secured on a floating charge over the company's assets; and (iii) as a shareholder for a return of capital once all the debts are paid off. In respect of the latter it is important to note that the shares in the company were allotted to him in respect of non-cash consideration. Since the company is a private company, there is no legal requirement for the business to be valued as would be the case for a public limited company. The company is entitled to place whatever value it likes on the assets transferred to it in the absence of fraud: *Re Wragg Ltd* [1897] 1 Ch 796.

Question 4

Paradise Ltd imports furniture from India. Adam is the managing director and there are three other directors. In 1999, the board decided to set up a retail business and created a wholly owned subsidiary, Indus Ltd, for the purpose. The registered office of Indus Ltd is the same as that of Paradise Ltd, and Adam is the sole director of Indus Ltd.

The retail business was successful until late 2006 when other suppliers continued to supply the company only on Adam's assurance that Paradise Ltd would give Indus Ltd financial support. By June 2006, Indus Ltd could not pay its debts as they fell due. It continued trading until February 2007 when it went into insolvent liquidation.

Advise the liquidator of Indus Ltd of any common law or statutory liability of Adam and Paradise Ltd and its directors for Indus Ltd's debts.

 Commentary

This problem raises issues relating to the veil of incorporation and the judicial and statutory exceptions to the rule when the veil is lifted or pierced. Although the context of the question is the liquidation of a company within a small group, the question does not require a discussion of liquidation as such. The possibility of a business failing and going into insolvent liquidation is in most cases the motivating factor for entrepreneurs to choose the form of a limited liability company limited by shares as a vehicle for their business. The context of the decision in *Salomon v A Salomon & Co Ltd* (1897) was the failure of the company and whether the founder and principal shareholder was liable to indemnify the company's creditors. The question does, however, require you to apply sections of the **IA 1986** relating to piercing the corporate veil.

Answer plan

- The rule in *Salomon v Salomon* and its application to a group of companies
- Judicial recognition of the separate identity of companies within a group
- Judicial exceptions to the rule as rationalized in *Adams v Cape Industries plc*
- Statutory piercing of the veil under the **Insolvency Act 1986** to make directors and other persons liable to contribute to the assets of a company in liquidation
- De facto and shadow directors

Suggested answer

The decision in *Salomon v A Salomon & Co Ltd* [1897] AC 22 is always cited as having established that a company is a separate legal person from its shareholders and enables persons to carry on trading without exposing them to the risk of personal insolvency in the event of the failure of the business. In effect, the separate nature of the corporation from that of its members had been recognized as early as the seventeenth century and the decision in *Foss v Harbottle* (1843) 2 Hare 461 is an earlier example. The true significance of the *Salomon* decision was in the context of the recognition of the private company, which was given statutory recognition in 1907. In the context of a group of companies, the rule also means that the companies of a group are all separate legal entities and that there is no liability on a company within a group if one of the other group companies collapses into insolvent liquidation. A frequently quoted statement which illustrates the general rule was by Templeman LJ in *Re Southard Ltd* [1979] 1 WLR 1198 at 1208: 'A parent company may spawn a number of subsidiary companies, all controlled directly or indirectly by the shareholders of the parent company. If one of the subsidiary companies, to change the metaphor, turns out to be the runt of the litter and declines into insolvency to the dismay of its creditors, the parent company and other subsidiary companies prosper to the joy of the shareholders without any liability for the debts of the insolvent subsidiary.'

There are, however, a number of judicial and statutory exceptions to this fundamental rule which operate to lift or pierce the corporate veil between the company and its shareholder and directors. An early example is *Re Darby, ex p Brougham* [1911] 1 KB 95 where the High Court treated a company formed by two fraudsters as 'merely an alias for themselves'. And in *Daimler Co Ltd v Continental Tyre and Rubber Co (Great Britain) Ltd* [1916] 2 AC 307 the corporate veil of a UK registered company was pierced to determine its nationality in time of war.

Throughout the twentieth century, there are numerous examples of judicial lifting or piercing of the veil. This culminated in decisions like *DHN Food Distributors Ltd v Tower Hamlets London Borough Council* [1976] 1 WLR 852 where the Court of Appeal treated the three companies in a group as a single economic entity. This much criticized decision marks the high point in judicial piercing of the veil of incorporation, and reinforced the demands for some principles to be established so that litigants could predict when the court would or would not lift the corporate veil.

The Court of Appeal decision in *Adams v Cape Industries plc* [1990] Ch 433 rationalized the judicial exceptions to the rule in *Salomon v A Salomon & Co Ltd*. The case involved a claim in respect of employees of an American subsidiary of Cape Industries to enforce a judgment against the subsidiary in respect of damages for exposure to asbestos against the UK parent. The claimants made three submissions in respect of piercing the corporate veil between the subsidiary and the parent: that the companies were a 'single economic unit', that the American subsidiary was a 'façade' created to allow the parent to escape liability, and that the subsidiary was the agent of the parent.

In rejecting the submissions, Slade LJ stated: 'Neither in this class of case nor in any other class of case is it open to this court to disregard the principle of *Salomon v A Salomon & Co Ltd* merely because it considers it just to do so.' This reflected a move away from the statement in *Re A Company* [1985] BCLC 333 where the Court of Appeal stated: 'In our view ... the cases show that the court will use its power to pierce the corporate veil if it is necessary to achieve justice ....'

The Court of Appeal rejected the submission that the companies were a single economic unit and limited this exception to cases concerning the interpretation of statutes, contracts, and other documents. It rejected the submission that the subsidiary was a façade because it was created solely to protect the parent company against future or contingent tortious liability in the USA: the group was entitled to organize its affairs to take advantage of *Salomon v A Salomon & Co Ltd*. The court rejected the agency argument on the grounds that agency will not be presumed merely because of the closeness of their operations. The decision was confirmed in *Yukong Line Ltd of Korea v Rendsburg Investments Corpn of Liberia (No 2)* [1998] 1 WLR 294.

As regards the promise made by Adam on behalf of Paradise Ltd assuring Indus Ltd's creditors of Paradise Ltd's financial support to Indus Ltd, this would not create any legal liability on Paradise Ltd. This type of statement is sometimes made in writing and is called a comfort letter. Such statements have been held not to be legally enforceable: *Kleinwort Benson Ltd v Malaysia Mining Corporation Bhd* [1989] 1 WLR 379.

Applying these principles to the facts of the case, it would appear that neither Paradise Ltd nor its directors have any liability for Indus Ltd's debts at common law.

Relevant statutory exceptions to the veil of incorporation in the **IA 1986** must be examined to see whether they offer any solution. Under **s. 212** there is the possibility of a summary remedy against delinquent directors. This applies where, in the course of the winding up of a company, an officer or a person who is or has been concerned, or has taken part, in the promotion, formation, or management of the company has been guilty of any misfeasance or breach of any fiduciary or other duty in relation to the company. If this is established, the court may compel him to contribute such sum as the court thinks just to the company's assets by way of compensation.

Section 213 creates the offence of fraudulent trading which provides that if, in the course of the winding up of a company, it appears that any business of the company has been carried on with intent to defraud creditors of the company or for any fraudulent purpose, the court may declare that persons who are knowingly parties to such conduct are liable to make such contribution to the company's assets as the court thinks proper.

There is an alternative offence of wrongful trading in **s. 214**. This operates where, in the course of the insolvent liquidation of a company, a person who was a director of the company at a time prior to the commencement of the winding up, knew or ought to have concluded that there was no reasonable prospect that the company would avoid insolvent liquidation and yet continued to trade. The court may order such a person to make a contribution to the company's assets as the court thinks proper: **IA 1986, s. 214**.

In respect of the summary remedy, when a company is insolvent or on the brink of insolvency, directors owe a general duty to the company's creditors as well as to the company to ensure that the company's property is not 'dissipated or exploited for the benefit of the directors to the prejudice of the creditors': *Winkworth v Edward Baron Development Co Ltd* [1987] 1 All ER 114 per Lord Templeman. Continuing to trade and exposing the creditors to increased risk of loss would constitute breach of the duty of care and could trigger an order under **s. 212**.

In respect of fraudulent trading, if it could be established that Adam continued to trade with suppliers in the knowledge that the company would be unable to pay for the goods or services when they fell due, this would constitute fraudulent trading. Paradise Ltd could also be liable for fraudulent trading. In this case, the necessary intention could be attributed to the company through the intention of Adam, the managing director of Paradise Ltd, by way of the identification theory: *Tesco Supermarkets Ltd v Nattrass* [1971] 2 All ER 127. In order for Paradise Ltd to be liable, it is necessary to establish that Adam, the sole director, is guilty of fraudulent trading: *Re Augustus Barnett & Son Ltd* [1986] BCLC 170. The problem would be establishing intent. Since there is also the criminal offence of fraudulent trading (**CA 2006, s. 993**), the proof required to establish civil liability under **s. 213** is the criminal test: beyond reasonable doubt.

It would be more straightforward to bring a claim against Adam under wrongful trading, where it is not necessary to establish any intention to defraud. The section catches 'honest but incompetent' directors. Since liability arises not only in respect of de jure directors but also de facto and shadow directors, the liquidator could potentially bring claims against Paradise Ltd and the other directors of Paradise Ltd. This would be more problematic since the liquidator would have to establish that Paradise Ltd and its directors qualified as shadow directors under **IA 1986, s. 251** or as de facto directors.

Question 5

'It seems, therefore, that almost exactly 100 years after *Salomon* was decided, the court may have settled down to the idea that it has to be followed, unless the situation can be brought within the "façade" test. It is likely that in future cases judges will find themselves focusing on what it is to mean' (Ben Pettet, *Company Law* (Harlow: Longman Law Series, 2nd edn, 2005)).

Analyse this statement and consider whether the veil of incorporation is too sacrosanct in the UK and whether the court should be given broader powers to lift or pierce the corporate veil.

 ## Commentary

This question recognizes the fact that since the 1970s, the attitude of the courts has moved towards a recognition of fact that the principle in *Salomon v A Salomon* should always be followed and only be departed from in cases where a company can be said to be a 'façade', in other words a company created specifically for the purpose of using the corporate veil to perpetrate a fraud or to avoid some existing—as against future or contingent—liability. It also raises the question of by what criteria the courts can identify a 'façade' company.

The courts in the UK have very limited powers to pierce the corporate veil since *Adams v Cape Industries Ltd* and you are required to consider whether the potential for judicial interference should be broadened. In this context, it is important for you to consider the position in other jurisdictions and EU proposals that favour a more interventionist approach.

 ## Answer plan

- History of the 'façade' company as a ground for piercing the corporate veil
- Identification of the criteria for establishing a company as a façade
- Scope for piercing the corporate veil in other jurisdictions
- EC proposals for broadening scope of intervention
- Analysis of adequacy or inadequacy of the UK position and recommendations

Suggested answer

On occasions, the *Salomon* principle can give rise to decisions that appear to be unfair and unjust and the courts are asked to ignore the principle and to lift or pierce the corporate veil. This was done in many cases, particularly in situations involving a group of companies. In *Smith, Stone & Knight v Birmingham Corporation* [1939] 4 All ER

116, the claimant company bought a partnership business, registered it as a company and carried on the business, apparently as a subsidiary company, but the business was never assigned to the new company. The claimant company held all the shares except for five which were held by the directors on trust for the claimant company. A manager was appointed but there were no staff and the books and accounts were all kept by the claimants who had complete control of the operations of the new company. Birmingham Corporation compulsorily acquired the premises on which the new business was carried on and the claimant claimed compensation. The corporation claimed that the subsidiary was the proper claimant in which case no compensation would be payable. The court held that the business was that of the parent company and that the subsidiary was its agent.

In the 1970s, the courts became increasingly prepared to pierce the corporate veil. In *DHN Ltd v Tower Hamlets London Borough Council* [1976] 1 WLR 852 the case concerned a group of three companies of which only DHN Ltd, the parent, carried on a business as cash and carry on premises owned by a wholly owned subsidiary; a second subsidiary owned the lorries and vans used by the parent. Tower Hamlets London Borough Council compulsorily acquired the premises and denied liability to compensate the parent company for the loss of its business since the parent only operated under a licence as opposed to a lease. Lord Denning held that the companies should be treated as one and that compensation was payable. The decision was criticized in an analogous situation in *Woolfson v Strathclyde DC* (1978) 38 P & CR 521. The House of Lords held that the corporate veil could only be lifted where the company is a 'façade'.

There were still many occasions on which the corporate veil was lifted, however, and in *Creasey v Beachwood Motors Ltd* [1992] BCC 638 it was held that the court could lift the corporate veil 'to achieve justice where its exercise is necessary for that purpose'. In *Adams v Cape Industries plc* [1990] Ch 433, CA however, the Court of Appeal signalled a much stricter approach: '[I]t is appropriate to pierce the corporate veil only where special circumstances exist indicating that it is a mere façade concealing the true facts'. The decision in *Adams* has been followed in a number of subsequent decisions. In *Re Polly Peck International plc* [1996] 2 All ER 433 PPI, a holding company at the head of a large group set up an overseas subsidiary, PPIF, to raise funds by way of a bond issue. PPIF had no separate management or bank account. The funds received were onward loaned to PPI, and PPI stood as guarantor in respect of the repayment by the subsidiary. Asked to treat PPI as the true borrower of the funds, the court rejected submissions to lift the veil on the grounds of 'group trading', 'agency', or 'sham' grounds. A similar line was observed in *Yukong Line Ltd of Korea v Rendsburg Investments Corporation of Liberia* [1998] 1 WLR 294.

If the corporate veil can only be lifted for a façade company, it is important to identify the criteria by which such companies are identified. The issue was raised in the Court of Appeal hearing of *Salomon*. In *Broderip v Salomon* [1895] 2 Ch 323 Lopes LJ stated: 'It never was intended that the company to be constituted should consist of one substantial person and six mere dummies, the nominees of that person, without any real interest in the company ... To legalise such a transaction would be a scandal.' The House of Lords rejected this argument; Lord Macnaghten stated: 'In order to form a company limited by shares, the Act requires that a memorandum of association should be signed by seven persons, who are each required to take one share at least. If those conditions are complied with, what can it matter whether the signatories are relations or strangers? There is nothing in the Act requiring that the subscribers to the memorandum should be independent or unconnected ... or that they should have a mind and will of their own ...'

A clear example is in *Gilford Motor Co Ltd v Horne* [1933] Ch 935 where Horne created a company solely for the purpose of avoiding a valid restraint of trade clause imposed on him by his ex-employer. In *Jones v Lipman* [1962] 1 WLR 832, L, seeking to a avoid specific performance of a contract for the sale of land, formed a company to which he transferred the property, offering nominal damages in breach of the sale contract. A variation on the theme is in *Coles v Samuel Smith Old Brewery (Tadcaster)* [2007] EWCA Civ 1461 where the respondent company sold a premises to a wholly owned subsidiary in order to defeat an order for specific performance. The Court of Appeal criticized the trial judge's failure to make an order against the subsidiary. In all of these cases, the company was used to avoid existing contractual liabilities. The company is also a façade where it is created specifically as part of a scheme for the purpose of sidestepping the rules of company law.

In *Re Bugle Press Ltd* [1961] Ch 270 90 per cent of the shares of the company were held by two individuals, and the remaining 10 per cent by a third. The two majority shareholders wished to remove the minority shareholder but could not compulsorily acquire his shares. They formed another company which then purported to make a takeover bid to the shareholders of *Bugle Press*. This was accepted by the two majority shareholders and the company then sought to compulsorily acquire the shares of the minority under **CA 1948, s. 209 (CA 2006, s. 979)**. Harman LJ regarded this as 'a barefaced attempt to evade that fundamental rule of company law which forbids the majority of shareholders, unless the articles so provide, to expropriate a minority'. *Acatos & Hutcheson plc v Watson* [1995] BCC 446 concerned the rule which prohibits a company from owning its own shares. A Ltd owned 30 per cent of the shares in the claimant company which then sought to purchase all the shares in A Ltd, resulting in it owning 30 per cent of its own shares. Allowing the acquisition, Lightman J added that he might have thought it appropriate to lift the veil and declare the transaction unlawful if A Ltd had been deliberately set up by the claimant to acquire the shares as a first stage in a single scheme to evade the rule in *Trevor v Whitworth*.

Thus it would appear that a company is classifiable as a façade where it has been created to avoid existing obligations or liabilities or as a deliberate stage in a scheme to avoid the rules of company law. The need for some form of impropriety linked to the use of the corporate structure is seen in the following decisions: *Trustor AB v Smallbone and Ors (No 2)* [2001] 1 WLR 1177, *Re K & Others* [2005] EWCA Crim 619, *Kensington International Ltd v Congo and Others* [2005] EWHC 2684 (Comm) and

Reed v Marriot [2009] EWHC 1183 (Admin). In *Adams v Cape Industries*, the Court of Appeal specifically made the point that groups are able to organize their affairs so that future or contingent liabilities will fall on another member of the group rather than the parent.

The UK courts' unwillingness to lift the corporate veil is in marked contrast to other jurisdictions where principles have been established to make other companies in a group liable for the obligations of a failing company. These include situations where the courts identify 'domination' by a company over another within the group, and the fact that the failing subsidiary was 'under-capitalized'. In New Zealand and Ireland the courts have the discretion of ordering that a company in a group should contribute to the assets of another company in insolvent liquidation or to order the joint liquidation of two associated companies and pooling of their assets and liabilities. The same is possible in France, where a parent company takes a dominant role in the business decisions of a subsidiary.

In the context of Europe, the veil of incorporation is not regarded with the respect accorded to it in the UK. In *ICI v EC Commission* [1972] ECR 619, ICI was liable to pay fines for the breach of competition law by an overseas subsidiary. In addition, in the Draft Ninth Directive on the Conduct of Groups of Companies, a dominant company in a group would in certain circumstances be liable for the losses of a dependent company.

The first academic to rail against *Salomon* was Kahn-Freund ((1944) 7 MLR 54). He called the decision catastrophic and argued for incorporation to be more expensive and for personal liability of members in small companies of fewer than ten members. In effect, the reverse has happened, with incorporation being easier and more available. On the other hand, statutory provisions in the **IA 1986**, in particular the creation of the offence of wrongful trading and provisions against 'phoenix companies', have provided a means by which unscrupulous or incompetent entrepreneurs can be controlled without disadvantaging honest persons. The possibility of disqualification under the **Company Directors Disqualification Act 1986** can also be cited as providing protection against abuse of the corporate veil.

It is a question of opinion as to whether these provisions—and many others—have adequately resolved the potential abuse of the corporate veil so that no further discretionary powers need to be given to the court. The main risk is that this would tend to increase confusion as to when the court will exercise that discretion, and a return to the confusion of the mid-twentieth century.

Question 6

Analyse the way in which the law has evolved to enable corporate bodies to be held liable for tortious and criminal offences requiring the establishment of intent or privity with particular regard to corporate manslaughter.

Commentary

This question requires the student to examine the development of the identification theory for the purpose of establishing tortious and criminal liability. The student should recognize the limitations of the common law approach as regards the successful prosecution of companies for manslaughter. The solution to this is the creation of a new statutory offence of corporate manslaughter and the scope of the legislation in moving from the doctrine of attribution to the gross negligence test.

Answer plan

- Explanation of the 'identification theory' and its application to tort and criminal offences
- Limitations on the application of the theory to cases of corporate manslaughter, particularly in the case of large companies
- Explanation of the scope of the statutory offence of corporate manslaughter
- Analysis of the effectiveness of the statutory offence

Suggested answer

Very early on, English law solved the problem of making a company liable in tort and crime in cases where it is necessary to establish criminal or tortious intention. The courts developed the identification theory, or alter ego doctrine, which attributes the requisite intention or knowledge of a person or persons controlling the company to the company, making the company tortiously or criminally liable.

In respect of tortious liability, in *Lennard's Carrying Co Ltd v Asiatic Petroleum Co Ltd* [1915] AC 705, the appellant shipowners were sued for damages for the loss of cargo caused by a ship running aground due to its being unseaworthy because of defective boilers. The House of Lords ruled that the necessary fault and privity to establish liability could be identified in respect of the company where the fault or privity existed in the mind of a person who was 'the directing mind and will' of the company.

Criminal liability of companies was established for the first time in 1944 when companies were convicted of intent to deceive: *DPP v Kent and Sussex Contractors Ltd* [1944] KB 146: and conspiracy to defraud, *R v ICR Haulage Ltd* [1944] KB 551. In *HL Bolton (Engineering) Ltd v TJ Graham & Sons Ltd* [1957] 1 QB 159, Denning LJ stated, 'Some of the people in the company are ... nothing more than hands to do the work ... Others are directors and managers who represent the directing mind and will of the company, and control what it does. The state of mind of these managers is the state of mind of the company and is treated by the law as such.' In *Stone & Rolls Ltd v Moore Stephens* [2009] UKHL 39 where a one-man company had been set up solely as a vehicle for defrauding banks, the House of Lords held that the company was primarily rather than vicariously liable for the frauds perpetrated by the sole member/ director.

The identification theory is restricted to cases where the intention is identified at the level of the board, the managing director and other superior officers or people to whom they have delegated full discretion to act independently of instructions. In *Tesco Supermarkets Ltd v Nattrass* [1971] 2 All ER 127 a branch manager was held not to be the company's representative for the purposes of liability for misleading pricing under the Trade Descriptions Act 1968.

Since there is a statutory penalty of life imprisonment, companies cannot be guilty of murder. It has been established, however, that a company can be guilty of manslaughter: *R v HM Coroners for East Kent, ex p Spooner* (1987) 3 BCC 636, DC. This case arose from the loss of the Herald of Free Enterprise and the deaths of nearly 200 passengers. Subsequently, P&O Ferries and five senior company managers were charged with manslaughter. The prosecution, however, failed to establish the guilt of the managers and the judge rejected prosecution arguments that the knowledge and intentions of the individual managers should be aggregated to establish the criminal intention of the company: *R v P&O Ferries (Dover) Ltd* (1991) 93 Cr App Rep 72.

The first conviction for corporate manslaughter arose from the deaths of four teenagers on a canoeing trip at sea against a one-man company operating an activity centre. The managing director's failure to heed previous warnings of potential danger by the company's instructors was attributed to the company and both were convicted of manslaughter: *R v Kite and OLL Ltd* [1996] 2 Cr App Rep (S) 295. The fact that it was easier to prosecute small companies was criticized in *Re Attorney-General's Reference (No 2 of 1999)* [2000] QB 796 (CA).

Public pressure to reform the law on corporate manslaughter finally resulted in the **Corporate Manslaughter and Corporate Homicide Act 2007** ('the 2007 Act') which came into force on 6 April 2008 and created a statutory offence of corporate manslaughter (corporate culpable homicide in Scotland).

The offence builds on the current common law offence of gross negligence manslaughter and is concerned with the way in which an organization's activities were managed or organized and whether an adequate standard of care was applied to the fatal activity. The offence is committed where an organization owes a duty to take reasonable care for a person's safety and the way in which activities of the organization are managed or organized by senior management amounts to a gross breach of this duty causing death of a person or persons. A substantial part of the failing must have occurred at senior management level, ie those making significant decisions about the organization or substantial parts of it, including those carrying out HQ functions as well as those in senior operational management roles. The identification of senior management will depend on the nature and scale of the organization's activities. Apart from directors and similar senior management positions, roles likely to be considered include regional managers in national organizations and managers of different operational divisions.

The Act applies to companies incorporated under the Companies Acts or overseas, and organizations incorporated by statute and by Royal Charter, including government departments and police forces. It extends to all partnerships, trade unions and employers' associations if the organization is an employer. It also applies to charities and voluntary organizations operating in forms covered by the 2007 Act. Parent companies cannot be convicted for failures within a subsidiary. The organization is legally represented and directors, managers, and employees can be called as witnesses. In the case of partnerships, the prosecution is brought in the firm's name and any fine is payable from partnership funds.

Individual directors, senior managers, or other individuals cannot be convicted of assisting in or encouraging the offence: **s. 18**. This excludes secondary liability but does not affect an individual's direct liability for gross negligence manslaughter, culpable homicide, or health and safety offences.

The 2007 Act applies across the UK and the new offence can be prosecuted if the harm occurs in the UK, as regards commercial or leisure craft, in the UK's territorial waters, on a British ship, aircraft or hovercraft and an oil rig or other offshore installation covered by UK criminal law. It does not apply to British companies etc responsible for deaths abroad.

The organization concerned must owe a 'relevant duty of care' to the victim in respect of systems of work and equipment used by employees, the condition of worksites and other premises occupied by an organization and products or services supplied to customers. These duties are set out in **s. 2** and include: employers' and occupiers' duties, duties connected to supplying goods and services, commercial activities, construction and maintenance work, using or keeping plant, vehicles or other things, and duties relating to holding a person in custody. The duty of care will apply to persons working or performing services for the organization and could include sub-contractors and persons supplying services other than employees. It is for the judge to decide whether a relevant duty of care is owed: **s. 2(5)**. Common law rules preventing a duty of care being owed by one person to another because they are jointly engaged in unlawful conduct or because a person has voluntarily accepted the risks involved are to be disregarded: **s. 2(6)**.

The 2007 Act sets out a number of exemptions covering deaths connected with certain public and government functions. The management of these functions involves wider questions of public policy and is already subject to other forms of accountability. Areas in which exemptions apply include military operations, policing, emergency response, child protection work, and probation. The offence will apply to the management of custody, but will only come into effect within three to five years.

Organizations convicted of the offence can receive: (a) an unlimited fine; (b) a publicity order requiring them to publicize the conviction and details of the offence; or (c) on the application of the prosecution after consultation with the appropriate regulatory authority or authorities, a remedial order requiring them to address the cause of the fatal injury. Failure to comply can lead to prosecution and an unlimited fine on conviction.

In England and Wales and in Northern Ireland the consent of the Director of Public Prosecutions is needed before a case can be taken to court. In Scotland all prosecutions are initiated by the Procurator Fiscal. Subject to this, in England and Wales and in Northern Ireland individuals can bring a private prosecution for the new offence, but it is no longer possible to bring proceedings for common law gross negligence manslaughter against an organization to which the 2007 Act applies: **s. 20**. In Scotland, the common law continues in force and the Procurator Fiscal will determine the appropriate charge according to individual circumstances.

Instead of identifying the individual guilty of the breach of care, the **2007 Act** identifies the senior management as those having a significant role in the decision-making, management, or organization of the whole or a substantial part of the organization's activities (**s. 1(4)(c)**) and avoids the problem with larger organizations where the complexity of the structure might otherwise lead to evasion of liability. In addition, the standard of gross negligence is an objective one whose breach falls below what can reasonably be expected of the organization in the circumstances: **s. 1(4)(b)**.

In conclusion, the new offence will have far-reaching implications for a larger group of organizations, including government departments previously covered by Crown privilege and senior individuals within those organizations.

Further reading

Craig, R., 'Thou shall do no murder: a discussion paper on the Corporate Manslaughter and Corporate Homicide Act 2006' [2009] Comp. Law., 30(1): 17.

Field. S., and Jones. L., 'Death in the workplace: who pays the price?' [2011] Comp. Law., 32(6): 166.

Griffin, S., 'Holding companies and subsidiaries—the corporate veil' [1991] Comp. Law., 12(1): 16.

Griffin, S., 'Limited liability: a necessary revolution?' [2004] Comp. Law., 24(4): 99.

Henning, J. J., 'Limited partnerships reform: Parts 1 & 2' [2011] Comp. Law., 32 (6):178 & 32(7): 208.

Hicks, A., 'Reforming the law of private companies' [1995] Comp. Law., 16(6): 171.

Hsaio, M. W. H., 'Abandonment of the doctrine of attribution in favour of gross negligence test in the Corporate Manslaughter and Corporate Homicide Act 2007' [2009] Comp. Law., 30(4): 110.

Krishnaprasad, K.V., 'Agency, limited liability and the corporate veil' [2011] Comp. Law. 32(6): 163.

Linklater, L., '"Piercing the corporate veil"—the never ending story?' [2006] Comp. Law., 27(3): 65.

Lower, M., 'What's on offer? A consideration of the legal forms available for use by small- and medium-sized enterprises in the United Kingdom' [2003] Comp. Law., 24(6): 166.

Makowicz, M. and Saifee, F., 'Societas Privata Europaea: The European Private Company' [2009] Comp. Law., 30(11) : 321.

Morse, G., *Partnership Law* (Oxford: Oxford University Press, 6th edn, 2006).

Randell, C., 'Joint ventures: an overview' (2005) PLC, 16(5): 29.

Scanlan, G., 'Partnership and quasi-partnership private limited company actions: some limitation issues' [2005] Comp. Law., 26(4): 111.

Slorach, J. S., and Ellis, J. G., *Business Law* 2009–2010 (Oxford: Blackstone Legal Practice Course Guide Series, 2009).

2

Constitution of the registered company

Introduction

The company's constitution was previously divided between the Memorandum of Association (external aspects) and the Articles of Association (internal aspects, including the balance of power between the board of directors and the general meeting). The Memorandum is now simply a statement of the subscribers' intention to form, and become members of, a company. The information previously contained in the memorandum is in application documents for registration sent to the Registrar of Companies including:

- (a) Company's proposed name
- (b) Situation of the registered office
- (c) Whether the members' liability is limited by shares or by guarantee
- (d) Whether the company is private or public: **Companies Act 2006 (CA 2006), s. 9**

For companies with a share capital, there must be a statement of capital and initial shareholdings (see **s. 10**). Memorandum provisions of existing companies are treated as articles: **CA 2006, s. 28.**

Under the **CA 2006**, references to a company's constitution include:

- (a) The company's articles, and
- (b) Any resolutions and agreements to which Chapter 3 applies (see **s. 29**): (**CA 2006, s. 17**)

This is a major area for examination questions—both problem and essay—with the emphasis on:

- (a) Alteration of the articles, and

(b) Legal effect of the articles on the company, its members and outsiders

(c) Shareholder agreements

Articles of association

Companies must register articles of association (**s. 18(1)**) contained in a single document divided into consecutively numbered paragraphs: **s. 18(3)**. The Secretary of State can set out model articles (**s. 19**) which may be adopted in whole or in part: **s. 19(3)**. As previously, if no articles are registered or they do not exclude or modify the model articles, the model articles apply by default: **s. 20**. The model articles for companies are contained in the **Companies (Model Articles) Regulations 2008 (SI 2008 No 3229)** which came into effect on 1 October 2009. The model articles for a private company limited by shares are set out in **Schedule 1** of the **Regulations** and the model articles for public companies are set out in **Schedule 3**. **Schedule 2** sets out the model articles for private companies limited by guarantee.

Alteration of the articles

Articles can be amended by special resolution (**s. 21(1)**) but, in a new development, certain provisions can be entrenched and can only be amended or repealed subject to more stringent conditions. Amendments must not:

- Conflict with the **Companies Act** eg directors removable only by special resolution
- Be illegal
- Deprive members of statutory protection (variation of class rights)
- Force members to take/subscribe for more shares or increase liability to contribute without written consent, and
- Be an abuse of majority power

The most important topic for examination question is abuse of majority power.

Binding effect of company's constitution

The constitution binds the company and its members as if there were covenants on the part of the company and each member to observe those provisions: **s. 33(1)**. See Figure 2.1, the constitution is enforceable by:

Company against member—A

Member against member—B

Member against company *in respect of membership rights*—C

Shareholder agreements

Articles can be supplemented by a formal contract on formation, or subsequently.

Figure 2.1

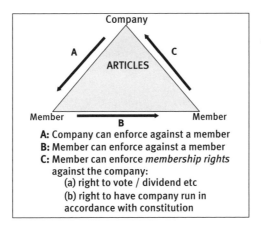

A: Company can enforce against a member
B: Member can enforce against a member
C: Member can enforce *membership rights*
against the company:
    (a) right to vote / dividend etc
    (b) right to have company run in
    accordance with constitution

An important point to remember is the non-enforceability of outsider rights.

Question 1

The **Companies Act 2006** provides that a company may alter its articles of association by special resolution: **s. 21(1)**. What restrictions are there on this power? Illustrate your answer with reference to decided cases.

 Commentary

This is a fairly standard essay question on the company's power to alter its articles. In order to achieve a pass you are required to be able to explain the statutory restrictions on alteration of the articles, including provisions of entrenchment and variation of class rights.

    The most important topic to cover is the court's power to police the company's power to ensure that alterations are bona fide for the benefit of the company as a whole and not simply an abuse of majority power. Where members claim that an alteration is an abuse of majority power, you need to know how the court approaches the identification of an abuse of power and the available remedies for the victim. This requires detailed knowledge of the relevant cases.

 Answer plan

- Inalienable right of companies to alter their articles by special resolution under **s. 21(1)**
- Statutory restrictions in respect of provisions of entrenchment, alterations imposing obligations on members to increase their capital contribution, and where alteration constitutes a variation of class rights

- Court's authority to police alterations and strike out alterations that are not bona fide for the benefit of the company as a whole
- The tests by which the court reaches its decisions
- Remedies available to injured parties

Suggested answer

In general, registered companies have the statutory right to alter their articles at any time by special resolution and cannot contractually restrict themselves from exercising this statutory right. This was decided in *Punt v Symons & Co Ltd* [1903] 2 Ch 506 where the company's articles contained provisions restricting the appointment of directors to Mr Symons (the company's founder) and after his death provided that the power was limited to his executors. The company entered into a contractual agreement that it would not alter its articles to remove this restriction. The court held that the restriction was illegal. Where a company does enter into such an agreement and then alters its articles in breach of the agreement, the injured party cannot prevent the alteration from being made by way of injunction, but can sue for damages for breach of the contract: *Southern Foundries (1926) Ltd v Shirlaw* [1940] AC 701; *British Murac Syndicate Ltd v Alperton Rubber Co Ltd* [1915] 2 Ch 186.

The articles of a company bind the company and its members (**s. 33(1)**) but members are not bound by an alteration to its articles after the date on which they became a member if and so far as the alteration requires them to take or subscribe for shares other than those held at the date of the alteration, or in any way increases their liability to contribute to the company's share capital or otherwise pay money to the company: **s. 25**.

Prior to the **Companies Act 2006**, the company's constitution was split between the memorandum of association and the articles of association. In addition to the clauses that were required to be in the memorandum, the company could include clauses in the memorandum and embed them against alteration. This was not possible for provisions contained in the articles which were always capable of alteration. In order to provide the same possibility of companies embedding provisions in their constitution, the law provides that a company's articles may contain provisions ('provision for entrenchment') to the effect that specified clauses of the articles may be amended or repealed only if conditions are met, or procedures are complied with, that are more restrictive than those applicable in the case of a special resolution: **s. 22(1)**. Provisions for entrenchment may only be made in the articles on formation, or by an amendment of the articles agreed to by all the members: **s. 22(2)**. Provision for entrenchment does not, however, prevent amendment of the articles by agreement of the members, or by order of the court or other authority having power to alter the company's articles: **s. 22(3)**. The registrar of companies must be notified of provisions for entrenchment and also of their removal: **s. 23**.

Companies in existence prior to the coming into effect of the **CA 2006** are subject to **s. 28**, which provides that provisions contained in the company's memorandum are to be treated as provisions of the company's articles, including provision for entrenchment.

Where the alteration of the articles constitutes a variation of class rights, the alteration cannot be made under **s. 21(1)** but only in accordance with **s. 630** which requires alteration in accordance with provision in the company's articles for the variation of those rights or, where the articles contain no such provision, if the holders of shares of that class consent to the variation either by (i) consent in writing of the holders of three-quarters of the issued shares, or (ii) a special resolution at a separate class meeting: *Cumbrian Newspapers Group Ltd v Cumberland & Westmorland Herald Newspaper & Printing Co Ltd* [1986] BCLC 286.

The most important restriction on companies' freedom to alter their articles is where the court decides that the alteration is not bona fide for the benefit of the company as a whole but is an abuse of majority power.

The power to police proposed alterations of the articles was established in *Allen v Gold Reefs of West Africa Ltd* [1900] 1 Ch 656. In this case, Z held both fully paid-up shares and not fully paid-up shares in the company. Under its articles, the company had a lien for all debts and liabilities of any member 'upon all shares (not being fully paid) held by such member'. Z was the only holder of fully paid shares in the company and, on his death, he owed the company arrears of calls on his unpaid shares but his assets were insufficient to pay this debt. By special resolution, the company then altered the article by omitting the words in parentheses and thus created a lien on Z's fully paid shares. In an action brought by Z's executor for a declaration that the alteration was void, the court held that the power of the company to alter its articles under what is now **CA 2006, s. 21(1)** had to be exercised, not only in the manner required by the law, but also bona fide for the benefit of the company as a whole. The fact that Z was, at the time, the only holder of fully paid shares did not mean that it was an abuse of majority power and that it was not for the benefit of the company as a whole. The fact that the alteration imposed a lien in respect of a previously contracted debt was not important.

The principal issue in this respect is how the court should decide whether the alteration is bona fide in the interests of the company as a whole. Initially there were two possibilities: an objective and a subjective test. Under the objective test, the court itself determined whether or not the proposed alteration was in the interests of the company, whereas under the subjective test the court is merely concerned to establish whether the shareholders, in voting for the alteration, believed that they were acting in the best interests of the company as a whole. The clash between these approaches can best be seen in *Sidebottom v Kershaw, Leese & Co Ltd* [1920] 1 Ch 154, which followed the subjective test, and *Dafen Tinplate Co Ltd v Llanelly Steel Co* [1920] 2 Ch 124, which applied the objective test. Both of these cases concerned an alteration of the articles to give the company the power to compulsorily acquire the shares of minorities who were competing with the company. In respect of the subjective test, all that the court has to determine is that the members, in voting in favour of the resolution, honestly believed that it was in the best interests of the company. In respect of the objective test, the court takes an interventionist approach and decides on the basis of whether the court believes that the alteration is in the company's best interests. The conflict between these two approaches was resolved in favour of the subjective test in *Shuttleworth v Cox Brothers*

& *Co Ltd* [1927] 2 KB 9. In *Greenhalgh v Arderne Cinemas Ltd* [1951] Ch 286, however, the court seems to suggest that there is an element of the objective test since that court was to consider whether the effect of the alteration was to discriminate between the majority and the minority shareholders.

The decision in *Clemens v Clemens Bros Ltd* [1976] 2 All ER 268, although not concerned with an alteration of the articles, is regarded as a classic example of an abuse of majority position. The company had two shareholders, a woman holding 55 per cent of the shares and her niece, holding 45 per cent. The aunt proposed to increase the company's capital by allotting shares to her fellow directors and establishing an employees' share scheme. The practical effect of the proposal was to reduce the niece's shareholding to below 25 per cent. In spite of the aunt's arguments that the increase of capital was required in the interests of the company, the court held that the proposed increase was an abuse of majority position.

Where a minority shareholder alleges that there has been an alteration of the articles which constitutes an abuse by the majority of their power, the claim should be brought as a claim of unfair prejudice under **s. 994**. If a claim is brought under this section and the court decides in favour of the claimant, the court has unlimited power to make orders under **s. 996(1)**. Without prejudice to the generality of its powers under that sub-section, the court may make specific orders under **s. 996(2)**. As regards the alteration of its articles, the court can require the company not to make any, or any specified, alterations in its articles without the leave of the court: **s. 996(2)(d)**.

Question 2

The articles of Able Limited contain the following clauses:

(a) Bertram should have the right to nominate a director for as long as he continues to hold a 10 per cent shareholding

(b) Claude should be the company secretary for life, and

(c) the company's sales manager shall receive an annual bonus equal to 5 per cent of the company's profits

David, the majority shareholder, has just sold his 75 per cent holding of shares to Edward. Edward proposes to alter the articles so that all the directors should be appointed by the general meeting, and that the annual bonus payable to the sales manager shall be reduced to 2 per cent. He also intends to appoint Frieda as company secretary. The sales manager has a contract with the company that makes no provision for the payment of any bonus. Bertram has a contract with the company stating that the company will not alter its articles so as to affect his rights without his consent.

Advise Edward.

Commentary

This question is a fairly common example of problem questions concerning the application of various judicial decisions concerning the nature of the contract contained in the articles of association between the company and its members. It involves explanation of **CA 2006, s. 33** and the application to the scenarios of judicial decisions on the section.

Answer plan

- Articles constitute a binding contract between the company and the members
- Relevant decisions concerning articles
- Recognition of issue of class rights and application of **CA 2006, s. 630**
- Relevant *case law* on outsider rights including directors' right to salary etc
- Indirect enforcement as implied term of service contract but still subject to variation on a prospective basis

Suggested answer

Section 33 of the Companies Act 2006 provides that 'the provisions of a company's constitution bind the company and its members to the same extent as if there were covenants on the part of the company and of each member to observe those provisions'. The contract is, however, an unusual one in that it can be unilaterally altered by a special resolution by the members of the company under **CA 2006, s. 21(1)** except where the proposed alteration relates to the variation of class rights, when s. 630 applies.

The scope of the contract is also restricted as a result of judicial decisions.

The legal positions of Bertram, Claude, and the sales manager are now considered in turn.

Bertram: The articles provide that Bertram has the right to nominate a director for as long as he continues to hold a 10 per cent stake in the company. In addition, the company has contracted with Bertram that the company will not alter its articles so as to affect his rights without his consent. The legal issue here is that the company has the statutory power under **s. 21(1)** to alter its articles and it has been held that this statutory power cannot be restricted contractually. This was established in *Punt v Symons & Co Ltd* [1903] 2 Ch 506. In this case, the defendant company was formed to carry on a business established by Symons. The articles provided that Symons was to be the governing director with full powers of management and the appointment of directors and that, after his death, these powers would be exercised by his trustees. The articles also provided that the company would not at any time alter or attempt to alter the articles in this respect. On Symons' death, the trustees appointed managing directors but, following a dispute between the managing directors and the trustees, the directors sought to alter the articles to deprive the trustees of their powers. The court held that the company could not contract out of its statutory right to alter its articles either by way of a separate contract or by a provision in the articles. Where the company has entered into a contract to that effect, the other party cannot, therefore, enforce his contract rights by way of an injunction, but can sue the company for damages where it proceeds to alter its articles in breach of the contract: *Southern Foundries* (1926) *Ltd v Shirlaw* [1940] AC 701.

The position in this case is further complicated by the fact that Bertram's right to appoint a director is conditional upon him continuing to hold a 10 per cent stake in the company. In *Cumbrian Newspaper Group Ltd v Cumberland & Westmorland Herald Newspaper & Printing Co Ltd* [1986] BCLC 286 the claimant was given various rights in respect of the defendant company contained in their articles. These included the right to nominate a director and pre-emption rights over new share issues conditional upon continuing to hold a 10 per cent stake in the defendant company. It was held that these rights constituted class rights, which could therefore not be varied under s. 21(1) but only in accordance with s. 630(2). This requires any variation of the rights to be made under the terms of a variation of rights clause contained in the company's articles or, failing that, the variation must be sanctioned by the holders of three-quarters in nominal value of the issued shares of that class in writing or by a special resolution passed at a separate class meeting. Since Bertram, who opposes the variation, is the sole shareholder of the class, the variation cannot proceed without his approval.

Claude: One of the major restrictions applicable to contracts contained in the memorandum and articles of association relates to enforcement of the contract by members against the company. Members are restricted in that they can only enforce against the company rights classified as membership rights. Rights in any other capacity are deemed outsider rights and cannot be enforced. A provision in the articles that Claude should be the company secretary for life is unenforceable by Claude, even though he is a member of the company, since the right to be the company secretary for life is not a membership right but an outsider right. The legal position that members can only enforce their rights as members was established in *Eley v Positive Govt Sec Life Assurance Co* (1876) 1 Ex D 88 in which Eley was named in the articles as the company's solicitor for life. The membership rights are defined as the personal rights enjoyed by the shareholders and include the right to attend meetings and to vote (*Pender v Lushington* (1877) 6 Ch D 70) and the right to receive payment of a dividend in cash where the articles so provide (*Wood v Odessa Waterworks Co* (1889) 42 Ch D 636).

In addition to these personal rights, they can also enforce their right for the company to be run in accordance with its constitution. Thus in *Re HR Harmer Ltd* [1958] 3 All ER 689 the shareholders of the company were able to enforce their right as members for the company to be run in accordance with its constitution, namely through decisions of the board of directors. Since they were also directors of the company, it also meant that they could also enforce their rights as directors. In *Quin and Axtens Ltd v Salmon* [1909] AC 442 the articles required the approval of both managing directors for certain transactions. When one refused to approve a particular transaction, the shareholders attempted to get round his refusal by passing an ordinary resolution authorizing the transaction. The court allowed the managing director's claim to enforce the company's compliance with its constitution.

Sales manager: This provision in the articles could not be enforced directly by the sales manager, even though he is a shareholder, for the same reasons as in the case of Claude. The law provides that provisions in the company's articles relating to such things as the salary rights of the company's directors are still to be regarded as outsider rights. In *Re New British Iron Co, ex p Beckwith* [1898] **1 Ch 324** the claimants had served the company as directors without any express agreement for remuneration, but Article 62 provided that the remuneration of the board of directors was to be the annual sum of £1,000, to be divided between them as they thought fit. On the company's liquidation, they claimed arrears of directors' fees. The court held that this provision did not constitute a contract between the company and the directors for the payment of fees to the directors. The court held, however, that, by accepting office on the understanding that the terms of the article applied, the article provision was impliedly incorporated in the contract of service between the company and the directors and they were entitled to payment. In the case of *Swabey v Port Darwin Gold Mining Co* (1889) **1 Meg 385** the company's articles provided that the directors were to be remunerated at the rate of £200 per annum. Subsequently, the company by special resolution altered the articles to provide that the directors should henceforth receive £5 per month. Swabey, a director, immediately resigned his office and claimed for three months' fees at the old rate. The Court of Appeal held in his favour on the grounds that, even though article provisions incorporated into a contract of service must be on the understanding that the articles are alterable, the alteration can only be prospective and not retrospective.

If we apply the law established by these decisions to the case of the sales manager, it is clear that, although Edward can alter the articles to reduce the bonus to be awarded to him, it can only be altered prospectively. If the sales manager has therefore completed a period of service prior to the alteration on the basis of the incorporation of the article provision prior to its alteration, he can sue for the bonus for that period to be calculated at the old rate of 5 per cent.

Question 3

Fred and Ginger are directors and majority shareholders of Funtimes Ltd, which organizes children's theme parties. They each hold 35 per cent of the issued share capital. Jerry, Lee, and Lewis each hold 10 per cent of the issued share capital. The articles contain inter alia the following provisions:

(a) Disputes between the company and members shall be referred to arbitration

(b) Fred and Ginger shall be directors for life

(c) If any member wishes to transfer his/her shares s/he shall offer them to the directors who will take them at a fair price

(d) The laundry service run by Jerry shall launder all table-linen etc of the company

Advise Jerry, Lee, and Lewis concerning the following situation:

(a) Jerry's laundry service has proved expensive, and Fred and Ginger have signed a new, exclusive contract for laundering with Spin & Tonic Ltd

(b) Lee has become a shareholder/director of 'Sixes and Sevens Ltd' which provides clowns and entertainers for private events including children's parties. Fred and Ginger have called an extraordinary general meeting (EGM) to propose the following, additional article: 'Any member must transfer his or her shares to the directors' nominee upon a request in writing by the holders of 75% of the issued shares'

(c) Lewis, upset by the breakdown in relationships, decides to sell his shares and offers them to Fred and Ginger who refuse to buy them

 Commentary

This problem question requires you to apply a number of principles of the law relating to the company's constitution. These include the enforceability of the contract contained in the articles and binding the members and the company and the restriction on the power to alter the articles where the alteration is an abuse of majority power.

 Answer plan

- Identification of the problems raised by the question
- Restriction on enforcement of outsider rights
- Alteration of the articles to compulsorily remove a shareholder
- Right of a member to enforce the articles against other members

Suggested answer

The problem raises issues concerning the nature of the contract contained in the articles and the restriction on the alteration of those articles where the proposed alteration constitutes an abuse of majority control.

In respect of Jerry, he would clearly wish to enforce the terms of the contract under which his business is designated as the launderer for the company's linens etc. While it would be unlikely for him to claim specific performance of such a contract, he would otherwise seek damages for the loss of the company's business.

In this situation, although Jerry is a member of the company holding 10 per cent of the issued share capital, the nature of the purported contract that he seeks to enforce against the company is a contract that is not in any way related to his membership rights in respect of the company since it is not concerned with his rights as a member. Neither is it concerned with the enforcement of a right that the constitution of the company be respected.

The relevant decision in this respect is *Eley v Positive Govt Sec Life Assurance* Co (1876) 1 Ex D 88 which decided that a person appointed as solicitor of a company for life could not, even as a member of the company, enforce this right against the company. The case established that members cannot enforce rights as outsiders contained in the articles. The scope of who is defined as an outsider for this purpose is very wide and includes the directors of the company in their capacity as directors. Thus in *Re New British Iron Co, ex p Beckwith* [1898] 1 Ch 324 the court held that directors could not claim enforceable contractual rights in respect of a statement of their right to remuneration contained in the articles, although they were indirectly allowed to enforce the right since it had become an implied term in the contract of service with the company.

In respect of Lee, the position is more complicated. He is faced with an alteration to the articles which will allow Fred and Ginger, the holders of 70 per cent of the issued shares of the company, to secure his enforced removal from the company if they gain the support of either Jerry or Lewis. Lee will try to contend that the proposed alteration of the articles is an abuse of majority power or, in another phrase, something which is not in good faith for the benefit of the company. In *Allen v Gold Reefs of West Africa Ltd* [1900] 1 Ch 656 it was established that the court could set aside proposed alterations of the articles that were not bona fide for the benefit of the company as a whole.

The question then was how to assess whether the proposed alteration was bona fide for the benefit of the company as a whole. In respect of this, there were two approaches taken by the court: the objective test (where the court decided whether or not the proposal was for the company's benefit) and the subjective text (where the court considered whether the members of the company, in voting for the proposed alteration, did so on the basis that it was for the benefit of the company).

In *Sidebottom v Kershaw, Leese & Co Ltd* [1920] 1 Ch 154 the defendant company altered its articles by introducing a provision allowing the directors to buy out at a fair price, members who competed with the company's business. The Court of Appeal took the view that, if the members acted in what they believed to be in the best interests of the company, the alteration was valid. However, in *Dafen Tinplate Co Ltd v Llanelly Steel Co (1907) Ltd* [1920] 2 Ch 124, Peterson J disagreed with this view in the following words: 'It has been suggested that the only question … is whether the shareholders bona fide or honestly believed that that alteration was for the benefit of the company. But this is not, in my view, the true meaning of the words of Lindley MR or of the judgment in Sidebottom's case. The question is whether in fact the alteration is genuinely for the benefit of the company.' The issue was resolved in *Shuttleworth v Cox Bros & Co (Maidenhead) Ltd* [1927] 2 KB 9 where Atkin LJ stated: 'The only question is whether or not the shareholders, in considering whether they shall alter the articles, honestly intend to exercise their powers for the benefit of the company ... It is not a matter of law for the court [to decide] whether or not a particular alteration is for the benefit of the company; nor is it the business of a judge to review the decision of every company in the country on these questions.'

The decision in *Greenhalgh v Arderne Cinemas Ltd* [1951] Ch 286 seems contradictory since, while agreeing to the correctness of the subjective test, it introduces a notion of the objective test in reference to discrimination in the following terms: 'a special resolution of this kind would be liable to be impeached if the effect of it were to discriminate between the majority shareholders and the minority shareholders, so as to give to the former an advantage of which the latter were deprived'.

In order to test this claim, Lee would now petition under **CA 2006, s. 994** on the grounds that alteration is unfairly prejudicial to him and ask for the court to block the alteration of the articles under **CA 2006, s. 996(2)(d)**. Since it would appear that Lee is in competition with Funtimes Ltd because of his association with Sixes and Sevens Ltd, the court is unlikely to think that his exclusion from Funtimes Ltd is unfair, even though prejudicial. In this case, however, the articles provide that all disputes between the company and members should be referred to arbitration. The company could seek a stay of proceedings in respect of any action by Lee: *Hickman v Romney Marsh Sheepbreeders' Association* [1915] 1 Ch 881. *In Fulham Football Club (1987) Ltd v Richards* [2010] EWHC 3111 (Ch) the court held that this would operate to stay a s. 994 petition.

The issue for Lewis is the ability to enforce an apparent obligation in the articles to the effect that the directors, Fred and Ginger, must purchase his shares in the company. Relevant to this issue is the decision in *Rayfield v Hands* [1960] Ch 1. In this case, the articles of a private company provided that 'every member who intended to transfer shares shall inform the directors who will take the said shares equally between them at a fair value'. In this case, the directors claimed that the articles merely created an option but not an obligation to take the shares. The court held that the articles bound the directors, as members, to take the shares and that this obligation was a personal one which could be enforced against them by other members directly without joining the company as a party to the action. This was in contradiction to the decision in *Welton v Saffery* [1897] AC 299 where Lord Herschell stated: 'It is quite true that the articles constitute a contract between each member and the company', but that 'such rights can only be enforced by or against a member through the company....'

In conclusion, I would advise Jerry that he cannot enforce his right to provide laundry services to the company. I would advise Lee that the company can compulsorily remove him as a shareholder since he is competing with the company; I would also advise Lewis that, in accordance with the decision in *Rayfield v Hands,* the directors have an obligation to purchase his shares.

Question 4

Unless the context otherwise requires, references in the **Companies Acts** to a company's constitution include—

(a) The company's articles, and

(b) Any resolutions and agreements to which **Chapter 3** applies (see **s. 29**). (**CA 2006, s. 17**)

Analyse the reference to resolution and agreements in this context and any other agreements which impact on the constitution of the company.

 Commentary

This question picks up the definition of the constitution of a registered company and considers the resolutions and agreements that have a bearing on the company's constitution. **Chapter 3** of **Part 3** replaces the equivalent provisions in the **1985 Act** on the registration of resolutions and agreements and on making these available to members. **Section 29** replaces s. **380(4)** and **(4A)** and lists the resolutions and agreements that must be forwarded to the registrar for registration under **s. 30** and made available to members on request (**s. 32**).

The most important point to discuss in this respect is the courts' willingness to bypass the strict legal formalities of the **Companies Acts** for small, incorporated firms on the basis of unanimity, estoppel, or waiver.

A further important issue raised by the question is the possibility of a shareholder agreement as a supplement to the articles.

These points are very important and knowledge of them is vital.

 Answer plan

- Need for compliance with formal requirements of the **Companies Acts** to achieve constitutional changes
- Exceptions to compliance where unanimous, informal consent of members
- Criticism of these exceptions
- Shareholder agreements and their enforcement

Suggested answer

In this essay it is necessary to identify and explain the resolutions and agreements that also constitute the company's constitution, in addition to the articles.

The definition of the constitution comes in **CA 2006, s. 17,** which refers to 'resolutions and agreements to which Part 3, Chapter 3 applies', with a forward reference to **CA 2006, s. 29** which sets out the resolutions and agreements affecting a company's constitution which are required to be notified to the Registrar.

The section includes any special resolutions (**s. 29(1)(a)**) and any resolution or agreement agreed to by all the members of a company that, if not so agreed to, would not have been effective for its purpose unless passed as a special resolution: **s. 29(1)(b).**

The reference to the constitution and the special resolution is obvious since the company may amend its articles—and thus its constitution—by special resolution: **s. 21(1).** The reference to agreements agreed to by all the members of a company that, if not so agreed to, would not have been effective for its purpose unless passed as a special resolution, refers to the possibility that the articles of a company can be changed by a unanimous decision of the members.

This links to a number of cases where the courts have been willing to bypass the strict legal formality of the **Companies Act.** Thus in *Re Duomatic Ltd* [1969] 2 Ch 365 Buckley J said: 'I proceed on the basis that where it can be shown that all shareholders who had a right to attend and vote at a general meeting of the company assent to some matter which a general meeting ... could carry into effect, that assent is as binding as a resolution in general meeting would be.' This was followed in *Cane v Jones* [1981] **1 All ER 533.** In this case, two brothers formed a company to run the family business. Each was a director and the shares were equally divided between the members of their family. The case concerned a claim that the constitution, which had originally given the chairman a casting vote, had been amended as a result of a unanimous decision of the members. The court held that the informal agreement had had the same effect as a special resolution altering the articles.

The decision in *Cane* was followed in *Re Home Treat Ltd* [1991] BCLC 705. where a company, in administration, was carrying on a business outside its objects. The administrator wished to continue the business and to sell it as a going concern. The court held that, since the company's only shareholder had agreed to the change of activity, it must be deemed to have changed its objects.

The **Companies Act 2006** also contains an equivalent provision to **s. 29(1)(b)** in respect of a decision by the members of a class of shareholders (**s. 29(1)(c)**) which presupposes that a unanimous decision of the members of a class could as effectively amend the class rights as the statutory requirements: consent in writing of the holders of three-quarters in nominal value of the issued shares of that class, or a special resolution passed at a separate general meeting of the holders of that class: **s. 630(4).**

Articles may be supplemented by a shareholders' agreement—usually a formal contract entered into at the time of the company's formation or subsequently. All of the members for the time being should be parties to the agreement, which restricts their use to small companies.

There are cases where the existence of a shareholder agreement is implied by the court. In *Pennell Securities Ltd v Venida Investments Ltd* (unreported, 25 July 1974) the directors proposed to call an EGM to increase the company's capital by a rights issue on a nine-for-one basis. They knew that the claimant (with a 49 per cent shareholding) would not be able to take up the issue, reducing his minority holding to below 10 per cent. The court granted injunctions against the directors as violation of a tacit agreement between the members that the claimant's minority stake should remain at 49 per cent unless they otherwise agreed.

The company itself may be a party, but there are dangers in that the company may be held to have fettered its statutory powers. In *Russell v Northern Bank Development Corpn Ltd* [1992] 3 All ER 161, a company was set up in 1979. Soon after incorporation, an agreement was entered into between the five shareholders and the company that no further share capital would be issued without the consent of each party. In 1988, the board proposed an increase in capital by way of a rights issue. Russell, a shareholder, obtained a declaration that the agreement was binding on his fellow shareholders (although not on the company itself since this would restrict the company's statutory right to increase its capital).

Agreement may be to the effect that each shareholder should be entitled to appoint a director. In *Re A & BC Chewing Gum Ltd* [1975] 1 All ER 1017 the agreement was that the petitioner, a corporate investor holding one-third of the capital, should have a fifty–fifty say in management. The agreement was in effect enforced on the equitable principles established in *Ebrahimi v Westbourne Galleries Ltd* [1973] AC 360 but it could and should have been enforced by injunction as a legally binding shareholder agreement. The terms may also provide that no shareholder should vote for alteration of articles or capital unless all members agreed, or that shareholders would not demand repayment of loans to the company except in certain circumstances. In *Snelling v John G Snelling Ltd* [1973] QB 87, the shareholders had lent money to the company and had agreed with each other that none of them would require repayment by the company while certain other funding arrangements were in place. The court refused to allow one of the shareholders to sue the company for repayment in breach of the agreement.

Shareholders may enter valid agreements restricting or determining the way in which they exercise their voting rights. These may be enforced by mandatory injunction. In *Greenwell v Porter* [1902] 1 Ch 530 the defendants agreed to do all within their power to secure election of two named persons as directors and to vote for their re-election. They later tried to oppose re-election on one of the two. The court granted an injunction restraining them from voting against the terms of their agreement.

The main advantage is that the terms of the agreement cannot be altered by majority vote or special resolution and that the terms are, in principle, enforceable as of right—where appropriate by injunction—whereas rights under the articles may not be enforceable by shareholder minority.

The disadvantage is that they are binding on immediate parties only—not persons subsequently becoming shareholders. Such agreements bind only the parties to the agreement. In *Greenhalgh v Mallard* [1943] 2 All ER 234 it was held: 'If the contract ... only imposes an obligation to vote in respect of whatever shares the parties happen to have available, it follows that directly they sell their shares the contract is at an end—until possibly they acquire more shares ... If the contract ... ceases to operate when the shares are sold, then in the hands of the purchaser there can be no question of a continuing obligation which runs with the shares' (Lord Greene MR at p. 239).

Shareholder agreements are standard practice for joint ventures and management buy-outs (MBOs).

Question 5

'By virtue of s. 14 [now CA 2006, s. 33] the articles of association become, upon registration, a contract between a company and members. It is, however, a statutory contract of a special nature with its own distinctive features' (per Steyn LJ: *Bratton Seymour Service Co Ltd v Oxborough* [1992] BCLC 693).

Discuss.

 ## Commentary

There are many ways in which it can be said that the contract contained in the articles is of a special nature. From the point of view of company law, there is the question that the terms of the contract can be varied by special resolution, that the members of the company can only enforce their contract rights to a limited extent: there is no recognition of outsider rights.

In addition, from the point of view of contract law, there are a number of ways in which the contract under **s. 33(1)** differs in a major way from any normal contract, although one of the anomalies has been removed.

These are important points that you need to be aware of and which can form the basis of essay and problem questions.

 ## Answer plan

- The articles as a binding contract
- Nature and limitations of the contract in respect of company law
- Nature and limitations of the contract as opposed to the usual rules of law of contract

Suggested answer

'The provisions of a company's constitution bind the company and its members to the same extent as if there were covenants on the part of the company and of each member to observe those provisions.' This is the nature of the legal effect of the articles of the company once registered as set out in **s. 33(1)**. This is the equivalent to the previous provision of the **Companies Act 1985** and only differs to the extent that the memorandum is no longer a part of the company's constitution.

The position is that the contract contained in the articles can be enforced by the company against the members of the company; by a member against a member; and by a member against the company but only in respect of membership rights including personal rights to attend meetings and to vote, rights to a dividend and also rights for the company to be managed in accordance with its constitution.

Thus the company can enforce compliance with an obligation to refer disputes between the company and a member to arbitration if the articles contain a valid ref erence to an arbitration clause. Thus in *Hickman v Kent or Romney Marsh Sheep-Breeders' Association* [1915] 1 Ch 881 the court upheld a clause requiring that disputes between the company and members should be referred to arbitration, while in *Beattie v E & F Beattie Ltd* [1938] Ch 708 the court refused a stay of action in a case brought against the company by the plaintiff, a director and shareholder, since the dispute was in his capacity as a director not as a member.

In respect of enforcement of the articles by a member against a member, *Rayfield v Hands* [1960] Ch 1 established that a member could enforce against another the obligation to acquire shares which that member wished to sell where such an obligation was contained in the articles.

In respect of members bringing an action against the company, this right is limited to purely personal membership rights. Thus in *Wood v Odessa Waterworks Co* (1889) 42 Ch D 636 the plaintiff successfully enforced his constitutional right for payment of a dividend in cash rather than in the form of debenture bonds. And in *Pender v Lushington* (1877) 6 Ch D 70 the plaintiff sued to enforce his right as a member to have his vote recorded. Members also have an enforceable right for the company to be managed in accordance with its constitution. In *Quin & Axtens Ltd v Salmon* [1909] AC 442 the company's two managing directors, Salmon and Axtens, held between them the bulk of the company's ordinary shares. The business of the company was delegated to the directors but there was an article to the effect that no resolution of a meeting of the directors for acquiring or letting premises would be valid if either Salmon or Axtens dissented. The directors resolved to acquire and let certain properties and Salmon dissented. At a subsequent EGM, the shareholders passed similar resolutions. The House of Lords held that the shareholders' resolutions were inconsistent with the articles and granted Salmon an injunction restraining the company from acting on them. In *Re HR Harmer Ltd* [1958] 3 All ER 689 the Court of Appeal held that the shareholder sons of the founder of the company, who were also directors, had the right as members for the company to be run in accordance with the proper procedure following the founder's disregard of board resolutions and the assumption of powers that he did not have.

The law does not recognize the enforcement of outsider rights against the company, even though they may be rights in respect of a member but not membership rights as such. This was established in *Eley v Positive Government Life Assurance Co Ltd* (1876) 1 Ex D 88 where the plaintiff tried to enforce a right contained in the company's articles that he should be the company's solicitor for life, only removable on grounds of misconduct. The definition of outsider rights is very broad and has been extended to include remuneration rights of directors contained in the articles. In *Re New British Iron Co, ex p Beckwith* [1898] 1 Ch 324 the court held that the articles did not constitute a contract between the company and the directors but that, since they had accepted office on the basis of the article, the terms were incorporated as an implied term in their contract of service. A similar decision was held in *Swabey v Port Darwin Gold Mining Co* (1889) 1 Meg 385 which held that the implied term was subject to prospective alteration in the normal way of any article.

In *Re Richmond Gate Property Co Ltd* [1965] 1 WLR 335 W, a member of the company, was appointed and worked as managing director of the company. The articles contained a provision that the board could fix the remuneration as they might determine. The company went into voluntary liquidation before any remuneration was fixed. W claimed for his services either on contract or in quasi-contract (quantum meruit). The court held that, because he was a member, a contract existed but that, as no remuneration had been determined, he was not contractually entitled to remuneration; neither was he entitled in quasi-contract since this was excluded by the valid contract. In *Craven-Ellis v Canons Ltd* [1936] 2 KB 403 the plaintiff successfully claimed for remuneration in quasi-contract because his contract of employment was a nullity.

In respect of the articles being subject to entirely different rules than other contracts, in *Scott v Frank F Scott (London) Ltd* [1940] Ch 794, the court rejected a request for the rectification of the articles to make them accord with the intention of the three brothers at the time of the company's registration. Luxmore LJ approved the statement of Bennett J that 'there is no room ... for the application to either the memorandum or the articles of association of the principles upon which a court of equity permits rectification of documents whether inter partes or not ...'.

As regards alteration by way of an implied term, the court will not imply a term to change the articles by implication from extrinsic facts known only to some of the people involved in the formation of the company. In *Bratton Seymour Service Co Ltd v Oxborough* [1992] BCLC 693, the company was set up to acquire and manage a property divided into flats. The property also included tennis courts, swimming pool and gardens. The Court of Appeal rejected a request to imply an obligation on the part of each flat owner to contribute to the expense of maintaining the amenity areas. Steyn LJ stated: 'Just as the company or an individual member cannot seek to defeat the statutory contract by reason of special circumstances such as misrepresentation, mistake, undue influence and duress and is furthermore not permitted to seek rectification, neither the company nor any member can seek to add to or to subtract from the terms of the articles by way of implying a term derived from extrinsic surrounding circumstances.'

A term can, however, be implied to give business efficacy to the language of the articles in their commercial setting: *Equitable Life Assurance Society v Hyman* [2002] 1 AC 408. In this case, the articles gave the directors a wide discretionary power to pay bonuses on members' policies and they had paid some policyholders larger bonuses than others contrary to guarantees given to certain of the members. Lord Steyn said the articles should be read as containing an implied term that the directors could not exercise their discretion 'in a manner which deprived the guarantees of any substantial value'. The power of the court to imply a term into the articles to give them business efficacy has been approved by the Privy Council in *Attorney General of Belize & Ors v Belize Telecom Ltd & Anor* [2009] **UKPC 10** and in *Cream Holdings Ltd v Davenport* [2010] **EWHC 3096 (Ch)** the court stated that articles were to be construed like any other contract in the context of their commercial purpose and implied into the articles a term that a transferor of shares could not unreasonably withhold his consent to the appointment of an accountant for the purpose of valuing his shareholding (see also *Cream Holdings v Davenport* [2008] **EWCA Civ 1363**).

Further reading

Cheung, R., 'The use of statutory shareholder agreements and entrenched articles in reserving minority shareholders' rights: a comparative analysis' [2008] Comp. Law., 29(8): 234.

Goldberg, G. D., 'The enforcement of outsider rights under s. 20(1) Companies Act 1948' [1972] 35 MLR: 362 and [1985] 48 MLR: 158.

Gregory, R., 'The section 20 contract' [1981] 44 MLR: 526.

Prentice, G. N., 'The enforcement of outsider rights' [1980] Comp. Law., 1: 179.

Savirimuthu, J., 'Thoughts on *Russell*—killing private companies with kindness' [1993] Comp. Law., 14(7): 137.

Scanlan, G., and Ryan, C., 'The accrual of claims for breach of contract under s. 14 Companies Act 1985 and s. 33 Companies Act 2006: the continuing obligation' [2007] Comp. Law., 28(12): 367.

Sealy, L. S., 'Shareholders' agreements—an endorsement and a warning from the House of Lords' [1992] CLJ 437.

Wise, E., 'If at first you don't succeed' (2010) Tax., 166(4272): 18/

3

Company contracts

Introduction

This chapter concerns the important topic of company contracts including pre-incorporation contracts, contracts beyond the company's capacity, and contracts beyond the directors' authority, all areas covered by the **First Company Law Directive 68/151/ EEC (9 March 1968)**. This was transposed into UK law by the **European Communities Act 1972** up to and including the **Companies Act 1989**. The legal position is largely unchanged by the **Companies Act 2006** except for contracts beyond the company's capacity where there have been major changes.

Pre-incorporation contracts

At common law, companies could not be bound by pre-incorporation contracts and neither could the contracts be ratified after incorporation. The position following implementation of **Article 7** of the **First Company Law Directive** is personal liability of 'the person purporting to act for the company or as agent for it': (**CA 2006, s. 51(1)**). But it is questionable as to whether the Directive has been completely implemented. The role of the **Contracts (Rights of Third Parties) Act 1999** is also of potential relevance in this area.

Contracts beyond the company's capacity

This is a vitally important topic and frequent subject of problem and essay questions. The *ultra vires* doctrine was imposed on registered companies by *Ashbury Railway Carriage & Iron Co v Riche* (1875) **LR 7 HL 653** which decided that contracts outside a company's objects were illegal, void, and unratifiable. Over the next century, lawyers drafting multi-objects clauses managed to limit its effect so that by the 1960s the doctrine could be said to have been largely sidestepped apart from the odd exceptional decision.

In addition to the traditional, multi-objects clause, the **Companies Act 1989** added **s. 3A** to the **Companies Act 1985** allowing companies to register 'to carry on a business as a general commercial company' and able to 'carry on any trade or business whatsoever', and 'do all such things as are incidental or conducive to the carrying on of any trade or business'.

The **Companies Act 2006** is claimed to amount to the removal of all that remains of the old *ultra vires* rule (Modernising Company Law (Cm 5553-1, part III, para. 5, 2002)) with companies having unrestricted objects unless specifically restricted by the articles: **CA 2006, s. 31(1)**. Companies incorporated under previous legislation retain their old objects (now in the articles: **s. 28**).

Contracts beyond the powers of directors to bind the company

Companies may restrict the directors' power to bind the company. At common law, companies could avoid contracts beyond the directors' authority, making third parties vulnerable unless protected by the rule in *Turquand's Case* and the doctrine of ostensible authority.

Statutory protection of third parties to contracts beyond company's capacity or the directors' authority

Article 9, First EC Council Directive required Member States to introduce legislation to protect third parties dealing with companies. The law regarding dealings beyond the company's capacity and directors' unauthorized acts is now in **CA 2006, ss. 39(1)** and **40(1)** respectively. Where the transaction's validity depends on **s. 40** and the parties include directors of the company or its holding company, or connected persons, the transaction is voidable by the company: **s. 41(2)**.

Contracts are made by a company, by writing under its common seal, or on its behalf by persons with express or implied authority: **CA 2006, s. 43**. Documents are executed by affixing its common seal or if signed by two authorized signatories or a director in the presence of a witness: **CA 2006, s. 44(2)**. The authorized signatories are every director or the company secretary. In favour of a purchaser, a document is deemed duly executed if it purports to be signed in accordance with **sub-s. (2)**. Thus in *Lovett v Carson Country Homes Ltd* [2009] EWHC 1143 (Ch) where a director forged the signature of another director on a debenture, the document was still valid. Companies are not required to have a common seal: **s. 45(1)**.

Question 1

Analyse how the law relating to pre-incorporation contracts has been reformed by the transposition into UK law of **Article 7** of the **First Company Law Directive** and the extent to which the Directive has been fully implemented.

Commentary

The topic of pre-incorporation contracts is relatively popular and, as here, can be a way of requiring you to analyse the position post-1972 and consider to what extent the UK has fully implemented the Directive. The main issue concerns the discrepancy between the wording of the Directive and the legislation purporting to implement it. The main problem arises due to the fact that there is no official English language text of the Directive since the UK was not at that time a Member State of the then EEC. In addition, whereas the civil law jurisdictions comprising the majority of the EEC members allowed companies to ratify pre-incorporation contracts, this was not the case for the UK.

Answer plan

- Common law position up to **European Communities Act (ECA) 1972**
- Analysis of the text of **Article 7** of the **First Company Law Directive** and comparison with text of **ECA 1972, s. 9(2)**
- Potential application of **Contracts (Rights of Third Parties) Act 1999**
- Application and interpretation of **CA 1985, s. 36C** (now **CA 2006, s. 51**)
- Conclusion

Suggested answer

At common law, companies cannot be bound by pre-incorporation contracts and cannot 'by adoption or ratification obtain the benefit of a contract purporting to have been made on its behalf before the company came into existence': *Natal Land Co & Colonization Ltd v Pauline Colliery and Development Syndicate Ltd* [1904] AC 120. The only protection for third parties who were parties to pre-incorporation contracts was that persons signing as agent on the company's behalf were personally liable on the contract and the contract could be enforced against them. This was the result of the decision in *Kelner v Baxter* (1866) LR 2CP 174 where the defendants contracted in January to buy stock on behalf of a proposed new hotel company, payment to be made on 28 February 1866. The goods were delivered and used in the business. The company was registered on 20 February but became insolvent before the money was paid. The court held that they purported to be agents of a non-existent principal and were therefore personally liable on the agreement which could not be ratified when the company came into existence.

The position became more complicated following the decision in *Newborne v Sensolid* (GB) Ltd [1954] 1 QB 45 where a contract for the sale of goods was signed in the name of the unincorporated company followed by the signature of the founder and 'director'. The court held that the contract was void and could not be enforced by the plaintiff: the contract purported to be made by the company through a future director and as the company was not in existence when the contract was signed it was a nullity.

This confusing situation was removed with the implementation of **Article 7** of the **First Company Law Directive 68/151/EEC (9 March 1968)**. The main aim of the article was to protect persons dealing with a company against the company being able to walk away from liability on the grounds that the contract was made before it was incorporated and to ensure that primarily the company would be liable but that, failing this, the persons acting on its behalf should be personally liable in all cases.

This was initially implemented in **s. 9(2) ECA 1972** and was later incorporated into the **Companies Act 1985**, post the **Companies Act 1989** as **s. 36C**. The provision, substantially unchanged, is in **CA 2006, s. 51**. This provides that: 'A contract that purports to be made by or on behalf of a company at a time when the company has not been formed has effect, subject to any agreement to the contrary, as one made with the person purporting to act for the company or as agent for it, and he is personally liable on the contract accordingly': **CA 2006, s. 51(1)**. This applies: (a) to deeds in England and Wales or Northern Ireland; and (b) to 'the undertaking of an obligation' in Scotland: **s. 51(2)**.

If we consider the English text of **Article 7**, a number of discrepancies can be seen between the text of the legislation and that of the article, which is as follows: 'If, before a company being formed has acquired legal personality, action has been carried out in its name and the company does not assume the obligation arising from such action, the persons who acted shall without limit, be jointly and severally liable therefor, unless otherwise agreed.'

The first thing to notice is the phrase 'a company being formed'. This phrase was the subject of the decision in *Phonogram Ltd v Lane* **[1982] QB 938** where counsel for the defence argued that the phrase should be interpreted in the light of the French text which referred to a *société en formation*, meaning that the provision only applied to a company that was already in the process of being incorporated and where the promoters had already signed the equivalent of the articles of association. In the case before the court, although there had been an intention to form the company, no steps had been or were ever taken towards its formation. Lord Denning MR rejected the submission that he should go by the French text of the Directive and held that the defendant was liable to refund money paid to him in negotiations on behalf of the unincorporated company. This would appear to widen the actual scope of the Directive beyond its literal meaning.

The Directive refers to 'action' not 'contract' which is the term used in **s. 51(1)**. The scope of the provision is however widened by the addition of **sub-s. (2)** to **s. 36C** by the **Companies Act 1989**, which extended the provision to cover deeds in England and Wales. This is repeated in the current legislation and Northern Ireland is included: **s. 51(2)(a)**. Also from the **Companies Act 1989**, the provision was extended to include the undertaking of an obligation under the law of Scotland, this too is repeated in the current legislation: **s. 51(2)(b)**. As a result, it is doubtful whether it has been fully implemented in English law but it could be regarded as fully implemented in

Scotland. In England the scope of the section was extended to cover quasi contract in *Hellmuth, Obata & Kassabaum Inc v Geoffrey King* (unreported 29 September 2000).

The Directive also presupposes the possibility of the company ratifying the contract in the phrase 'and the company does not assume the obligation arising from such action'. As a result, it has been argued that the intention of the article is that liability to the third party should primarily fall on the company and that it is only in the absence of this that the persons acting on its behalf should be personally liable. The Report of the Jenkins Committee (Cmnd 1749, 1962, paras 44, 54(b)) recommended that 'a company should be enabled unilaterally to adopt contracts which purport to be made on its behalf or in its name prior to incorporation, and thereby become a party thereto to the same extent as if the contract had been made after incorporation ...'. This has been adopted by many Commonwealth countries and was included in the abortive Companies Bill 1973. Nothing has since been done in this direction.

The **Contracts (Rights of Third Parties) Act 1999** could cover pre-incorporation contracts since it allows a non-party to enforce a contract provided that person is sufficiently identified. **Section 1(3)** of the 1999 Act specifically states that the person need not be in existence when the contract is entered into. The Law Commission acknowledged that changes to the doctrine of privity of contract could impinge on pre-incorporation contracts but was of the opinion that the matter should be left to be dealt with separately as part of the reform of company law. This matter was not in fact considered in the recent review of the subject, but the Act could enable a company to claim the benefit of contracts entered into on its behalf.

Section 51(1) CA 2006 deals exclusively with the liability of the parties in respect of pre-incorporation contracts and ignores the question of any rights of enforcement that these parties may have. This situation was resolved in *Braymist Ltd v Wise Finance Co Ltd* [2001] EGCS 35. The case concerned a contract for the sale of land on 28 January 1993 by Braymist Ltd, which was incorporated on 5 March 1993 and was a wholly owned subsidiary of Plumtree Ltd (the owner of the land), itself a wholly owned subsidiary of Pique Holdings plc, of which 75 per cent of the shares were owned by Colin Pool. Pool had instructed the solicitors to sign the contract on behalf of Braymist Ltd. The buyers claimed that they were not bound by the contract since Braymist had not been incorporated at the time. The court agreed that the contract was binding but held that only the solicitor could be the 'deemed contracting vendor' entitled to enforce the contract.

The section has been held not to apply where a company trades under a new name before the change is operative: *Oshkosh B'Gosh Inc v Dan Marbel Inc & Craze* [1989] BCLC 507; nor where a company had been described by an incorrect name: *Badgerhill Properties Ltd v Cottrell* [1991] BCLC 805; nor where a person contracted in the name of a company that had been struck off the register and a new company of the same name was incorporated to continue the business: *Cotronic (UK) Ltd v Dezonie* [1991] BCLC 721. The common law position still applies to companies registering outside

Great Britain (in this case Guernsey): *Rover International Ltd v Cannon Films Ltd* [1989] 1 WLR 912.

In conclusion, the current position regarding the law on pre-incorporation contracts is still an area of the law where reform could be introduced to fully protect third parties dealing with unincorporated companies. It is also questionable whether the spirit of the Directive has been fully transposed into UK law.

Question 2

Tardis Ltd carries on business as a travel agent. There is no restriction on the company's objects in the articles of association. The articles provide that the board may delegate authority to a managing director or to individual directors who may contract on behalf of the company up to a limit of £50,000, beyond which the board's prior authority must be obtained.

The following agreements have been entered into on behalf of the company:

(a) The board agreed to sponsor a local student to attend a three-year course at a nearby university at a cost of £10,000. The course is unrelated to the business of the company.

(b) Adam, who acts as the managing director without having been formally appointed as such, contracted with Itma Ltd for the installation of a computer network for £55,000. He had not obtained the prior authority of the board for this.

Advise about the validity of these transactions and of the liability of the company and/or the board and the individual directors.

 Commentary

This problem question requires you to apply the law relating to contracts beyond the company's capacity and beyond the authority of the directors. While it is relatively straightforward, it does require an analysis of aspects of the statutory rules and consideration of their effectiveness to achieve the intentions of the **EC First Company Law Directive** which they are intended to implement. In this respect, you are also called upon to consider whether it is necessary to fall back on the common law protection. Since the coming into force of the **CA 2006**, it is also necessary in this area to consider aspects of the general duties of directors.

 Answer plan

- Identification of the legal problems raised by the question and the relevant statutory provisions

- Consideration of the law relating to contracts beyond the company's capacity and the capacity of Tardis Ltd

- Application of relevant statutory provision and consideration of the validity of the agreement and the liability of the company and the directors

- Consideration of the effectiveness of the relevant statutory provision relating to contracts beyond the director's authority

- Discussion of the need to rely on common law protection of the rule in *Turquand's Case* and ostensible authority

- Application of relevant statutory provision relating to transactions involving directors or their associates and liability of the parties

- Conclusion

Suggested answer

This question requires discussion of contracts beyond the company's capacity and contracts beyond the director's authority.

In respect of contracts beyond the company's capacity, the objects of Tardis Ltd are in the form of **CA 1985, s. 3A**. This means that the object of the company is to carry on business as a general commercial company and that the company has the capacity 'to carry on any trade or business whatsoever', and the power to do 'all such things as are incidental or conducive to the carrying on of any trade or business by it'. Since the coming into effect of the **CA 2006**, companies already formed under the earlier **Companies Acts** will continue to have the same restrictions on their objects but the clause will now be deemed to be contained in the articles of the company under **s. 28**.

The agreement made by the board to sponsor a student for a three-year university course is an *ex gratia* agreement unrelated to the company's objects since it is unrelated to the company's business. In *Evans v Brunner, Mond & Co* [1921] 1 Ch 359, the company formed to carry on business as chemical manufacturers decided to distribute £100,000 to UK universities to further scientific education. The disbursements were only held to be valid because they were incidental or conducive to the main object.

The validity of the agreement is therefore subject to **CA 2006, s. 39**. This provides that the validity of an act done by the company shall not be called into question on the ground of lack of capacity by reason of anything in the company's constitution: **s. 39(1)**. The use of the term 'act' in the section covers both contractual and *ex gratia* payments. The validity of the agreement cannot be questioned.

The directors have, however, acted in breach of their general duties in that they have failed to act in accordance with the company's constitution under **s. 171(a)**. The consequences of this breach of their general duty would give rise to civil liability. The consequences of the breach are the same as would apply if the corresponding common law or equitable principle applied: **s. 178(1)**. This would mean that the directors would be liable to account to the company for the loss to the company as a result of the misuse of the company's assets.

If the members of the board of the company are also controlling shareholders of the company, the situation could be resolved without problem and without liability for the directors. Since the object now forms part of the articles of the company, it is possible for the company to ratify the agreement.

In respect of the contract with Itma Ltd for the computer system, Adam has clearly exceeded the limitation in the company's articles restricting the contractual authority of managing and individual directors to £50,000, beyond which the prior authority of the board is required. This is therefore an unauthorized contract which, at common law, is voidable by the company. The legal position is now potentially covered by **CA 2006, s. 40**. This provides: 'In favour of a person dealing with a company in good faith, the power of the directors to bind the company or authorise others to do so, is deemed to be free of any limitation under the company's constitution': **s. 40(1)**. For the purposes of the section a person deals with a company if he is a party to any transaction or other act to which the company is a party (**s. 40(2)(a)**); and a person dealing with the company is not bound to enquire as to any limitation on the powers of the directors to bind the company or authorize others to do so, is presumed to have acted in good faith, and is not regarded as having acted in bad faith even if he knew that the act was 'beyond the powers of the directors under the Company's constitution': **s. 40(2)(b)**.

From this it would appear that the company is liable on the contract to Itma Ltd. The only potential problem arises from the drafting of **s. 40(1)**. The law has always been claimed to be inadequate to protect third parties dealing with a company through an individual director (except the managing director) acting without board authority. It has been suggested that, in order to be effective, the wording should be 'the power of the directors or an individual director to bind the company, or authorize others to do so' (rather than 'the power of the directors to bind the company, or authorise others to do so'). This rather depends on the willingness of the court to interpret the section in the broadest possible way so as to implement the purpose of the Directive. A broad approach can be seen in the judgment of Browne-Wilkinson VC where, referring to **s. 9(1) ECA 1972**, he stated: 'the manifest purpose of both the directive and the section is to enable people to deal with a company in good faith without being adversely affected by any limits on the company's capacity or its rules for internal management' (*TCB Ltd v Gray* [1988] 1 All ER 108).

In contrast, in *Smith v Henniker-Major & Co* unreported, Ch D, transcript HC 0102108, Smith, the director of a company, sued a firm of solicitors for negligence in respect of a land acquisition claiming the company had suffered financial loss. Smith claimed that the company had assigned the cause of action to him. There were only two directors, and the articles required a quorum of two directors. The other director could not attend but Smith purported to act as the board and minuted the board's authorizing him to assign the cause of action to himself. On the question of whether Smith could rely on **s. 35A** to validate the assignment, Rimer J held that where an inquorate board attempts to transact business, the transaction will be a nullity.

In support of a generous interpretation of the section, it could be argued that the court has the legal obligation to interpret domestic legislation so far as possible in the light of the wording and purpose of any relevant directive: *Marleasing SA v La Comercial Internacional de Alimentación SA* [1990] I - 4135.

As a result, third parties may still need protection at common law of the Rule in *Turquand's Case* or the doctrine of ostensible authority.

Under *Turquand*, it could be argued that persons dealing with the company are entitled to assume that the internal management rules of the company have been complied with; and that Adam has obtained the prior authorization as required by the constitution. This would allow the third party to enforce the contract against the company.

In the alternative, the third party could argue that Adam has been held out as being the managing director of the company, that they acted in reliance on this holding out and that, since the contract would be within the potential authority of a managing director, it is enforceable against the company: *Freeman & Lockyer v Buckhurst Park Properties (Mangal) Ltd* [1964] 2 QB 480. However, it could be argued that the fact of allowing Adam to act as if he were the managing director of the company could constitute his implied appointment as such. In this case the company would be liable on the basis of Adam's actual authority: *Hely-Hutchinson v Brayhead Ltd* [1968] 1 QB 549.

Thus, in respect of the two situations the company would appear to be bound by the agreements but the directors could be liable to indemnify the company for any loss.

Question 3

Acts done by the organs of the company shall be binding upon it even if those acts are not within the objects of the company, unless such acts exceed the powers that the law confers or allows to be conferred on those organs.

However, Member States may provide that the company shall not be bound where such acts are outside the objects of the company, if it proves that the third party knew that the act was outside those objects or could not in view of the circumstances have been unaware of it; disclosure of the statutes shall not of itself be sufficient proof thereof.

(Article 9(1) of the **First Company Law Directive 68/151/EEC (9 March 1968)**)

Analyse the problems in transposing **Article 9(1)** into UK law and the extent to which the doctrine of *ultra vires* has been abolished for registered companies.

 Commentary

This essay question requires you to analyse the problems in the UK in implementing **Article 9(1)** of the **First Company Law Directive** and explain the current protection offered by the **CA**

2006 in this respect. This requires consideration of the previous attempts to legislate and an analysis of where and why this legislation failed.

Answer plan

- Historical introduction to the *ultra vires* doctrine and the evolution of the traditional multi-objects clause
- Implementation of **Article 9(1)** in the **ECA 1972, s. 9(1)** and problems arising from the drafting of the legislation
- External abolition of the doctrine following the **Companies Act** 1989 in respect of 'acts done'
- Internal retention in respect of proposed acts and liability of directors
- Analysis of the position post-**CA 2006**
- Continued liability of directors for breach of general duties under **CA 2006, s. 171**

Suggested answer

At common law, contracts outside a company's objects were illegal, void, and unratifiable: *Ashbury Railway Carriage & Iron Co v Riche* (1875) **LR 7 HL 653**. This led to the draftsmen of company memorandums developing the multiple objects clause by which, in a series of sub-clauses, the company's objects extended to all sorts of potential activities. In addition, things which had previously been left to be implied as powers ancillary to the company's objects were specified as independent objects. These included the power to borrow. The courts fought back against this development, ostensibly for the protection of investors and lenders, and where the court identified the company's main object and found that this had been abandoned, it was able to wind up the company on the grounds of the failure of its *raison d'être*. This approach was finally defeated in *Cotman v Brougham* [1918] AC 514 where the court was forced to recognize the validity of a clause to the effect that all of the objects in each of the sub-clauses of the objects clause were equal and independent. A further development in *Bell Houses Ltd v City Wall Properties Ltd* [1966] 1 QB 207 recognized the validity of the subjective objects clause whereby companies could carry on any other trade or business which 'in the opinion of the directors' could be carried on alongside the other business of the company. Finally, *Re Horsley & Weight Ltd* [1982] 3 All ER 1045 recognized the possibility of the inclusion into the objects clause of non-commercial objects: charitable and political donations etc. Political donations are now regulated by **CA 2006, Part 14, ss. 362–379.** *Ex gratia* payments to employees and ex-employees are also covered by statute: **s. 247.**

As a result, it could be said that by the end of the twentieth century—and even before—the problem of the *ultra vires* doctrine had been largely drafted out of existence apart from some problems. Thus in *Re Introductions Ltd* [1970] **Ch 199**, a company that had started out providing facilities for foreign visitors to the 1951 Festival of Britain and which was now engaged in pig farming, borrowed money on a secured loan from a bank for the purpose of this new, *ultra vires*, activity. In seeking to enforce its rights as a secured creditor, the bank relied on an independent object contained in a sub-clause empowering the company to borrow. The court held that the power to borrow could not be an independent object in itself, it was merely a power that had to be exercised for the legitimate purposes of the company. The distinction between objects and powers was largely removed by the decision in *Rolled Steel Products (Holdings) Ltd v British Steel Corpn* [1986] Ch 246. In effect, had the bank in *Re Introductions* been properly advised, they would have based their case on the validity of a subjective objects clause within the company's objects.

The impetus for reform came from **Article 9(1)** of the **First Company Law Directive**. Since the UK was not a Member State of the then EEC at this time, there was no official English text of the Directive and—more importantly—no input concerning UK company law. As a result, the transposition of the Directive into UK law has taken a long time and it is still questionable as to whether it has been effectively implemented. The main problem concerned the term 'organs' of the company, which is a direct translation of the French '*organes*'. Since English company law limits the concept of directors as 'organs' to the identification theory for corporate criminal and tortious liability, the term was translated as 'directors' and also as 'board of directors'.

Article 9 was first transposed into English law by **ECA 1972, s. 9(1)** which referred to 'any transaction decided on by the directors' as being deemed to be within the capacity of the company. It also stated that the power of the directors to bind the company shall be deemed to be free of any limitation under the memorandum or articles of association. The use of the word 'directors' was held to exclude acts by one or some members of the board (except where there was only one board member) but was later extended to cover acts by the 'sole effective director'. The reference to a 'transaction' was held to exclude *ex gratia* payments, while the requirement of good faith was only resolved by way of a broad interpretation of the text in the light of the spirit of the Directive: *TCB Ltd v Gray* [1986] Ch 621. In spite of being regarded as generally ineffective, it was, however, replaced in virtually the same terms in **CA 1985, s. 35**.

The legislation was significantly revised by the **Companies Act 1989** with a revised **s. 35** and the removal of the doctrine of deemed notice in **CA 1985, s. 35B** and **s. 711A** (the latter not implemented for various reasons). The section was largely effective in abolishing the external aspects of the doctrine in so far as they related to third parties dealing with a company, largely by way of ignoring the concept of 'organs' and leaving it untranslated. Thus the provision became: 'The validity of an act done by a company shall not be called into question on the ground of lack of capacity by reason of anything in the company's memorandum.'

The *ultra vires* doctrine was not, however, abolished on an internal level and the section provided that a member of a company 'may bring proceedings to restrain the doing of an act which, but for sub-s. (1) would be beyond a company's capacity': **s. 35(2)**. The section further provided that the company could ratify an *ultra vires* action by special resolution, but that the directors were liable to indemnify the company in respect of any loss suffered by it irrespective of this ratification unless relieved of their liability by a separate special resolution: **s. 35(3)**.

The legislation failed to take advantage of the second paragraph of **Article 9(1)** and recognized the validity of all acts done in respect of third parties, even where they were aware of the fact that the act was beyond the company's capacity. The only exception was in respect of contracts where the third parties dealing with the company included the directors of the company (or its holding company) and persons connected with them: **s. 35(4)**. In such a situation the company could avoid the contract and, whether avoided or not, the parties to the contract were obliged to indemnify the company for any loss suffered by it and to account for any profits made—directly or indirectly—as a result of the transaction: **CA 1985, s. 322A**.

Thus, after the implementation of the **Companies Act 1989**, the *ultra vires* doctrine no longer posed a problem for third parties who had dealt with the company, and those contracts were able to be enforced by and against the company, but the company's directors were liable to indemnify the company in respect of losses. Members could still, however, prevent proposed actions by the company as being beyond the company's objects. The *ultra vires* doctrine continued to operate in respect of registered companies that were charities: **s. 35(4)**.

The **Companies Act 2006**, based on a recommendation of the Company Law Review (Final Report, paras 9, 10) has adopted a completely different approach. Instead of companies being required to state their objects, companies will have unrestricted objects unless the objects are specifically restricted by the articles. This will mean that unless a company makes a deliberate choice to restrict its objects, the objects will have no bearing on what it can do. Where the company has objects and acts beyond its capacity, the position is now covered by a simplified replacement to **s. 35** which states: 'The validity of an act done by a company shall not be called into question on the ground of lack of capacity by reason of anything in the company's constitution': **s. 39(1)**. In place of imposing liability on the directors in further subsections, the issue of liability of the directors is now covered by **Chapter 2** of **Part 10** relating to the general duties of directors. Under **s. 171**, directors of a company must 'act in accordance with the company's constitution'. Should they enter into any dealings beyond the capacity of the company, liability to account to the company for any losses will now arise under this section.

An exception to this is charitable companies which will need to restrict their objects under charities legislation and in addition some community interest companies may also choose to restrict their objects. The Act makes separate provision for charitable companies which are covered by **CA 2006, s. 42**.

In conclusion, it took the UK government 17 years to draft legislation to implement the **First Company Law** directive in respect of contracts beyond the company's capacity. This is continued in the **Companies Act 2006** which in a radical step, sidesteps the problem by offering companies the possibility of unlimited capacity.

Question 4

Jerry set up Ecotours organizing ecological tourism in the UK. Jerry brought in Lewis, an investor who did not want to be involved in the business. It was agreed to buy an off-the-shelf company and rename it Ecotours Ltd. Jerry was the principal shareholder and managing director; Lewis a non-executive director. The articles required the board's prior consent for contracts over £10,000.

Jerry found an ideal location for the agency and agreed to acquire the lease. He instructed Lee, his solicitor, to take the assignment in the name of Ecotours Ltd. The assignment was completed in January 2008 and a company was acquired and renamed Ecotours Ltd in February 2008.

The assignor, having received a better offer, sought to avoid the assignment in March.

In February, without the board's prior approval, Jerry contracted with Infocon Ltd for a £15,000 computer system. Jerry's wife is a major shareholder in Infocon Ltd.

Advise Jerry and Lewis of the legal position regarding these dealings.

Would your answer be different if, when the assignment was completed, an off-the-shelf company had already been acquired but the company's name had not been changed, and if the major shareholder in Infocon Ltd had been the child of Jerry's girlfriend from her previous marriage?

 ## Commentary

This problem question concerns the topic of pre-incorporation contracts and contracts beyond the authority of directors where the parties include a director of the company or persons connected with him. In respect of pre-incorporation contracts, this requires the application of **CA 2006, s. 51** and decisions based on the **Companies Act 1985**. For contracts beyond the authority of directors, you are required to apply the appropriate sections of the **Companies Acts**, including those concerning the identification of persons connected with directors.

 ## Answer plan

- Identification of the problems raised by the question
- Application of **s. 51(1)** to the assignment of the lease to Ecotours Ltd
- Application of the decision in **Re Braymist** concerning the enforcement of the contract
- Application of **s. 40(1)** to the contract between Ecotours Ltd and Infocon Ltd and recognition of the potential application of **s. 41**
- Analysis of the sections relating to the identification of Infocon Ltd as a person with whom the director of Ecotours Ltd is connected
- Application of **s. 41** and recognition of the legal position of Ecotours Ltd and the liability of the contracting parties
- Consideration of the changed circumstances

Suggested answer

This problem raises the issue of pre-incorporation contracts and their validity and enforceability and the issue of directors acting beyond their authority in respect of transactions with directors or their associates.

In respect of the assignment of the lease, the solicitor has been instructed by Jerry, the managing director of Ecotours Ltd, to take the assignment in the name of Ecotours Ltd at a time before the acquisition by Jerry and Lewis of an off-the-shelf company and its renaming as Ecotours Ltd. This is clearly a pre-incorporation contract, however, on the interpretation of the equivalent section of the **Companies Act 1985** in the case of *Phonogram Ltd v Lane* [1982] **QB 938**. The current equivalent section of the **Companies Act 2006** will apply making the person purporting to act for the company or as agent for it personally liable: **s. 51(1)**.

The legislation merely deals with the issue of liability on the contract and does not concern itself with the issue of the validity and the enforceability of the contract. This was, however, settled by the decision in *Braymist v Wise Finance Co Ltd* [2002] **2 All ER 333**. In a similar situation to this, concerning a contract for the sale of property by an as yet unincorporated company, the buyers attempted to escape from the contract by arguing that, as a pre-incorporation contract, it was void. The court rejected this argument and held that the contract was validated by **CA 1985, s. 36C** (now **CA 2006, s. 51(1)**).

The main issue then to be resolved was whether the person was able to enforce the contract on behalf of the unincorporated company. In that case, on behalf of the company, it was argued that the contract should be enforceable by—among others—the controlling shareholder of the group of companies who had instructed the solicitor to draw up the contracts in the name of the unincorporated company. This was based on the 'identification theory' and the claim that he represented the mind and will of the company: *Tesco Supermarkets Ltd v Nattrass* [1971] **2 All ER 127**. The court rejected this argument and held that the solicitor alone was the 'deemed contracting party' to the contract and that only he could enforce the contract.

Applying this decision to the facts of the present case, the assignment of the lease is valid and it can be enforced against the assignor by Lee, the solicitor instructed by Jerry.

The second aspect of the question involves an unauthorized contract since it is beyond the authority of Jerry as managing director but not beyond the company's capacity. The articles of the company require the prior approval of the board for contracts in excess of £10,000. Jerry has contracted with Infocon Ltd for a computer system costing £15,000. In this respect the contract can only be validated under **CA 2006, s. 40**. This section provides that in favour of a person dealing with the company in good faith, the power of the directors to bind the company, or authorize others to do so, is deemed to be free of any limitation under the company's constitution: **s. 40(1)**.

A further complication here, however, is that the section applies subject to **s. 41** in respect of transactions with directors or their associates: **s. 40(6)**. Where a company enters into a transaction whose validity depends on **s. 40**, and the parties to the transaction include: (a) a director of the company or of its holding company; or (b) a person connected with any such director, the transaction is voidable by the company at the instance of the company: **s. 41(2)**.

Persons connected with directors are as specified in **Part 10 CA 2006, ss. 252–256: s. 41(7)**. Under **s. 252**, connected persons include members of the director's family (**s. 253**) and a body corporate with which the director is connected (as defined in **s. 254**): **s. 252(2)(a)** and **(b)**. Members of the director's family include the director's spouse or civil partner: **s. 253(2)(a)**. As regards a body corporate with which the director is connected, **s. 254** provides that a director is connected with a body corporate if, but only if, he and the persons with whom he is connected: (a) are interested in shares comprised in the equity share capital of that body corporate of a nominal value to at least 20 per cent of that share capital; or (b) are entitled to exercise or control the exercise of more than 20 per cent of the voting power at any general meeting of that body: **s. 254(2)(a)** and **(b)**.

The question informs us that Jerry's wife is a major shareholder in Infocon Ltd. If this shareholding amounts to more than 20 per cent of the equity, Infocon Ltd is a body corporate connected with Jerry and **s. 41** applies. The result of this is that the contract is voidable by Ecotours Ltd (**s. 41(2)**). Whether the contract is avoided or not, Jerry and Infocon Ltd are liable to account to Ecotours Ltd for any direct or indirect gain, and to indemnify the company for any loss or damage: **s. 41(3)**. In respect of Infocon Ltd there is the possibility that the company would escape liability if it could be established that at the time of the transaction it did not know that Jerry was exceeding his powers: **s. 41(5)**.

If, when the assignment had been completed, Jerry and Lewis had already acquired an off-the-shelf company but had not yet changed the company's name to Ecotours Ltd, the position would be as in the case of *Oshkosh B'Gosh Inc v Dan Marbel Inc & Craze* [1989] BCLC 507 and there would be no application of **s. 51(1)**. In that case, Craze acquired an off-the-shelf company, E Ltd, and later changed its name to DM Ltd. Before the change was registered, the company acting through Craze bought goods from the plaintiff. In an action under **s. 9(2) ECA 1972** (now **CA 2006, s. 51(1)**), it was held that the section could not be applied to make Craze personally liable because the company had been formed when the contract was made. The issue of an amended certificate of incorporation did not imply that the company had been re-formed or reincorporated. If this was the case, the assignment of the lease in the question case could be enforced by the company under its new name, Ecotours Ltd.

If the major shareholder in Infocon Ltd had been the son of Jerry's girlfriend's previous marriage the situation would be different, depending on the child's age. Jerry's girlfriend would be connected with him if they lived together in an enduring family relationship: **s. 253(2)(b)**. In addition, any children or step-children of Jerry's girlfriend would also be connected with Jerry, but only if they live with the director and have not attained the age of 18: **s. 253(2)(d)**. If this was the case, the situation would still fall within **CA 2006, s. 41**; otherwise the situation would be that the validity of the contract would be covered by **s. 40(1)**.

Further reading

Ferran, E., 'The reform of the law on corporate capacity and directors' and officers' authority: Parts 1 and 2' [1992] 13 Comp. Law., 124: 177.

Gilmore. P., 'The execution of deeds by a company: the current position in England and Wales' [2010] Comp. Law., 31(1): 3.

Hicks, A., and Goo, S. H., *Cases and Materials on Company Law* (Oxford: Oxford University Press, 6th edn, 2008).

Savirimuthu, J., 'Pre-incorporation contracts and the problem of corporate fundamentalism: are promoters proverbially profuse?' [2003] Comp. Law., 24(7): 196.

Talbot. L.E., 'A contextual analysis of the demise of the doctrine of Ultra Vires in English company law and the rhetoric and reality of enlightened shareholders' [2009] Comp. Law., 30(11): 323.

4

Share capital

Introduction

This chapter deals with:

(a) The categories of share capital

(b) The concept that share capital account (SCA) does not represent the fluctuating net worth of the business, and

(c) Share capital as the creditors' guarantee fund and the doctrine of raising and maintenance of capital

These are complex areas of the law requiring familiarity with the detailed provisions of the **Companies Act 2006 (CA 2006)**.

Categories of share capital

The **Companies Act 2006** abolished the requirement of authorized share capital and companies registered under the Act must include a statement of capital and initial shareholdings as part of the documentation submitted to the Registrar of Companies (ROC). A fresh statement is required on a variation of class rights and any alteration to its share capital.

The different categories of share capital are defined in **CA 2006**: issued and unissued capital (**s. 546(1)(a)**); called-up capital (**s. 547**); and uncalled capital (**s. 257**). They can be illustrated in the diagram on facing page (Figure 4.1).

The share capital account (SCA) and the net worth of the company

The aggregate nominal value of the issued share capital is credited to the share capital account (SCA). On formation, this is equal to the net assets of the company. Once the company begins to trade, the net assets fluctuate according to the success or otherwise of the business. The SCA, however, remains unchanged until the company formally increases or reduces its capital in accordance with powers in the **Companies Act 2006**.

Share capital as the creditors' guarantee fund

Creditors of limited liability companies can only claim against the company's capital, the doctrine of raising and maintenance of capital ensures: (a) the company has raised the capital it claims to have raised; and (b) the capital is not subsequently returned, directly or indirectly, to the shareholders.

Figure 4.1

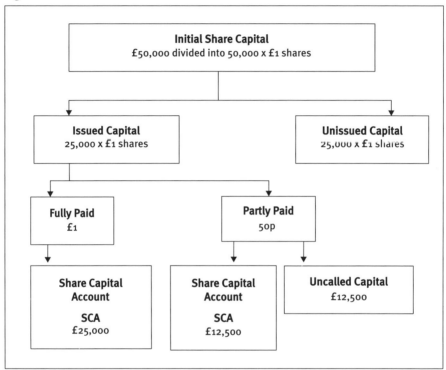

Raising capital

The most important topic under this heading is the issue of the allotment of shares for non-cash consideration. The legal position for public and private companies can be illustrated as set out below.

Public companies

    (a) No issue against performance of future personal services (**s. 585**)

    (b) Minimum payment pre-allotment—one-quarter of nominal value and all of any premium paid up (**s. 586**)

    (c) Time limit for long-term undertaking, performed or performable within five years (**s. 587**)

    (d) Valuation, report to company six months before allotment (**ss. 593 and 597**)

Private companies

(a) Shares can be issued in consideration of an undertaking to perform future services

(b) No minimum payment on issue/allotment

(c) No time limits for transfer of assets/performance of undertaking

(d) No control on valuation: *Re Wragg Ltd* [1897] 1 Ch 796

Capital maintenance

The rule in *Trevor v Whitworth* (1887) **12 App Cas 409** established that a company could not buy its own shares. The rule, now subject to important exceptions, is restated in CA 2006, **s. 658(1)**. The exceptions are:

- Acquisition of fully paid shares otherwise than for valuable consideration: **s. 659(1)**
- Acquisition of shares in a reduction of capital: **ss. 641–657**
- Purchase in pursuance of a court order under various sections including **ss. 994–996** (protection of members against unfair prejudice): **s. 659**
- Purchase of own shares as treasury shares: **ss. 724–732**

The rules also cover:

- The payment of dividends: **ss. 830–847**
- Financial assistance for the acquisition of shares in a public company: **ss. 678–680**

Shares may be issued for more than their nominal value: shares issued at a premium. The aggregate amount or value of the premiums must be transferred to a Share Premium Account (SPA): **s. 610(1)**. This account is also subject to the capital maintenance provisions (**s. 610(3)**) subject to statutory exceptions. The same is true for the Capital Redemption Reserve (CRR): **s. 733**. You must be aware of these two quasi-capital accounts and the doctrine of capital maintenance.

Question 1

Commenting on the procedure laid down in the **Second EC Directive (Companies Act 1985, ss. 96–116; Companies Act 2006, Part 17, Chapter 6, ss. 593–597)** regulating the issue of shares in a public company for a non-cash consideration, L.S. Sealy (2001) calls it 'a very elaborate (and costly) procedure ...: a pretty large sledgehammer to crack a fairly small nut'.

Explain the procedure and the consequences of their breach for the company, the allottees, and subsequent shareholders and consider to what extent Sealy's comment is fair.

Commentary

This question picks up the topic of raising capital and the regulation of the allotment of shares for non-cash consideration with particular concern for the position of public companies. You are required to be aware of the slack regulation of this area at common law from the end of the nineteenth century right up to the implementation in the **Companies Act 1980** of the **Second EC Directive on Company Law**. In addition to explaining the operation of the regulatory system now in **CA 2006**, you are called upon to comment on whether indeed such complex and expensive regulation can be justified.

 Answer plan

- The regulation that existed at common law prior to the **Companies Act 1980** for both private and public companies
- The post-1980 position introduced by the **Companies Act 1980** and how the regulations ensure that the company actually raises the capital that it claims to have raised including discussion of the position of the allottee and subsequent holders
- The possibility of relief against liability on application to the court
- The stricter controls applicable during the initial period of a company's existence
- Analysis of the applicable regulations in the light of LS Sealy's comment

Suggested answer

The courts in the nineteenth and twentieth centuries recognized the importance of a company's share capital as the creditors' guarantee fund even before the decision in *Salomon v Salomon & Co Ltd* settled the fact that the incorporators of a company were not liable to indemnify the company's creditors. They elaborated detailed rules to ensure that companies raised the capital they claimed to have raised and then retained that capital in the business and did not return it—directly or indirectly—to the shareholders.

In relation to raising capital, *Ooregum Gold Mining Co of India v Roper* [1892] AC 125 established that companies could not issue shares at a discount to their nominal value. In this case, the company sought to raise capital by issuing preference shares credited as paid up to 75 per cent of their nominal value since the company's ordinary shares were already trading below their nominal value. In a subsequent decision, the court held that companies could not allot their shares for past consideration since past consideration was no consideration: *Re Eddystone Marine Insurance Co* [1893] 3 Ch 9. The protection offered by these decisions was weakened, however, by decisions during the 1870s to the effect that companies could allot shares in return for property and services. This issue was settled by the Court of Appeal which endorsed the practice and held that, in the absence of fraud, the value received by the company in respect of its shares could not be inquired into: *Re Wragg Ltd* [1897] 1 Ch 796.

This continued to be the position until the UK was obliged to implement the strict capital raising regulations imposed on Member States in respect of public companies by the **Second European Directive on Company Law**. It remains the position for private companies. The Second Directive was implemented in the Companies Act 1980 and the provisions are now in **CA 2006, Chapters 5** and **6** of **Part 17, ss. 580–609.** The rationale of the rules is to ensure that the company receives the aggregate nominal capital and any premium.

The legal position for all companies, public or private, is that shares cannot be allotted at a discount: **s. 580(1)**. If shares are allotted in contravention of this section, the allottee of the shares is liable to pay the company an amount equal to the discount, with interest at the appropriate rate: **s. 580(2)**. The appropriate rate is fixed at 5 per cent: **s. 592**.

Additional rules cover the position for public companies. Thus, shares taken by the subscriber to the memorandum of a company, and any premium, must be paid up in cash: **s. 584**. More importantly, public companies cannot accept in payment of their shares or any premium an undertaking to work or perform services for the company or for another person: **s. 585(1)**. If a company acts in breach of this provision, the holder of the shares is liable to pay an amount equal to their nominal value and any premium plus interest at the appropriate rate: **s. 585(2)**.

Public companies are also prohibited from allotting their shares unless they are paid up at least as to one quarter of their nominal value and the whole of any premium: **s. 586(1)**. In the event of breach of this provision, the share is to be treated as if one-quarter of its nominal value plus the whole of any premium had been received and the allottee is liable to pay the minimum amount which should have been received by the company, with interest at the appropriate rate: **s. 586(3)**. Public companies are further restricted in that they must not allot shares otherwise than in cash if the consideration is or includes an undertaking which is to be, or may be, performed more than five years from the date of the allotment: **s. 587(1)**. In the event of breach of this provision, the allottee is liable to pay the company an amount equal to the aggregate of their nominal value and the whole of any premium, with interest at the appropriate rate: **s. 587(2)**.

The Act further provides for the joint and several liability of subsequent holders of any shares issued in breach of these provisions with the exception of persons who are purchasers for value of the shares who, at the time of their acquisition, did not have actual notice of a contravention of the law, or who acquired the shares from a subsequent holder who was not liable: **s. 588(1)** and **(2)**.

The harshness of the law is softened by a statutory power of the court to grant relief in the event of liability in respect of contravention of **ss. 585, 587,** and **588: s. 589(1)**. The court can grant exemption to applicants but only if and to the extent that it is just and equitable having regard to whether the applicant has paid or is liable to pay any amount in respect of any other liability in respect of those shares under **Chapter 5** or **6,** or arising by virtue of any undertaking in connection with the payment of the shares; whether any other person has paid or is likely to pay any such amount or whether the applicant or any other person has performed in whole or in part, or is likely to perform any such undertaking, or has done or is likely to do any other thing in payment or part payment for the shares: **s. 589(3)**. An example of an unsuccessful application for relief under **CA 1985** is *Re Bradford Investments plc* (No 2) **[1991] BCLC 688**. In this case, four members of a partnership converted a dormant private company into a public company and transferred the partnership business to it in consideration of the allotment of 1,059,000 fully paid £1 ordinary shares. Subsequently, the company claimed £1,059,000 from them as the issue price. Their application for relief was rejected as the court was not satisfied that the business had any value when it was transferred to the company. In addition, the Act provides that the breach of any provision in **Chapter 5** constitutes an offence by the company and every officer of the company in default and that persons convicted are liable to a fine: **s. 590**.

A further control over public companies is the legal requirement for the valuation of any non-cash consideration. Thus a public company must not allot shares as fully or partly paid up as to nominal value or any premium unless the consideration has been independently valued, with a copy of the valuer's report given to the company within six months immediately preceding the allotment and a copy to the allottee: **s. 593**. The legal regulations relating to the valuation are laid down in **s. 596** and must be complied with. In addition, a copy of the valuation report must be sent to the registrar of companies at the same time as it is delivered to the company: **s. 597**. In the event of breach of **s. 593**, the allottee is liable to pay the company an amount equal to the aggregate of the nominal value of the shares, the whole of any premium plus interest at the appropriate rate (5 per cent—**s. 609**): **s. 593(3)**. The valuation requirement is subject to exceptions under **s. 594** (arrangement with another company) and **s. 595** (merger).

Even more stringent regulations apply to agreements for transfer of a non-cash asset to a company within the company's initial period where the transferor is a subscriber to the memorandum and where the transfer is equal in value to one-tenth or more of the company's issued share capital: **s. 598**. The initial period is two years from the date of the issue of a trading certificate under **s. 761**. The conditions to which the section refers are a requirement for independent valuation (**s. 599**) and approval of the members (**s. 601**). The independent valuation must comply with **s. 600** and also **ss. 1150–1153**. The need for independent valuation under **s. 599** does not affect the need for an independent valuation under **s. 593** where the transfer is in consideration of shares.

In respect of non-compliance with **s. 593**, the Act makes subsequent holders of the shares jointly and severally liable with any other person so liable subject to exemption for a purchaser for value without notice or a person acquiring from such a person: **s. 605**. The court has power to grant relief from liability equivalent to **s. 589** and the Act also provides for the criminal liability of the company and every officer in default: **s. 607**.

The question of whether the current regulation of public companies is excessive in this respect will probably depend upon the stance of the commentator. The law certainly imposes complex and costly obligations on the company which will be seen as excessive by company officers. In the light of the current stress on transparency and corporate governance, however, the rules can be seen as great progress and a means of ensuring investor confidence—something that is completely lacking in the case of private companies.

It is clear that the regulations provide protection against obvious areas of potential abuse and, in so doing, ensure that the company does receive the capital that it declares it has received.

There are aspects of the provisions which seem at odds with the aims of the legislation. The need for copies of the valuation report under **s. 593** to be circulated to the allottee seems unnecessary. In addition, the fact of making the company criminally liable for breach of provisions under both **Chapters 5** and **6** is illogical and contradictory. While imposing a fine on officers in default can be defended, there is no logic in fining the company.

Question 2

In March 2008, Utopia plc issued 2,500,000 £1 ordinary shares to Adam in consideration of the transfer to the company of four printing machines valued at £750,000 each and Adam's services as a design consultant for one year valued at £50,000. The first machine was delivered when the shares were allotted, but the others are to be delivered over the next two years as Adam's own printing business is run down. Adam transferred 500,000 of these shares to his wife, and 100,000 to each of his four children.

Consider the legality of the share issue and the potential liability of the parties.

Commentary

This problem question requires you to apply the law relating to the allotment of shares in a public company for non-cash consideration to a factual situation. In particular it concentrates on the requirement that a public company cannot allot shares unless it receives as a minimum one-quarter of the aggregate nominal value and all of any premium.

Answer plan

- Statement of the law relevant to the question: issue of shares at a premium, issue for less than the statutory minimum, absence of statutory valuation
- Liability of the allottee and subsequent holders
- Possibility of relief by the court
- Criminal liability of company and directors in default

Suggested answer

The legal issues raised by this question are the law relating to the allotment of shares by a public company for non-cash consideration. The relevant law is contained in **Chapters 5** and **6** of **Part 17 CA 2006** and in particular in **ss. 585, 586, 588, 589,** and **590**. The question also requires consideration of **ss. 593** and **596** and **s. 610**.

In this case, a public company has agreed to allot shares to Adam with an aggregate nominal value of £2.5m in return for a transfer to the company by Adam of four printing machines valued at £750,000 each and an undertaking to act as a design consultant for one year valued at £50,000. The aggregate value of the consideration for the share issue is on the face of it £3,050,000. Since the aggregate nominal value of the shares allotted is less than the apparent value of the non-cash consideration, it is clear that this is an issue of shares at a premium of £550,000.

In accepting an undertaking to do work or perform services as consideration for the allotment, the company is in breach of **s. 585(1)**. As a result, Adam would be liable to pay to the company an amount equal to the nominal value of the shares, together with the whole of the premium, and to pay interest at the appropriate rate as fixed by **s. 592: s. 585(2)**.

In the immediate, the company has allotted 2.5 million shares to Adam against the transfer to it of only one of the machines, with the remaining three machines to be transferred to it over the next two years. The performance of the service as a design consultant is also postponed to a future date. The company has as a result transferred shares with an aggregate nominal value of £2.5m in return for an immediate consideration of £750,000. As a result, the company is also in breach of a prohibition from allotting shares except as paid up at least to one-quarter of their nominal value and the whole of any premium: **s. 586(1)**. If the company allots shares in breach of this provision, the shares are to be treated as if one-quarter of their nominal value, together with the whole of any premium, had been received and the allottee is liable to pay the company the minimum amount which should have been received in respect of the allotment: **s. 586(3)**. The minimum amount that should have been transferred to the company on allotment is one-quarter of £2.5m, namely £625,000 plus the total amount of the premium of £550,000, ie a total of £1,175,000. The company must credit the amount of £625,000 to the Share Capital Account and £550,000 to the Share Premium Account and Adam must pay an amount to bring his contribution to the company up to the required minimum—a contribution of a further £425,000.

A further complication is that we are told that the machines are valued at £750,000 each but there does not appear to have been a valuation report in accordance with **s. 593** in respect of an independent valuation in accordance with **s. 596(1)**; a valuer's report to the company in the six months immediately preceding the allotment of the shares and a copy of the report to the allottee. There is also no mention of a copy of such a report having been delivered to the Registrar in accordance with **s. 597**. If there has been a breach of **s. 593(1)**, Adam, the allottee, is liable to pay the company the aggregate amount of the nominal value of the shares, the whole of the premium, and interest at the appropriate rate: **s. 593(3)**.

Adam's wife and four children have since received 900,000 of these shares. The fact that some of these shares have been transferred to Adam's wife and children means that the wife and children will be jointly and severally liable along with Adam in respect of the amounts for which he is liable under **ss. 585** and **586** unless they are purchasers for value without notice of the shares: **s. 588**. There is also joint and several liability for breach of **s. 593**: **s. 605**. The court has power to grant relief to Adam and his wife and children under both **s. 589** and **s. 606** and the sections clearly rule out any double jeopardy for Adam and his wife and children.

If this agreement to transfer four machines and to provide advice as a design consultant has been honoured or is likely to be honoured, there is a probability that Adam, his wife and children will be exempt from liability in whole or in part. The burden of proof would be on Adam and his family to establish that the company has received either total or partial consideration for the share allotment. A successful claim was made under *Re Ossory Estates plc* [1988] BCLC 213. In this case the vendor of property to the company received eight million shares as part of the consideration for the sale. No report and valuation of the property had been made in accordance with **CA 1985, s. 103** (equivalent to **CA 2006, s. 593**) and a claim was made against the allottee for payment of £1.76m for the price of the shares. The court, however, granted relief under **CA 1985, s. 113** (now **CA 2006, s. 606**) on the grounds that the company had sold some of the property at a substantial profit and had undoubtedly received at least money or money's worth equal to the aggregate nominal value of the shares and any premium.

Even if Adam and his family escape liability in whole or in part, the company and any officers of the company in default have committed criminal offences for contravention of the provisions against allotment in return for personal services, non-compliance with the minimum payment requirement, and the failure to undertake a valuation in accordance with **s. 593**. This means that they are liable to a fine on conviction under **s. 590** (for offences in **Chapter 5** of **Part 17**) and **s. 607** (for offences in **Chapter 6, Part 17**).

Question 3

The rules relating to maintenance of capital of a limited liability company with a share capital are designed to protect the company's creditors for whom the company's capital is a guarantee fund.

In this context, analyse the function of the law relating to—

(a) The role of the capital redemption reserve in the redemption or purchase by a company of its own shares, and

(b) Controls on the payment of dividends for public and private companies

Commentary

This question relates to the rule in *Trevor v Whitworth* since the passing of the **Companies Act 1981.** This allows companies to acquire their own shares but subject to stringent rules to ensure that there is no breach of the doctrine of maintenance of capital. As an aspect of the same doctrine, it also concerns the regulation of the payment of dividends post the **Companies Act 1980** recognizing the legal distinction between private and public companies.

You are required to show understanding of the common law rules that operated before 1980/1981 and the ways in which those rules were deficient in that they were either too rigid (in the case of companies acquiring their own shares) or too lax (in respect of the payment of dividends).

Having analysed the pre-1981 common law position, you must cover the reform of the law and show in what way it is relevant to and acts to promote the protection of creditors.

Answer plan

- The doctrinal basis of the common law rule in *Trevor v Whitworth* and the regulation of the payment of dividends
- The changes introduced post **Companies Act 1981** and the relaxation of the rule in *Trevor v Whitworth*
- The need for the Capital Redemption Reserve where the company redeems or buys its shares out of distributable profits as opposed to the proceeds of a fresh issue of shares
- The position regarding companies holding shares as treasury shares
- The basis of the reform of the law relating to the payment of dividends and the relevance of the distinction made between the regulation of public and private companies
- As a conclusion, an analysis of how effectively the regulation of these two areas operates to protect the company's creditors

Suggested answer

The rules relating to capital maintenance have their origin in the common law. The rule in *Trevor v Whitworth* (1887) **12 App Cas 409** established that a company could not buy its own shares since this would be a reduction of capital which could only be achieved through a formal, statutory procedure. The common law also established that companies were prohibited from paying dividends out of capital since this was also a way of returning capital to shareholders: *Re Exchange Banking Co, Flitcroft's Case* (1882) **21 Ch D 519**. The common law rules relating to dividends were flawed, however, in that there was no restriction against the payment of dividends out of current trading profits without making provision for the depreciation of fixed assets: *Lee v*

Neuchatel Asphalte Co (1889) **41 Ch D 1**. Companies could also pay dividends out of profits without making good losses in fixed capital: *Verner v General & Commercial Investment Trust* [1894] **2 Ch 239**; or to make good past revenue losses: *Ammonia Soda Co Ltd v Chamberlain* [1918] **1 Ch 266**. The court also decided that dividends could be paid out of unrealized profits: *Dimbula Valley (Ceylon) Tea Co Ltd v Laurie* [1961] **Ch 353**.

The position changed when the **Second EC Directive (No 77/91/EEC)** was transposed into UK law in the **Companies Act 1980**. This imposed stringent controls over public companies. In respect of the payment of dividends, the common law rules were replaced by statutory provisions which distinguished between private and public companies with the latter being more severely regulated to ensure capital maintenance.

The **Companies Act 1981** created a further radical change in the law by allowing companies to purchase their own shares in controlled circumstances. The rule in *Trevor v Whitworth* had already been modified in 1929 when the law was changed to allow companies to redeem (buy back and cancel) shares issued as redeemable preference shares. After the **Companies Act 1981**, the power to issue redeemable shares was extended to cover shares of all categories: ordinary, preference, and deferred. A further modification to the rule came in the decision in *Re Castiglione's Will Trusts* [1958] **Ch 549** where fully paid shares gifted to the company but held by a nominee on the company's behalf were held not to violate the rule in *Trevor v Whitworth*. In a further major change to the law, the blanket prohibition on companies acquiring their own shares was made subject to numerous exceptions when companies could buy their own shares subject to complex regulatory rules. The effect of these regulations was to ensure creditor protection while allowing companies greater flexibility.

The Capital Redemption Reserve (CRR) relates to the cancellation of shares redeemed under **s. 688(b)** or the cancellation of shares purchased under **s. 706(b)(ii)** and is designed to ensure respect for the capital maintenance rules.

Companies redeeming or purchasing their own shares can finance the purchase by the proceeds of a fresh issue of shares or out of distributable profits, defined as profits out of which the company could lawfully make a distribution: **s. 736**.

If the shares are purchased or redeemed out of the proceeds of a fresh issue of shares, then there is no reduction in the company's share capital account since the new issue takes the place of the old. Thus, if a company wishes to redeem an issue of 1 million 7 per cent preference shares and does so by issuing 1 million 3 per cent preference shares and using the capital raised to redeem the 7 per cent issue, the company's capital is maintained since the aggregate nominal value of the new issue replaces the cancelled issue.

Where, however, the redemption or purchase is out of distributable profits, the company's capital is reduced. In order to maintain its capital, the company must transfer the aggregate nominal value of the redeemed or purchased issue to the CRR: **s. 733(2)**. The same is true where the redemption or purchase is wholly or partly out of the proceeds of a fresh issue and the aggregate amount of those proceeds is less than the aggregate nominal value of the shares redeemed or purchased. In that event, the amount of the difference must be transferred to the CRR: **s. 733(3)**. The CRR is a capital account and the provisions relating to the reduction of a company's share capital apply as if the capital redemption reserve were part of its paid up share capital: **s. 733(6)**. The company may, however, use the capital redemption reserve to pay up new shares to be allotted to members as fully paid bonus shares: **s. 733(5)**.

Companies may hold their own market traded shares as treasury shares subject to **s. 724**. The holding is limited to 10 per cent of the nominal value of the issued capital of the company where the company has only one class of share (**s. 725(1)**) or to 10 per cent of the aggregate nominal value of each class of shares where the share capital is divided into shares of different classes: **s. 725(2)**. If the company subsequently cancels shares held as treasury shares, the company's capital is reduced by the nominal amount of the shares cancelled: **s. 729(4)**. In this event, the company is also required to transfer to the CRR the amount by which the company's share capital is diminished: **s. 733(4)**.

The statutory rules relating to distributions: the payment of dividends, is now in **CA 2006, Part 23**. Distributions can only be made out of profits available for the purpose: **s. 830(1)**. These are its 'accumulated, realised profits, so far as not previously utilised by distribution or capitalisation, less its accumulated, realised losses, so far as not previously written off in a reduction or reorganisation of capital duly made': **s. 830(2)**. There are special rules for investment companies—accumulated revenue profits see **ss. 832–835**.

For the purposes of identifying realized profits, the Act provides that where, on the revaluation of a fixed asset, an unrealized profit is shown to have been made, and on or after the revaluation, a sum is written off or retained for depreciation of that asset over a period, an amount equal to the amount by which that sum exceeds the sum that would have been so written off or retained for the depreciation of that asset over that period, if that profit had not been made, is treated as a realized profit made over that period: **s. 841(5)**.

This is the position for private companies. Public companies are subject to more stringent rules and may only make a distribution if: (a) the amount of its net assets is not less than the aggregate of its called-up share capital and undistributable reserves; and (b) if, and to the extent that, the distribution does not reduce the amount of those assets to less than that aggregate: **s. 831(1)**. A company's undistributable reserves are its:

(a) share premium account

(b) capital redemption reserve

(c) the revaluation reserve (the amount by which its accumulated, unrealized profits exceed its accumulated, unrealized losses), and

(d) other reserves that the company is prohibited from distributing:

  (i) by any enactment, or

  (ii) by its articles: **s. 831(4)**

Shareholders are liable to repay any distribution if they know or have reasonable grounds for believing that the distribution was illegal: **s. 847(2)**.

In conclusion it can be seen that the function of the capital redemption reserve serves to maintain the company's share capital in the event of the company redeeming or purchasing shares wholly or partly out of distributable profits by ensuring that the company transfers the aggregate of that amount to an account that is subject to the rules on capital reduction. In so doing, it operates to protect the company's creditors. In respect of the payment of dividends, public companies cannot make a distribution that would reduce their net assets to below the aggregate of their undistributable reserves. This operates so as to maintain the company's capital. The position for creditors of private companies is less protected but certainly the anomalies of the position under the common law by which distributions could potentially be made out of capital have been removed.

Question 4

Owen, the MD of Grand Designs (GD) plc, a property development company, is the major shareholder with 5 million shares. In negotiations to bring into the company Peter, a wealthy businessman, Owen agrees on behalf of GD plc to acquire a property with planning permission for commercial development from Peter for £3m. Peter then obtained an unsecured loan of £2m from the South Bank and purchased 50 per cent of Owen's shareholding in GD plc for £5m.

Peter joined the board of GD plc, and shortly after, GD plc created a floating charge over its property portfolio to secure Peter's loan from the South Bank.

Consider:

(a) the legality of these transactions entered into by GD plc, and

(b) the rights and liabilities of Owen, Peter, and the South Bank

 Commentary

This question calls upon you to show familiarity with and the ability to apply the law prohibiting public companies from giving financial assistance for the acquisition of their shares or the shares in their holding company. The law in this area has been greatly simplified by **CA 2006** but many of the judicial decisions under previous **Companies Acts** are of relevance in analysing the situation and reaching a conclusion.

The question requires you to recognize and distinguish between contemporaneous and subsequent financial assistance and of the principal purpose defence that can be raised by the company. It also requires you to consider the criminal and civil liability of the parties and the validity of charges issued in the course of any financial assistance.

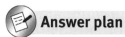

Answer plan

- Definition of financial assistance and the distinction between contemporaneous and subsequent financial assistance
- Identification of the transactions that are potential breaches of the law and the possibility of their falling within the scope of the principal purpose defence
- Analysis of the limitations imposed on this defence by the decision in *Brady v Brady*
- Civil liability of the parties and the validity of the floating charge
- Criminal liability of the company and directors in default

Suggested answer

This problem raises the question of whether GD plc has been guilty of the offence of financial assistance in respect of facilitating the financing of Peter's purchase of 50 per cent of Owen's shareholding in the company. There are two situations which could constitute financial assistance: the purchase by GD plc of the commercial property from Peter for £3m and the creation of a floating charge over the company's property portfolio to secure Peter's previously unsecured loan of £2m from the South Bank.

Financial assistance is defined in **s. 677** and the definition includes financial assistance given by way of a guarantee, security, or indemnity: **s. 677(1)(b)(i)** (which covers the creation of the floating charge) and any other financial assistance given by the company where the net assets of the company are reduced to a material extent by the giving of the assistance: **s. 677(1)(d)(i)** (this could potentially cover the purchase of Peter's property if the purchase price is in excess of the value of the property acquired). In *Belmont Finance Corpn Ltd v Williams Furniture Ltd* [1979] Ch 250 four directors of the defendant company, with the connivance of two of the three directors of the plaintiff company, had sold its property worth £60,000 for the price of £500,000. The four directors then used the money to purchase all the issued shares in the plaintiff company for £489,000. The Court of Appeal held that the transaction was illegal financial assistance and a breach of what is now **CA 2006, s. 678(1)**. Even if the purchase of the property is at a fair value, it could be argued that, if the principal purpose of the purchase was to provide Peter with the funds to acquire Owen's shares, this could constitute illegal financial assistance. This was the point made by Hoffmann J in *Charterhouse Investment Trust Ltd v Tempest Diesels Ltd* [1986] BCLC 1.

The law recognizes two types of financial assistance: contemporaneous financial assistance and subsequent financial assistance, and both are prohibited: **s. 678**.

As regards contemporaneous financial assistance, the offence is described as follows. Where a person is acquiring or proposing to acquire shares in a public company, it is not lawful for that company, or a company that is a subsidiary of that company, to give financial assistance directly or indirectly for the purpose of the acquisition before or at the same time as the acquisition takes place: **s. 678(1)**. This could potentially cover the purchase of the commercial property from Peter which occurred prior to Peter's acquisition of Owen's shares.

Subsequent financial assistance is where a person has acquired shares in a company, and a liability has been incurred for the purpose of the acquisition by that or another person. In such a situation, it is not lawful for that company, or a subsidiary of that company, to give financial assistance directly or indirectly for the purpose of reducing or discharging the liability if, at the time the assistance is given, the company in which the shares were acquired is a public company: **s. 678(3)**. By issuing a floating charge to secure Peter's previously unsecured loan from the South Bank, GD plc is guilty of subsequent financial assistance since, in the event of Peter defaulting on the loan, the South Bank could enforce the floating charge against GD plc's assets. This is an example of indirect financial assistance in that the charge is created in favour of the South Bank rather than the actual person benefiting from the financial assistance.

Exceptionally, the law does not prevent a subsidiary which is a foreign company from giving financial assistance for the acquisition of shares in its holding company: *Arab Bank plc v Mercantile Holdings Ltd* [1994] 2 All ER 74.

Both of these offences are subject to the principal purpose defence under which the company can escape liability on the ground that the company's principal purpose in giving the assistance is not to give it for the purpose of any such acquisition (in the case of contemporaneous financial assistance) or to reduce or discharge any liability incurred (in the case of subsequent financial assistance), or that the giving of the assistance (or the reduction or discharge) is only an incidental part of some larger purpose of the company, and the assistance is given in good faith in the interests of the company: **s. 678(2) and (4)**.

The scope of this defence was severely restricted by the House of Lords' decision in *Brady v Brady* [1989] AC 755 where it rejected the decision of the High Court and the Court of Appeal that financial assistance as part of a major company reorganization to resolve the conflict and deadlock between the two brothers who controlled it and to avoid its likely liquidation fell within the exception. The House of Lords held that the larger purpose must be something more than the reason why the transaction was entered into.

It would not be possible, therefore, for GD plc to argue that the financial assistance is to achieve the larger purpose of bringing Peter and his expertise into the company.

In respect of the purchase of Peter's property, if this was a purchase at a substantial overvaluation, Owen could be liable to account to the company for any loss to the company in breach of his fiduciary duties. In addition, if Peter received the consideration knowing that the transaction was improper and an abuse of Owen's fiduciary duties, he could also be liable as a constructive trustee to account to GD plc: *Belmont Finance Corpn Ltd v Williams Furniture Ltd* (No 2) [1980] 1 All ER 393; *Royal Brunei Airlines Sdn Bhd v Tan Kok Ming* [1995] 2 AC 378. It is also possible for the company to sue Owen and Peter for damages for conspiracy, despite the company being a party to the transaction: *Belmont Finance Corpn Ltd v Williams Furniture Ltd* [1979] Ch 250. It could also be illegal financial assistance even where the purchase was not at an over-value if the principal purpose behind the purchase was not the acquisition of a property for the company but to facilitate Peter's share acquisition.

In respect of the creation of the floating charge over GD plc's assets to secure the unsecured loan obtained by Peter from the South Bank, the charge will be illegal and unenforceable against the company by the bank: *Heald v O'Connor* [1971] 1 WLR 497.

Prohibited financial assistance is a criminal offence committed by the company and every officer of the company who is in default: **s. 680(1)**. A person convicted on indictment is liable to imprisonment for a term not exceeding two years and/or a fine. On summary conviction they are liable in England and Wales to imprisonment for a term not exceeding 12 months and/or a fine not exceeding the statutory maximum: **s. 680(2)**.

Further reading

Daehnert, A., 'The minimum capital requirement—an anachronism under conservation: Parts 1 & 2' [2009], Comp. Law., 30(1): 3 and 30(2): 34.

Judge, S., 'When is the capital maintenance rule breached?' [2011] F. & C.L. May: 5.

Pickering, M. A., 'Shareholder voting rights and company control' [1965] 81 LQR: 248.

Proctor, C., 'Financial Assistance: new proposals and new perspectives?' [2007] Comp. Law., 28(1): 3.

5

Loan capital

Introduction

This chapter deals with long-term borrowing by companies and introduces the following important topics:

(a) The legal nature of and the various forms of debentures issued by companies

(b) The legal distinction between fixed and floating charges created by companies over their assets as security for loans

(c) The registration of charges and the consequences of non-registration or late registration, and

(d) The priority of charges in an insolvency and the avoidance of charges under the **Insolvency Act 1986 (IA 1986)**

This is a complex area of the law largely as a result of the fact that there is no real legal or commercial definition of a debenture, and that the distinction between fixed and floating charges has become blurred since 1979 with the result that it is not always clear whether a particular charge is fixed or floating. The criteria for identifying fixed and floating charges is an area of great importance for students of company law.

The topic of the registration of charges presents less of a problem but there are interesting legal aspects relating to the conclusive nature of the certificate of registration issued by the Registrar of Companies (ROC). There was an attempt at major reform of this area of the law in the **1989 Companies Act** but this was never implemented and the **Companies Act 2006 (CA 2006)** largely re-enacts the position under the **Companies Act 1985**.

This topic overlaps with that of corporate insolvency in the sense that it is possible for the liquidator of a company to set aside charges created by companies in the run up to the commencement of insolvency. The importance of this is that it releases assets that would otherwise be the preserve of the secured creditor to be distributed to unsecured creditors. In this respect, it is important to understand the increased vulnerability of floating charges as against fixed charges. In the context of corporate insolvency, it is also important to be aware of the clear advantage of the secured creditor with a fixed charge over the secured creditor with a floating charge. The former ranks above all other creditors, including the expenses of the liquidation, while the latter ranks in a lowly position just above the ordinary, unsecured creditors.

Question 1

'In my opinion a debenture means a document which either creates a debt or acknowledges it, and any document which fulfils either of these conditions is a 'debenture'. I cannot find any precise legal definition of the term, it is not either in law or commerce a strictly technical term, or what is called a term of art.'

(Per Chitty J: *Levy v Abercorris Slate and Slab Co* (1887) 37 Ch D 260)

Discuss.

 ## Commentary

This essay question requires you to consider this definition of a debenture and compare and contrast it to the statutory definition in order to see whether something more precise can emerge. In effect, the statutory definition is even less informative than this judicial pronouncement of 120 years ago. The problem essentially is the wide range of debentures that can be identified and you need to analyse the differences between them. An essential area of confusion is that the term can be used to cover the acknowledgement of unsecured loans as well as referring to a document that identifies and creates a charge over the company's assets as security for the charge.

 ## Answer plan

- Statutory definition of debenture and different types of debenture: single, debentures in a series, and debenture stock
- Secured and unsecured debentures
- Perpetual, redeemable, and convertible debentures
- Registered and bearer debentures
- Priority of debenture holders in company insolvency

Suggested answer

The statutory definition of a debenture as including 'debenture stock, bonds and any other securities of a company, whether or not constituting a charge on the assets of the company' (CA 2006, s. 738) is every bit as non-informative as this judicial attempt at a definition at the end of the nineteenth century. The source of the problem in establishing a clear definition is that the term 'debenture' covers an enormous spectrum of instruments in connection with corporate borrowing—simply any document evidencing a debt of any kind.

The most confusing aspect of the definition is the reference to the existence of an instrument as a debenture 'whether or not constituting a charge on the assets of the company'. In spite of this, both in commercial usage and as generally understood, the term refers to a document evidencing a loan secured by charges over the company's assets. In recognition of this, the Listing Rules require that any issue of unsecured debentures should be referred to as an 'unsecured debenture' and in practice it is more common in that situation to avoid the term altogether and use a term such as 'loan stock' or 'loan notes' as an alternative.

The definition also encompasses single debentures where the company issues an instrument acknowledging its indebtedness to a single lender. This is a typical transaction between a company and the company's bank and the instrument will generally be in the standard form of the bank. A debenture can also be created in favour of a single loan raised from a number of creditors. In this case there will be a number of instruments issued by the company in a series evidencing the company's indebtedness and usually secured by charges over the company's assets. This is called a debenture in a series and the individual debenture holders will rank as creditors equally (*in pari passu*) in the event of the default or insolvency of the company. If this form of loan is secured on the company's assets, the instrument will create charges in favour of a trustee for the debenture holders; normally a trust corporation or an insurance company by means of a trust deed.

The most complex form of debenture is debenture stock (sometimes referred to as bonds). This will concern a quoted company whose securities are listed on the Stock Exchange or a secondary market. The company will raise a loan which will be converted to stock in the sense that the total loan will be divided into units of currency (£1). Investors advancing money to the company will be issued debenture stock certificates evidencing their total personal loan to the company forming part of the total loan. The advantage to the investor is that the debenture stock can be traded on the stock market in the same way as shares. The statutory provisions for transfer of securities apply to shares and debentures: ss. 770–778 and ss. 783–787. If the issue is secured, the company will once again create charges over its assets by way of a trust deed to a trust corporation or insurance company which will hold the charges on trust for the debenture stock holders.

The advantage of a trust deed in both debentures in a series and debenture stock is that the company can deal with the trustee should it wish to amend the details of the charged property. It is also an advantage to the debenture holders since the trustee could also be appointed a director of the company to oversee and protect the debenture holders' interests.

The major difference between a debenture secured by a charge over the company's property rather than a mortgage is that a debenture can be perpetual. The **Companies Act** provides that debentures or a deed for securing debentures is not invalid simply because the debentures are: (a) irredeemable; or (b) redeemable only: (i) on the happening of a contingency (however remote); or (ii) on the expiration of a period (however long), any rule of equity notwithstanding: **CA 2006, s. 739.**

The reference to the rule of equity is to the rule against 'clogging' the equity of redemption of a mortgage. This refers to inserting terms into the mortgage restricting the mortgagor's right to redeem the mortgage beyond a reasonable time. In *Knightsbridge Estates Trust Ltd v Byrne* **[1940] AC 613,** the House of Lords held that a mortgage of a freehold property by the appellants to Byrne, with a covenant to repay the money by 80 half-yearly instalments, was a debenture and not a mortgage, and that the postponement of the right to redeem for 40 years was not void as a clog on the equity of redemption.

A further distinction is that there can be registered debentures and bearer debentures, although bearer instruments are extremely rare in the UK. If the debentures are registered, then the company has a legal obligation to register an issue of debentures as soon as practicable but in any event within two months of their allotment: **s. 741.** Where the company issue is debenture stock, the company must issue debenture stock certificates within two months of the allotment: **s. 769.** There is no statutory requirement for companies to keep a register of debenture holders, but if such a register is kept then it must be available for inspection at the company's registered office or a place permitted under regulations made under **s. 1136: s. 743.** (The same applies to the obligatory registers of members: see **s. 114.**)

Debentures (more normally debenture stock) can be expressed to be redeemable or convertible into shares. Redeemable debentures allow the company to buy them back in and cancel them in accordance with the terms of the debenture. Convertible debentures have the possibility of being converted into shares of the same nominal value. If debentures are convertible, they cannot be issued at discount in order to ensure compliance with the rules of raising and maintenance of share capital. Non-convertible debentures can be issued at a discount to their nominal value.

In respect of debentures and debenture stock, the debenture holder/debenture-stock-holder will receive a return on the loan in the form of fixed interest. This is a charge on the company and is payable by the company whether or not the company has made a profit and can therefore pay out a dividend in respect of its shares.

The priority of the debenture holder as a creditor in the event of the insolvent liquidation of the company depends on the nature of the charges—if any—securing the loan. Where the loan is secured by a fixed charge over specific assets of the company, the debenture holders will rank ahead of all the other creditors of the company, including the expenses of the liquidation. Where secured by a floating charge over the company's assets, the debenture holder will rank after the preferential creditors of the company and above the ordinary unsecured creditors of the company. In many cases the debenture will be secured by a combination of fixed and floating charges.

Question 2

'A specific charge, I think, is one that without more fastens on ascertained and definite property or property capable of being ascertained and defined; a floating charge, on the other hand, is ambulatory and shifting in its nature, hovering over and so to speak floating with the property which it is intended to affect until some event occurs or some act is done which causes it to settle and fasten on the subject of the charge ...'

(Per Lord Macnaghten: *Illingworth v Houldsworth* [1904] AC 355)

Analyse the judicial application of the distinguishing characteristics of fixed and floating charges, particularly in the context of fixed charges over fluctuating assets and book debts.

 Commentary

This is one of the most complex aspects of company borrowing. Creditors will generally require some form of security in respect of advances to the company and companies (and limited liability partnerships—LLPs) have the choice of creating fixed and/or floating charges over their assets as opposed to sole traders and general partnerships which cannot create floating charges. Once floating charges were recognized and their characteristics were identified at the beginning of the twentieth century, there was for a long time no problem in distinguishing between and identifying fixed as opposed to floating charges. This all changed in the 1980s when creditors tried to create fixed charges over fluctuating assets including book debts and chattels. You need to analyse the problems faced by the court regarding attempts by legal draftsmen to extend fixed charges beyond their original scope and the final decision of the House of Lords in this respect.

 Answer plan

- Distinction between fixed and floating charges
- Identification of crystallizing events in connection with floating charges
- Function of the court to distinguish and identify fixed and floating charges
- Problems with attempts to create fixed charges over fluctuating assets

Suggested answer

Fixed charges are legal or equitable charges created by the company over specific, identified assets. The fundamental characteristic of fixed charges is that the company cannot deal with or dispose of the charged asset without the chargee's consent. A fixed charge can be created over present and future assets but in the case of future assets, the asset must be sufficiently described so as to be identifiable when it is finally acquired.

A fixed charge is generally created over freehold or leasehold property, fixed plant and machinery although since 1979 fixed charges have been created over less permanent assets including receivables (or book debts).

The floating charge was first legally recognized in *Re Panama, New Zealand and Australian Royal Mail Co* (1870) 5 Ch App 318 where the court recognized a debenture giving the holders a charge on the proceeds of sale of the company's ships and other assets, in priority over the claims of the ordinary unsecured creditors in the winding up. This recognition was followed by several judicial attempts to define the essential characteristics of the floating charge. The most commonly accepted definition is given by Romer LJ in *Re Yorkshire Woolcombers Association Ltd* [1903] 2 Ch 284 who said: 'if a charge has the three characteristics that I am about to mention, it is a floating charge: (1) If it is a charge on a class of assets of a company present and future; (2) if that class is one which, in the ordinary course of the business of the company, would be changing from time to time; and (3) if you find that by the charge it is contemplated that, until some future step is taken by or on behalf of those interested in the charge, the company may carry on its business in the ordinary way as far as concerns the particular class of assets I am dealing with'. This can be simplified to the following points:

(a) It is a charge on a class of assets (or the whole of the assets) of the company present and future, and

(b) Assets change in the ordinary course of the company's business, and

(c) Until crystallization a company may treat assets as if uncharged

Crystallization is the event that causes the charge to cease to float over the body of assets covered by the charge and to attach to the assets of that description in the possession of the company at the time of crystallization. This will usually be a formal act taken by the chargeholder but it can also be the happening of an event not directly triggered by the chargeholder. The following events cause floating charges to crystallize:

(a) The appointment by the chargeholder of a receiver in respect of a class of assets or the appointment of an administrator where the floating charge is over the whole or substantially the whole of the company's assets. The right to appoint a receiver or administrator will generally be contained in the instrument creating the charge. Failing this, the chargeholder will have to apply to the court for the appointment to be made.

The trigger for the appointment of a receiver will depend on the specific terms in the charging instrument. These will usually include: (a) the appointment of a receiver by another chargee; (b) the levy of execution or distress on company's assets by an unsecured creditor; and (c) the inability of the company to pay its debts under **IA 1986, s. 123**. The debt in respect of which the charge is created must be unpaid. In the case of a bank overdraft repayable on demand, the bank must make demand prior to the appointment of a receiver but there is no obligation to give extended time to the company for repayment: *Cripps (Pharmaceuticals) Ltd v Wickenden* [1973] 1 WLR 944.

(b) The commencent of winding up.

(c) Where the company ceases to be a 'going concern': *Re Woodroffes (Musical Instruments) Ltd* [1985] 3 WLR 543.

Cessation may also occur on the crystallization of another floating charge over the company's assets but only if the company ceases business as a result. See also criticized decision in *Griffiths v Yorkshire Bank plc* [1994] 1 WLR 1427

(d) Under the terms of an automatic crystallization clause or notice. The validity of the automatic crystallization clause was recognized in *Re Brightlife Ltd* [1987] Ch 200 but by the time the decision was reported the decision had been overtaken by IA 1986 which, under s. 40, s. 175, and s. 251, preserves the priority over floating charge holders of preferential creditors and provides that charges created as floating charges always rank as such and cannot, due to having crystallized prior to the commencement of the liquidation or receivership of a company, jump in the order of priority of creditors to that of the holder of a fixed charge.

It is for the court to determine whether a charge is a fixed charge or a floating charge, irrespective of the description of the charge in the instrument creating the charge: *Re Armagh Shoes Ltd* [1984] BCLC 405. This is particularly important in respect of attempts to create fixed charges over a range of assets not previously thought capable of being so charged. In *Siebe Gorman & Co Ltd v Barclays Bank Ltd* [1979] 2 Lloyd's Rep 142, the court recognized a fixed charge over receivables (book debts) due to the fact that the charging instrument required the debts to be credited to a specific bank account and restricted the company's right to dispose of the monies paid into this account. In this case, there was no problem since the chargeholder was a bank. Even for banks, however, the situation has not always been straightforward. In *Royal Trust Bank v National Westminster Bank plc* [1996] 2 BCLC 682 the chargee bank was given the right under the charging instrument to demand that the company should open a dedicated account into which it should pay all monies received on collection of debts. In effect, the monies collected went into the company's ordinary trading account. As a result, the charge was held to be a floating rather than a fixed charge. In *William Gaskell Group Ltd v Highley* [1994] 1 BCLC 197 it was held that a charge on book debts requiring them to be paid into an account from which withdrawals could only be made with the chargee's consent was a fixed charge.

There were problems with creditors seeking to obtain fixed charges over receivables where the chargeholder, not being a bank, was unable to restrict the chargor's right to deal with or dispose of the funds once paid: *Re Brightlife Ltd* [1987] Ch 200.

Problems in creating fixed charges over receivables led to attempts to create hybrid charges. These were recognized in *Re New Bullas Trading Ltd* [1993] BCC 251 where the court approved a charging instrument creating a fixed charge over receivables while they remained outstanding but a floating charge over the monies once they had been collected by the company. In *Agnew v Commissioner of Inland Revenue* [2001] 1 BCLC 353 the Judicial Committee of the Privy Council, on an appeal from the New

Zealand Court of Appeal, held that *New Bullas* was wrongly decided. In *National West-minster Bank plc v Spectrum Plus Ltd* [2005] 2 BCLC 269 the House of Lords made up of seven judges overruled *Siebe Gorman* and *New Bullas*. In a unanimous decision, their Lordships held that a debenture which required the proceeds of book debts to be paid into a bank account, but which placed no restriction on the use of the balance of the account, had to be regarded as a floating charge. The decision means that, in order to create a fixed charge, the relevant assets must be permanently appropriated to the payment of the debt for which the charge is a security. The decision is complicated by the fact that their Lordships refused to make the overruling prospective. This means that many charges created in reliance on *Siebe* and *New Bullas* are now vulnerable.

Attempts to create fixed charges over chattels have generally been recognized as float-ing charges in the absence of a restriction of chargor's right to deal in or dispose of assets charged. However, in *Re Cimex Tissues Ltd* [1994] BCC 626 a charge over plant and machinery was held to be a fixed charge even though the charge envisaged that some of the charged items might be changed from time to time as they wore out. In *Re GE Tunbridge Ltd* [1994] BCC 563 the charging instrument creating a charge over certain items of office furniture, prohibited the company from disposing of the assets without the chargee's consent but there was no requirement that, if they were sold, the proceeds should be paid into a designated account. This was held to be a floating charge.

In *Re CCG International Enterprises Ltd* [1993] BCLC 1428 a contract giving a bank a floating charge on a company's assets required the company to insure the charged property and required any money received under the policy to be paid into an account designated by the bank and used as the bank directed either to reduce the debt secured by the charge or the replacement of the lost assets. It was held that this created a fixed charge over the insurance money.

It is clear that the third aspect—the trading power—of the definition of floating charges is more important than the other two, which can be seen as non-essential char-acteristics. Thus in *Re Bond Worth Ltd* [1980] Ch 228 the assets affected by the charge were not 'present and future' but present in respect of the goods and future in respect of the proceeds of sale. Equally, in *Welch v Bowmaker (Ireland) Ltd* [1980] IR 251 a charge over land held by the company was held to be a floating charge although there was no anticipation of the assets being turned over in the course of the company's business.

Question 3

With regard to the registration of charges critically analyse the effect of:

(i) The registration of charges under **s. 860**

(ii) The conclusive nature of the certificate issued by the Registrar of Companies, and

(III) Late registration and priority

Commentary

The topic of the registration of charges is a fairly straightforward one in some respects but it is also a vital topic that can be the subject of essay and problem questions. Of particular importance are the consequences of the failure to comply with the registration requirements and the possibility of late or out-of-time registration which has great significance in respect of the priority of the charge where there have been intervening charges prior to the late registration. Another vital topic is the conclusive nature of the certificate of registration issued by the Registrar of Companies. This has led to some extraordinary situations in the past.

Answer plan

- Identification of registrable charges as opposed to non-registrable charges and the period allowed for registration
- The effect of registration and the consequences of the failure to register
- The conclusive nature of the certificate of registration and judicial decisions relating to it
- Rectification of the register and the legal consequences of late registration regarding the priority of the charge

Suggested answer

Charges created by a company falling within the scope of **s. 860** must be registered before the end of the period allowed for registration: **s. 860(1)**. Failure to register is an offence by the company and every officer in default: **s. 860(4)**. The section applies to nine charges ((a)–(i)) including—

(a) a charge on land or any interest in land, other than a charge for any rent or other periodical sum issuing out of land

(b) a charge for the purpose of securing any issue of debentures, and

(c) a charge on book debts of the company

Category (a) covers legal and equitable mortgages even if the land is overseas. Thus an equitable charge created by memorandum and deposit of title deeds is registrable, otherwise it is void and the chargee cannot claim a lien over the deeds and documents: *Re Molton Finance Ltd* [1968] Ch 325. An agreement to create a mortgage or charge over land is registrable as an equitable mortgage, and any subsequent mortgage or charge is also registrable. Where an equitable charge is registered and later converted to a legal charge, the legal charge does not require registration: *Re William Hall (Contractors) Ltd* [1967] 2 All ER 1150.

Category (b) refers to the issue of a series of debentures rather than operating to catch any form of charge not specifically mentioned. Book debts (c) are also referred to as receivables and defined as: 'any amounts due or to become due to a company in respect of goods supplied or to be supplied or services rendered or to be rendered by a person ... in the course of that person's business'. Charges over the company's bank account are not book debts: *Re Brightlife Ltd* [1987] **Ch 200**. Rights of escrow in respect of a bank account are not a registrable charge: *Lovell Construction Ltd v Independent Estates plc* [1994] 1 BCLC 31. Registration is not required where a company charges a holding of shares.

The period allowed for registration of charges created by the company is 21 days from the day after the day on which the charge is created, or if created outside the UK, 21 days from the day after the day on which the instrument by which it is created or evidenced could, in due course of post, have been received in the UK: **s. 870(1)**. The period for existing charges on property acquired by the company is 21 days from the day after the day of completion of the acquisition except where the property and the charge were created outside the UK, when it is 21 days from the day after the day on which the charging instrument could have been received in the UK: **s. 870(2)**.

The registration period for a series of debentures is either 21 days from the date of the execution of the deed containing the charge or from the day after the day on which the first debenture is executed: **s. 870(3)**. A copy of the certificate is endorsed on every debenture or certificate of debenture stock issued by the company: **s. 865**.

One of the grounds for the proposed reform of the registration of charges in the **Companies Act 1989** was the fact that, where a charge is registered within 21 days of its creation, it operates as a valid charge from the date of its creation. This means that there is in effect a 21-day period when a subsequent chargee, inspecting the register, will find no evidence of the charge's registration but it will take priority over any subsequent charge created within that 21-day period. Failure to register a charge results in the charge being void against a liquidator, an administrator, and a creditor of the company: **s. 874(1)**. On becoming void, the money secured becomes immediately repayable: **s. 874(3)**.

Registration constitutes deemed notice of the charge's existence and, in respect of fixed charges, whether legal or equitable, priority depends on order of registration. Floating charges, also rank in the order in which they are registered, except that a floating charge over the whole undertaking may be postponed to a later floating charge over a part of the assets where the earlier charge allowed subsequent floating charges over a part of the assets, ranking in priority to it: *Re Automatic Bottlemakers Ltd* [1926] Ch 412.

Where there is a combination of fixed and floating charges, the floating charge will always be postponed to fixed charges even though created subsequently. It is, however, common for floating charges to contain a clause restricting the company from creating subsequent charges ranking in priority above it. The mere fact of the restriction being contained in the floating charge will, however, have no validity against the holder of a subsequent fixed charge, since there is no constructive notice of the contents of the charge. If the restriction is endorsed on the registered particulars, some degree of inferred knowledge could be argued but, generally, a subsequent chargee, aware of the existence of a floating charge, will request a copy of the charge and have knowledge of the restriction. Where the subsequent chargee has knowledge, s/he will not rank in priority over the floating charge.

The Registrar of Companies is required to keep a register of charges for each company and the particulars of the charge required by the law must be entered in the register: **s. 869(1)**. The Registrar must issue a certificate of the registration of any charge (**s. 869(5)**) and the certificate is conclusive evidence that the requirements of the Act have been satisfied: **s. 869(6)(b)**. The effect is that inaccuracy in the registered particulars and the certificate do not affect the charge's validity. The proposed reform of the registration procedure in the **Companies Act 1989** would have removed the conclusive characteristic of the certificate. This caused an outcry in the legal profession.

The significance of the conclusive nature of the Registrar's certificate can be seen in *Re Eric Holmes (Property) Ltd* [1965] Ch 1052. In this case, formal charges were executed on 5 June but the date was not inserted in the charge instruments. Subsequently the date 23 June was entered and the charges were registered within 21 days of 23 June and the Registrar issued certificates of registration. The company went into liquidation on 4 August. The liquidator sought a declaration that the charges were void on the ground of defective registration. In respect of the defective registration, the court held that the Registrar's certificate was conclusive evidence of compliance with the statutory requirements as regards registration, even though the wrong date was stated on the charges.

In *Re CL Nye Ltd* [1971] Ch 442 a charge was created on 28 February 1964 and left undated. The solicitor charged with registering the charge failed to do so. This was noticed on 18 June and the charge was registered on 3 July as if created on 18 June. The company went into liquidation on 16 July. The charge was held to be validly registered since the certificate issued by the Registrar was conclusive evidence of compliance with the statutory requirements. In *Re Mechanisations (Eaglescliffe) Ltd* [1966] Ch 20 a company mortgaged its property up to the sum of £16,000 plus interest and sums becoming due from the company for goods supplied. The registered particulars omitted the reference to the interest and the subsequent amounts. The liquidator claimed that the charge was void in respect of sums in excess of the £16,000 as registered. The court held, however, that the terms and effect of the charge must be looked for in the document creating the charge and not in the entry on the register. The mortgagees were therefore entitled to be treated as secured creditors for the full sums due.

On the application of the company or an interested person, the High Court may order that the time for registration shall be extended, or that the omission or misstatement of any registered particular shall be rectified on such terms and conditions as are just and expedient. The court must be satisfied that the failure to register, or the omission or misstatement was accidental or due to inadvertence or to some other sufficient cause, or is not of a nature to prejudice the position of creditors or shareholders of the company, or that on other grounds it is just and equitable to grant relief: **s. 873**. In the case of extension of the registration period, the effect will be that the charge will be regarded as void until registered which will affect the priority of the charge in respect of other secured creditors whose charges have been created and registered in the period during which the charge was void: *Re Teleomatic* [1994] 1 BCLC 90.

The failure to register within 21 days causes the charge to become void *ab initio* until registered under an order made under s. 873, when it becomes valid from the date of registration. The court will refuse an application for late registration if the application follows the passing of a resolution for the voluntary winding up of the company or after an order for its compulsory liquidation. It will also be refused if the company is in administration and it is clear that it will proceed to an insolvent liquidation: *Re Barrow Borough Transport Ltd* [1990] Ch 227.

Question 4

Hernando's Hideaway Ltd (HH Ltd) operated a nightclub. In June 2007, Lola Bank plc (LB plc) agreed to allow HH Ltd an overdraft on the security of a combination fixed and floating charge over the whole of HH Ltd's assets. The debenture was executed on 21 June 2007. The company secretary of HH Ltd meant to register the debenture but forgot to do so. The failure to register the debenture was discovered in January 2008.

In December 2007, HH Ltd created a second fixed charge over its leasehold premises in favour of Ravers (R Ltd) Ltd to finance the installation of a sound system. R Ltd were informed of the earlier charge to LB plc and noticed that the charge had not been registered when it applied for registration of its charge.

Advise the company secretary of HH Ltd how best to secure the validity of the charge to LB plc and of the priority in respect of the two charges and of any unsecured creditors to whom the company became liable before the charge was late registered.

 Commentary

This is a problem concerning the consequences of failure to register within the requisite period and the possibilities open to the company secretary of HH Ltd to rectify the matter. It also raises the issue of the priority of charges. You are required to consider the occasions when out of time registration is possible and consider any alternative course of action open to the company secretary and the consequences for LB plc.

 Answer plan

- Identification of the legal problems raised by the question
- Discussion of the possibility of late registration and the effect of such action

- Consideration of the possibility of inserting a new date and registering the charge within 21 days of the new date
- In respect of Ravers (R) Ltd, discussion of the significance of R Ltd being aware of the existence of LB plc's charge and its non-registration prior to the registration of their own charge
- Application of the law to the problem and advice concerning the legal position of the parties and unsecured creditors

Suggested answer

This question raises legal issues concerning the effect of failure to register charges within the requisite statutory period, the possibility and legal effect of late registration and the topic of priority of charges.

In respect of the charge to Lola Bank (LB) plc, the charge was created on 21 June 2007 and, as a category of charge registrable under **s. 860**, should have been registered with the Registrar of Companies within the period of 21 days from the day after the date of its creation. In effect, this has not been done and as a result the charge is void and the money advanced by the bank against the security of the charge is immediately repayable. The failure to register the charge is also a criminal offence and the company and every officer in default is liable on conviction to a fine: **s. 860(4) and (5)**.

There are two possible courses of action open to the company secretary to salvage the situation. The most obvious solution would be to apply to the court for late registration of the charge under **s. 873**. A high court judge can only order that the period allowed for registration can be extended if satisfied that the failure to register the charge falls within the terms of **s. 873(1)**. In this respect, the situation would appear to be covered by **s. 873(1)(a)(i)** in that it was accidental or due to inadvertence. It would be necessary to satisfy the court that the failure to register the charge was not motivated by the desire to delude persons dealing with the company into thinking that it was in a better financial position than was in fact the case.

In *Re Kris Cruisers Ltd* [1949] Ch 138, the company secretary of the company thought that the solicitor had registered the charge and the solicitor thought the company secretary had done so. In the event, the charge was unregistered. The court, however, allowed its late registration under the equivalent of **s. 873(1)(a)(i)**. Where none of the five grounds is established, late registration is refused: *Re Teleomatic* [1994] 1 BCLC 90.

The effect of late registration is that the charge becomes void through failure to register and that it remains void until it is registered. The effect of this would be that, whereas the charge held by LB plc would have enjoyed priority from the date of its creation, the charge will only become valid once the late registration is achieved. This is important in respect of priority over subsequent charges.

Out-of-time registration can be on such terms and conditions as are just and expedient and is generally subject to the following formula: 'That ... this order is to be without prejudice to the rights of any parties acquired prior to the time when the said debenture is to be actually registered.'

The effect of this formula was considered in *Watson v Duff Morgan and Vermont (Holdings) Ltd* **[1974] 1 All ER 794**. The company in January 1971 created a first debenture in the plaintiff's favour to secure £10,000 and a second debenture in favour of the defendant to secure £5,000. The debentures were secured by floating charges covering all undertakings and property, present and future including uncalled capital. The second charge was made subject to and ranked immediately after the first charge. The second debenture was registered within 21 days but the first was not registered. In October 1971, the plaintiff applied for late registration and the order was made subject to the above condition. In the event, the company went into liquidation with insufficient assets to provide even £5,000. The plaintiff successfully claimed that his debenture ranked in priority to the other, the proviso only applied to the period when the first debenture was void for non-registration. The defendant's rights had not been acquired during that period but when the second debenture was executed.

In spite of this formula, if other chargees have agreed that their charges are to rank after a charge that was not registered through inadvertence etc, the court will respect the contractually agreed priorities between the parties: *Barclays Bank plc v Stuart Landon Ltd* **[2001] 2 BCLC 316**. There is no protection to persons becoming unsecured creditors of the company during the time that the charge was unregistered. The court takes the view that unsecured creditors run the risk that the company might subsequently create a charge over its assets: *Re MIG Trust Ltd* **[1933] Ch 542**.

If the charge to LB plc were not dated except in pencil, it would always be open for the company secretary to falsify the date on which the charge was created and to register it within 21 days of the false date. In *Esberger & Son Ltd v Capital and Counties Bank* **[1913] 2 Ch 366**, the company deposited with its bank an undated but signed memorandum of charge on 17 September 1910. On 14 June 1911, the bank manager filled in that date onto the document and registered it with the Registrar of Companies on 3 July. The court held that the charge was void as not having been registered in time.

It was only in *National Provincial and Union Bank of England v Charnley* **[1923] 1 KB 431** that the matter of the conclusive nature of the Registrar of Companies' certificate of registration was raised and recognized. The conclusive nature of the ROC's certificate has subsequently been recognized in *Re Eric Holmes (Property) Ltd* **[1965] Ch 442** where the court recognized the validity of a charge created on 5 June and not registered within the 21 days of its creation but subsequently dated 23 June and registered within 21 days of that date. This could also be a route for the company secretary. It is important, however, to realize that the failure to register within the 21 days constitutes a criminal offence (**s. 860(4)**), and that the priority of the charge will be adversely affected.

In respect of the charge created in favour of Ravers (R) Ltd over the leasehold premises in December 2007, the fact that R Ltd was aware of the existence of the unregistered combined fixed and floating charge in favour of LB plc does not affect the validity and priority of their registered charge. A registered charge has priority over an earlier unregistered charge, even though the holder of the registered charge has notice of the unregistered security: *Re Monolithic Building Co* [1915] 1 Ch 643.

As regards the priorities between the two charges, the charge in favour of LB plc is only registered after January 2008 whereas the charge in favour of R Ltd is registered within 21 days of its creation in December 2007. This means that the fixed charge in favour of R Ltd will rank in priority over the fixed charge of LB plc. Since the charge to LB plc is a combined fixed and floating charge, the floating charge will always rank after a subsequent fixed charge over the same asset. Any persons who became unsecured creditors of the company between the charge to LB plc becoming void for non-registration and being registered out-of-time under **s. 873** will not be protected by the subsequent validation of the charge.

Question 5

Paradise Ltd is a wholly owned subsidiary company of Eden Ltd which is itself controlled by Adam, the principal shareholder and managing director. Paradise Ltd suffered a financial crisis in 2004 and it was agreed in January 2005 that Eden Ltd would pay off its outstanding debts and advance a further £50,000 on the security of a floating charge on Paradise Ltd's assets. Eden Ltd settled the debts and made the first payment to Paradise Ltd in March 2005, although the debenture containing the charge was not actually executed until July 2005. The charge was registered within 21 days of its creation.

The company had a major supplier, Viper plc, which in September 2005 refused to make further deliveries to Paradise Ltd on credit since it was already owed £40,000 for previous deliveries. Following talks between the directors of Paradise Ltd and Viper plc, Viper plc agreed to continue to supply Paradise Ltd on condition that Paradise Ltd created in its favour a fixed charge over its freehold premises to cover the existing debt of £40,000. The charge was created in October 2005 and registered within 21 days.

Paradise Ltd went into voluntary creditors' liquidation in March 2006. Advise the liquidator of the validity of the charges to Eden Ltd and Viper plc.

 Commentary

This problem question shows how great an overlap there is between the topics of charges and corporate insolvency where the company creating the charge becomes insolvent after having created the charge. In spite of this overlap, it is relevant for you to be aware of the consequences of such an event under the heading of company borrowing and charges. In reality, you are not being asked to discuss issues relating to insolvency proceedings but merely to consider how they can impinge on the validity of company charges.

Answer plan

- Identification of the legal problems raised by the question
- Discussion of the law relating to the avoidance of floating charges and the interpretation of **s. 245(2)**
- Application of the law to the facts of the case involving Paradise Ltd and Eden Ltd
- Discussion of the law relating to voidable preferences and cases concerning the interpretation of **s. 239**
- Application of the law to the fixed charge created by Paradise Ltd in favour of Viper Ltd

Suggested answer

This question raises problems connected with the avoidance of floating charges under **IA 1986, s. 245** and charges being avoided as voidable preferences under **IA 1986, s. 239**.

Floating charges created in favour of outsiders within one year before the onset of insolvency are invalid under **s. 245(3)(b)** unless the chargee can prove that the company was not unable to pay its debts at that time or became so as a consequence: **s. 245(4)(a)** and **(b)**. For connected persons, the period is extended to two years (**s. 245(3)(a)**) and is not conditional upon the company being unable to pay its debts at the time of the creation of the charge. The onset of insolvency is precisely determined for administrations and liquidations: **s. 245(5)**. Connected persons are defined in **IA 1986, s. 249** and by reference to **IA 1986, s. 435**.

There are exceptions to the charges being avoided as regards the extent of the aggregate of:

(a) the value of money paid, or goods or services supplied to the company at the same time as, or after, the creation of the charge

(b) the value of the discharge or reduction, at the same time as or after, the creation of the charge of any debt of the company, and

(c) any interest payable in pursuance of (a) or (b): **s. 245(2)(a)**

The exceptions under (a) and (b) are both subject to the proviso that the cash, goods and services paid or supplied to the company, or the value of the discharge or reduction of any debt of the company took place 'at the same time as, or after, the creation of the charge'.

In an early decision under earlier equivalent sections, the court took a very relaxed view of the definition of 'at the same time'. Thus in *Re F & E Stanton Ltd* [1929] 1

Ch 180 M advanced money to an insolvent company on the security of debentures creating a floating charge. The company passed a resolution to issue the debenture before the loan was advanced but the debentures were not issued until five days after the last instalment of the advance and fifty-four days after the first instalment. The company went into liquidation within five days of the creation of the charge. The court nevertheless held that the charge was created 'at the same time' as the advance and the charge was valid.

In interpreting this proviso in respect of **IA 1986, s. 245** in *Re Shoe Lace Ltd* [1992] **BCLC 636**, the court decided that the degree of contemporaneity depended upon the ordinary meaning of the words used. On that basis, although loans had been made between April and early July in consideration of the proposed creation of a debenture, they could not be said to have been made at the same time as the creation of the debenture, which was finally executed on 24 July 1990. The floating charge was therefore invalid. This decision was criticized by the court in *Re Fairway Magazines Ltd* [1993] **BCLC 643** where the judge followed the approach of *F & E Stanton*. The Court of Appeal, however, endorsed the High Court's decision in *Shoe Lace* on appeal under the name *Power v Sharp Investments Ltd* [1994] **1 BCLC 111**.

The result of this is that an advance made before the formal execution of a debenture but in anticipation of it will not be regarded as being made at the same time as the creation of the charge unless the interval is so short that it can be regarded as minimal.

In respect of the floating charge to Eden Ltd by Paradise Ltd, Eden Ltd is a person connected with Paradise Ltd since it is the parent company of Paradise Ltd. The floating charge is therefore vulnerable under **IA 1986, s. 245(2)** for a period of two years from the date of its creation in July 2005 in the event of Paradise Ltd going into liquidation within that period. In the event, Paradise Ltd went into insolvent liquidation in March 2006. As a result, the floating charge is avoided unless it falls within one of the exceptions in **s. 245(2)(a)–(c)**. Since Paradise Ltd's debts were discharged and money was advanced to it by way of a loan before the date of the creation of the charge, the liquidator can avoid the charge under **s. 245(2)**.

The result is the Eden Ltd is no longer a secured creditor of Paradise Ltd and the charged property is released for the benefit of unsecured creditors.

In respect of the fixed charge created in favour of Viper plc to secure an existing debt, the charge is potentially vulnerable to be set aside as a voidable preference under **IA 1986, s. 239**. Under this provision, administrators or liquidators can set aside payments and charges created in the period prior to the onset of insolvency which have been made to put a creditor or guarantor or surety of a creditor into a better position in the event of the company going into an insolvent liquidation or administration. Changing the status of Viper plc from that of an unsecured creditor to a secured creditor with a fixed charge is a major improvement in status.

In order to be set aside, such transactions must have taken place within the relevant time prior to the onset of insolvency, which is two years for connected persons and six months for outsiders: **s. 240(1)(a)** and **(b)**, and the company must at the time of the transaction have been unable to pay its debts within the meaning of **IA 1986, s. 123**. The section also catches transactions made between the making of an administration application and the making of the order: **s. 240(1)(c)** and the filing with the court of a notice of intention to appoint an administrator under **para. 14** or **22** and the making of an appointment.

Preferences are only voidable where it can be established that the company creating the charge or making the payment was motivated by a desire to confer a benefit on the person preferred. For connected person, an intention to advantage the person is presumed: **s. 239(6)**; *Re DKG Contractors Ltd* [1990] BCC 903; and *Re Beacon Leisure Ltd* [1991] BCC 213. In the event of charges or payments being avoided, the court may order retransfer of property, release or discharge of security, repayments to administrator or liquidator, revival of guarantees, and so on: **s. 241**. Third parties who are bona fide purchasers in good faith and for value are protected: **s. 241(2)** and **(2A)**. Proceeds of a successful claim are held on trust for the unsecured creditors: *Re Yagerphone Ltd* [1935] 1 Ch 392.

In *Re MC Bacon Ltd* [1990] BCLC 324, the company had an unsecured overdraft limit of £300,000. In 1986 it lost its major customer and two of the directors retired from active management. In May 1987 a bank report found the company to be technically insolvent. As a condition of continuing to operate the bank account, the bank demanded fixed and floating charges over the company's assets. In September 1987 the company went into liquidation and the liquidator sought to set aside the charge as a transaction at an undervalue or as a voidable preference.

Having rejected the submission that the charge could be avoided as a transaction at an undervalue, the court considered the question of whether it was void as a voidable preference. It concluded that the company did not necessarily desire that which it intended to achieve and held that the charge was not voidable. In *Re MC Bacon Ltd (No 2)* [1990] 3 WLR 646, the liquidators were held unable to claim the costs of the abortive action as part of the expenses of the liquidation.

Banks and suppliers under the terms of a current account are in an advantageous position in respect of this. In *Re Yeovil Glove Co Ltd* [1965] Ch 148, a bank met company cheques totalling some £110,000 subsequent to the creation of a secured debenture to secure an existing debt. This was held to be a new advance even though the overdraft remained virtually unchanged. This was due to the operation of the rule in *Clayton's Case* (1816) 1 Mer 572 in the bank's favour. The rule provides that credits to a current account discharge debts in the order in which they were incurred in the absence of specific appropriation.

In conclusion, the floating charge in favour of Eden Ltd can be avoided by the liquidator of Paradise Ltd. The fixed charge in favour of Viper plc is, however, valid since it was created as a result of pressure from the chargee which prevents the liquidator claiming that Paradise Ltd intended to prefer Viper plc as required by the legislation.

Further reading

Atherton, S. and Jameel Mokal, R., 'Charges over assets: issues in the fixed/floating jurisprudence' [2005] Comp. Law., 26(1): 10.

Capper, D., 'Fixed charges over book debts—the future after *Brumark*' [2003] Comp. Law., 24(11): 325.

Pennington, R., 'The vulnerability of debenture holders' [2004] Comp. Law., 25(6): 171.

Pennington, R., 'Recent developments in the law and practice relating to the creation of security for companies' indebtedness' [2009] Comp. Law., 30(6): 163.

Smart, P., 'Fixed or floating? *Siebe Gorman post-Brumark*' [2004] Comp. Law., 25(11): 331.

Walters, A., 'Statutory redistribution of floating charge assets: Victory (again) to Revenue and Customs' [2008] Comp. Law., 29(5): 129.

Wild, L., '*Spectrum* and *Leyland DAF*: the spectre of new claims' [2006] Comp. Law., 27(5): 151.

6

Shares and shareholders

Introduction

'Share' means a share in the company's share capital: **s. 540(1)**. Shares are personal property (**s. 541**) and must have a fixed nominal value: **s. 542**. This can, however, be in any currency, and different classes of shares in the same company may be in different currencies: **s. 542(3)**.

An important legal distinction is the difference between registered and bearer shares as regards title, transfer and the legal significance of the share certificate (share warrant for bearer shares). In practice, bearer shares are rarely met in the UK.

In this area of the company law syllabus, it is particularly important to understand the rights associated with the different classes of share that can be issued by a company: ordinary, preference, and deferred shares. Examination questions generally concentrate on the distinctions between ordinary and preference shares (deferred shares are relatively rare) and it is important to realize at the outset that the preference share—despite its name—is one whose holders are generally disadvantaged. They have sometimes been described as 'hybrid securities' meaning that they combine the characteristics of shares and debentures. This is due to the fact that the holders of preference shares have few of the powers of shareholders—generally no voting rights—while enjoying few of the advantages as creditors—security and priority in liquidation.

Associated with this, is the major topic of variation of class rights—concerning statutory restrictions on the right of the company directors to vary the rights of a particular class of share without the consent of the majority of the holders of that class of share. In respect of this, you must realize the significance of the judicial definition of what constitutes variation of class rights and its damaging effect on the statutory protection.

Other important topics in this area of the syllabus include:

(a) Existing shareholders rights of pre-emption in respect of new issues of equity shares: **s. 560–577**

(b) Restrictions on the directors' power to allot shares: **s. 549–551**

(c) Certification and transfer of shares: **s. 768–782**

(d) The register of members: **s. 113–128**

The **Companies (Shareholders' Rights) Regulations 2009 (SI 2009 No1632)** implement **Directive 2007/36/EC** on the exercise of certain rights of shareholders of listed companies (OJ L184/17, 14/07/2007) and became effective on 3 August 2009. The rationale for the Directive was that existing legislation at EU level does not adequately address sufficiently cross-border voting issues. The Directive lays down a framework of rules facilitating the rights of shareholders—in particular it seeks to ensure that shareholders in companies registered in another Member State may vote without difficulty at these companies' company meetings. The intention is to improve shareholder rights and corporate governance in particular, and ultimately improve the conditions for cross-border investment and business competitiveness.

Question 1

Distinguish between ordinary shares and preference shares. Why are preference shares described as a hybrid between debt and equity?

 Commentary

This is a very important topic that you can expect to appear in an examination paper, generally in the form of an essay question. You need to have the distinctions between the shares at your fingertips and to be able to make the distinction between the two classes of share in a cogent fashion. While preference shares only represent a small percentage of the number of shares issued, it is important to realize how they are used, particularly in respect of venture capital and corporate financing of quoted companies where they are frequently issued as an alternative to borrowing. In all cases, however, because of the rights generally attaching to them, preference shares are always a hybrid between debt and equity.

 Answer plan

- General introduction and characteristics of ordinary and preference shares
- Dividend rights of preference and ordinary shares
- Rights to return of capital of preference and ordinary shares
- Voting rights of preference and ordinary shares
- Function of preference shares as an alternative to borrowing
- Characteristics rendering all preference shares a hybrid between debt and equity

Suggested answer

Many companies divide their share capital into different classes of shares and refer to one class or more as preference shares as opposed to the ordinary shares issued by the company. Shareholder rights relate to dividend, return of capital, and voting rights. The rights will depend entirely on the terms of issue or the articles; there are no statutorily defined rights in the UK.

The characteristic of preference shares is that they will rank ahead of ordinary shares as to either dividend or return of capital or both. Thus the preference dividend will be paid in priority to the ordinary dividend and, on the company's dissolution, the preference shareholders will have priority in respect of the return of their capital. This can be simply established by formula that preference shareholders carry 'priority as to dividend and capital': *Re EW Savory Ltd* [1951] 2 All ER 1036.

The preferential dividend payable on a preference share is generally a fixed percentage of the nominal value of the share and is an identifier of the share: '7 per cent preference shares'. If the shares were issued at a premium, however, the dividend is normally expressed in pence per share or as a percentage of the total subscription price.

Occasionally, particularly for venture capital transactions, preference shares may have a right to a particular percentage of the company's profits. There must be a clear definition of profits in the document creating the rights which must set out how the percentage of profits should be divided. This will usually be proportionately according to the shareholding.

In addition, unless otherwise stated, the shares are deemed to be cumulative preference shares so that the failure to pay a dividend in a financial year means that the right will be carried forward or 'accumulate' until it is paid. The presumption against dividends being cumulative can be rebutted by providing that the dividend is only 'payable out of net profits of each year': *Staples v Eastman Photographic Materials* Co [1896] 2 Ch 303.

The date at which the dividend is due depends on the articles. Dividends can become payable: by resolution of the shareholders, by a resolution of the directors, automatically on specified dates provided that (and to the extent that) the company has profits available for distribution. The advantage of the latter is if the company has distributable profits, the dividend becomes a debt due on the specified date and the shareholder can sue the company if it is not paid.

If a company is wound up with arrears of preference dividend, difficulties arise as to whether a right to arrears of dividend has arisen. Preference shareholders may have no right to a dividend at least until it has been declared and arrears of undeclared dividend will not be paid on a winding up. In *Re Roberts and Cooper Ltd* [1929] 2 Ch 383 the holder of 4 per cent cumulative preference shares was entitled on winding up to be paid the amount paid up on their shares and arrears of dividend due at the date of winding up. The company went into liquidation with surplus assets; it was held that the shareholders were not entitled to payment of arrears since dividends were not due until declared. To avoid this, the rights should provide for the payment of arrears of preference dividend 'whether declared or not'. The problem would still arise if the dividend fell due on a specified date if the company had distributable profits.

In contrast, ordinary shares have unlimited rather than fixed dividend rights and those rights are not cumulative. Thus, if the company is successful, there is no limit to the amount of dividend that can be declared but if it is unsuccessful the shareholder loses the dividend for that financial year. The right to a dividend arises where the company makes a distributable profit and declares a dividend.

In respect of return of capital, all shares are presumed to have equal rights to a return of capital unless specifically provided. If the preference shareholders enjoy a priority, however, the effect is that they have no right to a share of surplus assets: *Scottish Insurance Corporation Ltd v Wilsons & Clyde Coal Co Ltd* [1949] 1 All ER 1068. Repayment of capital is limited to the nominal value of the shares and not to any premium element unless there is a right to be paid the issue price in priority to the other shareholders.

Ordinary shareholders will generally be postponed to any preference shareholders in respect of return of capital but will then have the sole right to share in any surplus assets unless there are deferred or founders' shares in issue. These have a deferred right of return of capital and exclusive claims over surplus assets.

As regards voting rights, preference shareholders will be deemed to have equal voting rights with all other shareholders. In practice, the right to vote at general meetings of the company will generally be restricted to certain specified matters: if the preference dividend is in arrears beyond a specified period; if the shares are redeemable and redemption has not taken place on a specified date; and if there is a proposal to wind up the company. In respect of the non-payment of a dividend, if the articles are appropriately drafted, the voting rights can arise even where the company was unable to pay the dividend because there were no available profits: *Re Bradford Investments plc* [1990] BCC 740.

Preference shares will often be a preferred way for a venture capital firm to invest in companies. The company's bankers and creditors may find the issue of preference shares more acceptable than a large loan and the preference shares rank after all creditors in a winding up. In addition, the company's balance sheet will be less highly geared and look more solid to potential suppliers and customers. For the venture capitalist the advantages are a potential dividend stream and the possibility of weighted, voting rights in given situations so that they will be able to vote down a resolution to wind up the company or be able to appoint and remove directors on the company's failure to achieve performance targets. The risk is that if a corporate preference shareholder has a majority of the votes or can remove or appoint a majority of the board, the company could become a subsidiary of the corporate preference shareholder: CA 2006, s. 1159(1).

Ordinary shareholders generally enjoy voting rights in the general meeting and will participate in the decision making. In the event of a takeover bid for the company, their shares will be sought after and will potentially show an increase in value.

Listed companies can issue preference shares as part satisfaction of consideration due in respect of a share or business acquisition or as a means of raising capital at cheaper rates than for a loan. They are also sometimes issued on a company refinancing with debt being converted into preference shares. For the issuing company, preference shares have the advantage that the dividend payable may be lower than the rate of interest that would have been incurred had the capital been borrowed (although interest payments are tax deductible whereas dividends are not). The absence of voting rights prevents the preference shareholders from acquiring a voting stake in the company. The issue of preference shares may not count towards the calculation of gearing ratios under the company's finance documents. In addition, the issue of preference shares may be made without a pre-emptive offer to existing shareholders unless they are convertible into ordinary shares: **CA 2006, ss. 560–561.**

Even if not issued as an alternative to a loan, all preference shares are hybrid securities. In having a right to a fixed dividend they, like creditors, do not benefit materially from the company's success in respect of earnings. But unlike creditors with a right to interest on their loan, the dividend is only payable if the company has available distributable profits, whereas interest payments are a charge on capital and payable even where the company makes a loss. As has been shown, even if the dividend is cumulative, in the event of the company's liquidation, the arrears of cumulative dividend may not be provable in the liquidation.

The same is true as regards capital value since the price of the preference share will only fluctuate in value during the company's lifetime in relation to the level of the fixed dividend as against the market rate of interest. On the company's liquidation, even if they enjoy priority in return of capital over ordinary shares, they are still below creditors in priority who can even be protected by charges over the company's assets.

Finally, the lack of voting rights mean they have no right to participate in the decision making of the company. This is true for most creditors but important creditors may be given the right to nominate a director to represent their interests.

When one considers their vulnerability to selective reduction of capital and the lack of protection they receive in respect of variation of class rights, we can but agree with the statement in Gower's *Principles of Modern Company Law* (6th edn, 1997): 'Suspended midway between true creditors and true members they [preference shareholders] may get the worst of both worlds, unless the instrument creating the preference shares is carefully drafted.'

Question 2

Nick held registered shares in Diabolo Ltd. Mick stole the certificate from Nick's study and, pretending to be Nick, deposited the certificate and a signed blank transfer form with South Bank as security for a loan. When Mick defaulted on the loan, South Bank transferred the shares to Paul. On receipt of the share certificate and the transfer form, Diabolo Ltd replaced Nick with Paul on the register of members and issued a share certificate to him. Paul later transferred the shares to Quentin.

Nick noticed that he had not received any dividends from Diabolo Ltd and was informed that he was no longer a shareholder.

Advise Diabolo Ltd of the legal position of Nick, Quentin, and South Bank.

Commentary

This question deals with the topic of estoppel by share certificate and requires an understanding of the rights and liabilities of the parties where a forged transfer has been used in a sequence of share transfers. This is a fairly frequent problem scenario.

Answer plan

- Legal position of Nick
- Legal position of Quentin
- Legal rights of Diabolo Ltd against South Bank

Suggested answer

This question concerns the topic of estoppel by share certificate and situations in which a company can be liable to third parties for statements made on share certificates issued by the company. Share certificates contain two statements of fact: the name of the registered holder, and the extent to which the shares are paid up.

In order for liability to arise, the company must issue certificates which contain an incorrect statement as to the registered holder or the degree to which the share is paid up and the statements must be relied upon by a third party. If this occurs, the company is estopped from denying the truth of the statement contained on the certificate.

In *Re Bahia and San Francisco Rly Co* (1868) LR 3 QB 584, T, the registered holder of five shares, left the share certificate with her broker. Later a forged transfer purporting to be executed by T in favour of S and G was sent to the company for registration and the company issued a share certificate to S and G. They later sold the shares to B having produced the share certificate showing them as the registered holders of the shares. The court held that, in giving the certificate to S and G, the company was making a representation that S and G were the true holders of the shares and the company intended that purchasers in the market should act upon this. The company was ordered to restore T's name to the register of members since the transfer form was forged and to pay damages to B. B having acted in reliance on the representation contained in the share certificate, the company was estopped from denying that S and G were the legal holders.

There must be an act in reliance on the false statement; thus the company is not generally liable to persons to whom the share certificate is issued. If, however, the registered holder of the shares then acts in reliance on the representation contained in the share certificate, the company will be estopped from denying the truth of the representation. In *Balkis Consolidated Co v Tomkinson* [1893] AC 396, Tomkinson, acting in reliance on his supposed title to the shares as represented by a share certificate issued in his name, entered into a contract to sell them. When the company refused to register the transfer, he purchased more shares to honour his contract and successfully claimed damages against the company.

In *Ruben v Great Fingall Consolidated* [1906] AC 439, Rowe, the company secretary of the defendant company, applied to the plaintiff stockbrokers for a loan to enable him to buy shares in the company. As security he issued what purported to be a valid share certificate of the company to the brokers' bank. The certificate bore the forged signatures of two directors and the company seal and was countersigned by Rowe. The company refused to register the brokers as holders and they sued for damages. The House of Lords held that the defendant company could not be liable as the forged certificate was a pure nullity. The same decision was reached in *South London Greyhound Racecourses Ltd v Wake* [1931] 1 Ch 496.

The position now appears to be that a company would be bound where a share certificate is authenticated by a company officer acting within the scope of his authority. At the time of this decision, the company secretary was a mere servant of the company with no implied authority as agent to bind the firm. *Panorama Developments (Guildford) Ltd v Fidelis Furnishing Fabrics Ltd* [1971] 2 QB 711, however, held that a company secretary had implied authority to bind the company in respect of administrative matters. A company secretary is also an authorized signatory to company documents under **CA 2006, s. 44(3)**. However, in *Northside Developments Pty Ltd v Registrar-General* (1980) **170 CLR 146** a mortgage of the company's land was purportedly executed by one of the three directors and a person purporting to act as the company secretary to secure the debts of other companies controlled by the director, not to those of the issuing company. The High Court of Australia held that the mortgage was a forgery and did not bind the company. In contrast, in *Lovett v Carson Country Homes Ltd* [2009] **EWHC 1143 (Ch)** a debenture issued by a company where one director had forged the signature of another was held to validated under **CA 2006, s. 44(5)**.

Bloomenthal v Ford [1897] AC 156 is a decision where the company was estopped in respect of a statement that the shares were fully paid. The appellant lent money to a company on the security of 10,000 £1 shares in the company. Certificates issued to him stated that the shares were fully paid. When the company went into liquidation, it was discovered that nothing had been paid on the shares which were part of the company's unissued shares and the liquidator, therefore, sought payment for the shares from Bloomental as a contributor. The court held that he should be removed from the list of contributories since the company had obtained the loan by representing that the shares were fully paid and was estopped from denying it.

In *Longman v Bath Electric Tramways Ltd* [1905] 1 Ch 646, B became the registered holder of shares but two certificates made out in his name were not sent to him since, on the same day, B presented to the secretary for certification a transfer of the shares to H and M. Subsequently the secretary, by mistake, returned the original certificates to B, who lodged them with L as security for a loan. In an action by L to be registered as holder, the court held that the company owed a duty of care only to the transferee in respect of a share certificate lodged for certification, and that the proximate cause of the loss was the improper use by B of the certificates.

Where the company has acted in reliance on a forged transfer, it can claim an indemnity from the person sending in the forged transfer, even though the person is totally innocent. In *Sheffield Corporation v Barclay* [1905] AC 392 T and H were joint hold-ers of corporation stock. T forged a transfer and borrowed money from a bank on the security of the stock. The bank sent the transfer to the corporation and was registered as holder. The bank then transferred the stock to a third party and new certificates were issued. On T's death, H discovered the forgery and sued the corporation who were ordered to buy H an equivalent amount of stock and pay him the dividends he had missed. The court held that the bank should indemnify the corporation against any loss. This was followed in *Yeung Kei Yung v Hong Kong & Shanghai Banking Corpn* [1981] AC 787.

Applying the law to the facts of the problem, since the forged transfer was a nullity, Nick is still the registered holder of the shares now registered to Quentin. Diabolo Ltd must either pay damages to Nick, including dividend payments not received, or retransfer to his name the shares currently registered to Quentin. In respect of Quentin, however, Diabolo Ltd is estopped from denying that Paul was the registered holder of the shares and Diabolo Ltd must issue him with equivalent shares or pay damages.

Diabolo Ltd will be entitled to claim indemnity from South Bank Ltd in respect of the losses arising from the sending in of the forged transfer. South Bank Ltd could poten-tially claim indemnity against Mick if they can trace him.

Question 3

Explain the reasons behind and analyse the effectiveness of the restrictions on directors' powers to allot shares and the pre-emption rights of existing shareholders.

 Commentary

This question requires you to consider why the law stripped away from the board of directors the power to allot shares and introduced a statutory right of pre-emption for existing share-holders. The reasons behind both moves were to prevent the board from abusing its power to allot shares. Previously, directors had misused their powers to allot shares to fight off unwelcome takeovers for the company and to perpetuate their control. By making the right to allot shares dependent upon a power in the articles or subject to a prior resolution of the members, the potential for abuse was largely controlled.

At the same time, introduction of the right of pre-emption for existing shareholders meant that directors could not simply issue shares to third parties and crush the existing power base within the company.

Answer plan

- Statutory duty of directors not to abuse powers and examples of abuse in connection with share issues
- Statutory regulation of directors' power to allot shares
- Statutory right of pre-emption in respect of equity shares of existing shareholders
- Exclusion and disapplication of the statutory controls

Suggested answer

One of the general duties of the directors is the requirement that directors must 'only exercise powers for the purposes for which they are conferred': **s. 171(b)**. This new statutory formulation merely reflects the earlier equitable principle that directors could not abuse their powers. A major potential area for abuse was the power to allot shares to create or destroy majorities or to perpetuate the directors' power.

In *Piercy v S Mills & Co Ltd* [1920] 1 Ch 77, P had been appointed manager and, having acquired a majority of the shares, he wished to become a director. He asked the directors to call a general meeting to pass a resolution proposing himself and his two brothers to the board. The existing directors were against this. P was dismissed and the directors allotted shares to themselves and another to obtain a majority over P and retain control. As a result, P's resolutions were defeated. P acquired more shares and the directors allotted further shares to two new directors to give them majority control. The court held that the directors were not entitled to use their powers to maintain their control over the company. The issue was an abuse of their fiduciary duty and void.

The abuse has frequently been in connection with frustrating take-over bids. In *Hogg v Cramphorn Ltd* [1967] Ch 254 the directors were faced with a takeover bid which they honestly believed to be against the company's interest. The directors and their supporters held 37,000 of the 126,181 shares issued. They devised a scheme to give themselves effective control and issued 5,707 preference shares carrying a right to 10 votes per share to a trust for the benefit of employees. The court held that the issue was an improper use of their fiduciary powers and the issue was liable to be set aside. A similar situation occurred in *Bamford v Bamford* [1970] Ch 212.

In *Howard Smith Ltd v Ampol Petroleum Ltd* [1974] 1 All ER 1126, the directors were faced with a takeover by the defendant company and an associate company which currently controlled the company. The aim was to convert it into a wholly owned subsidiary. The directors preferred to be taken over by the claimant company and issued shares to the claimant. The court held that this was an abuse of the directors' powers.

This potential for abuse was curtailed when the board's power to allot shares was restricted by **CA 1985, s. 80,** and pre-emption rights were given to existing shareholders over new issues by **CA 1985, s. 89.** These powers are now in modified form in the **Companies Act 2006 (CA 2006).**

For private companies with one class of shares, the directors may exercise the company's power: (a) to allot shares; or (b) to grant rights to subscribe for or to convert any security into such shares, except to the extent that they are prohibited from doing so by the company's articles: **s. 550.**

Otherwise, the directors may exercise a company's power (a) to allot shares, or to grant rights to subscribe for or to convert any security into shares, if authorized to do so by the company's articles or by resolution of the company: **s. 551(1).**

Authorization may be particular or general, and may be unconditional or conditional: **s. 551(2).** It must state the maximum amount of shares that may be allotted, and the date on which it will expire, which must not be more than five years from: (a) in the case of authorization in the articles, the date of original incorporation; (b) in any other case, the date on which the resolution is passed: **s. 551(3).** Authorization may be renewed or further renewed for a further period not exceeding five years, and be revoked at any time by resolution of the company: **s. 551(4).** A resolution to give, vary, revoke, or renew authorization may be an ordinary resolution, even though it amends the company's articles: **s. 551(8).**

In respect of existing shareholders, they are given statutory pre-emption rights in respect of an allotment of equity securities. 'Equity securities' means (a) ordinary shares, or (b) rights to subscribe for, or to convert securities into, ordinary shares. 'Ordinary shares' are defined as shares other than those with limited rights of participation in respect of dividends and capital in a distribution: **s. 560.**

A company must not allot equity securities to a person on any terms unless it has made an offer to each person holding ordinary shares to allot to him on the same or more favourable terms a proportion of those securities that is as nearly as practicable equal to the proportion held by him of the ordinary share capital, and the period for acceptance of such an offer has expired or the company has received notice of the acceptance or refusal of every offer made: **s. 561.** Shares held by the company as treasury shares are disregarded for the purposes of this section: **s. 561(4).**

As regards the communication of the right of pre-emption, the methods of communication of the offer are laid down in **s. 562(2) and (3).** The offer must state a period during which it may be accepted and the offer cannot be withdrawn before the end of that period. The period is of at least 21 days beginning with the date of the communication of the offer depending on whether it is made in hard copy form, electronic form, or by publication in the *London Gazette*: **s. 562(5).**

In the event of contravention of **ss. 561/562,** the company and every officer who knowingly authorized or permitted the contravention are jointly and severally liable to compensate the person to whom an offer should have been made for any loss, damage, costs, and expenses sustained or incurred as a result: **s. 563(2).**

Section 561 is subject to exceptions in relations to the issue of bonus shares (**s. 564**), issues for non-cash consideration (**s. 565**), and securities held under employee share schemes: **s. 566**.

In addition, the articles of a private company can exclude all or any of the statutory requirements regarding the right of pre-emption and the communication of pre-emption offers to shareholders: **s. 567(1)**. These can be excluded generally in relation to the allotment by the company of equity securities, or in relation to allotments of a particular description: **s. 567(2)**. Any requirement or authorization contained in the articles of a private company that is inconsistent with the pre-emption right and the making of pre-emption offers is treated as a provision excluding that section.

Private companies can also exclude the pre-emption rights of existing members if the company's articles contain a corresponding right in accordance with **s. 568**.

The pre-emption rights can also be disapplied in the case of private companies with only one class of shares. The directors may be given power by the articles, or by special resolution, to allot equity securities as if **s. 561** did not apply to the allotment, or applied as modified by the directors: **s. 569(1)**.

Pre-emption rights can also be disapplied for directors acting under general authorization: **s. 570**. Where the directors are generally authorized, they may be given power by the articles to allot equity securities as if **s. 561** did not apply to the allotment, or applied to the allotment subject to as modified by the directors: **s. 570(1)**. This power ceases to be effective when the authorization is revoked or would (if not renewed) expire. But if the authorization is renewed, the power may also be renewed by special resolution for no longer than the period for which the authorization is renewed: **s. 570(3)**.

A further area of disapplication applies where the directors are authorized to allot shares, whether generally or otherwise. The company may by special resolution resolve that **s. 561** does not apply to a specified allotment of equity securities to be made pursuant to that authorization, or applies as modified by the resolution: **s. 571(1)**. A special resolution ceases to have effect when the authorization to which it relates is revoked or would (if not renewed) expire, but if the authorization is renewed the resolution may also be renewed by a special resolution, for no longer than the period for which the authorization is renewed: **s. 571(3)**.

A special resolution must be recommended by the directors, who must have made a written statement giving their reasons for making the recommendation, the amount to be paid in respect of the equity securities, and their justification of that amount. If it is to be proposed as a written resolution, the statement must be sent or submitted to every eligible member at or before the time the proposed resolution is sent or submitted to him; or if proposed at a general meeting, be circulated with the notice of the meeting: **s. 571(5)–(7)**. Persons who knowingly or recklessly authorize or permit the inclusion of misleading, false, or deceptive matters in the statement are guilty of an offence: **s. 572**. There is also the possibility of disapplication in respect of the sale of shares held by the company as treasury shares: **s. 573**.

In conclusion, the position is more closely regulated in the case of public companies or private companies with more than one class of shares. The important points to note are the fact of time limitations under **s. 551**, which also apply in respect of the disapplication of the section, except for private companies with one class of share. In addition the criminal and civil liability in the event of breach of the statutory requirements would appear to be more than sufficient to ensure that directors comply with the statutory rules.

Question 4

Utopia plc has a share capital of two million £1 ordinary shares and one million £17 per cent cumulative preference shares. The preference shares have the following rights under the articles:

  (a) to participate rateably with the ordinary shareholders in the profits of the company, and

  (b) a preferential right to dividends and repayment of capital on winding up, and

  (c) no right to attend meetings and to vote

Following the sale of its chain of 'Paradiso Hotels', the company has capital surplus to its requirements and the directors of Utopia plc decided that, operating a reduced business following the disposal, it will be difficult to support the payment of the preferential dividend. The board decided, therefore, to formally reduce the company's capital by buying in and cancelling the preferential shares.

In accordance with the procedure under **CA 2006, s. 645**, Utopia plc passed a resolution to reduce the issued share capital by repaying the preference shares at par. The preference shareholders did not receive notice of the meeting and the vote was passed by the holders of the ordinary shares. The preference shareholders have not yet received a dividend in respect of the previous financial year.

Advise the preference shareholders whether:

  (a) They can prevent Utopia plc from going through with the reduction, and otherwise

  (b) Whether they are entitled to arrears of cumulative dividend prior to being bought out

 Commentary

This problem raises the issue of the rights of preference shareholders, particularly the fact that, where shareholders are given preferential rights in respect of dividend and return of capital, these are held to be an exhaustive statement of their rights. This means that a preferential right to a return of capital on a winding up excludes the preference shareholders from a right to a share of surplus assets. This has been established in numerous decisions since the 1950s and you are required to show your familiarity with them and to understand their significance.

The question also raises the issue of the right of shareholders to claim arrears of undeclared preferential dividend.

 Answer plan

- Rule relating to the interpretation of class rights and recognition of the exhaustive nature of any preferential right

- Explanation of the significance of the application of this rule of interpretation which makes the preference shareholder vulnerable to a selective reduction of company capital

- Recognition that such a selective reduction does not constitute a variation of class rights, neither would it enable a petition on the grounds of unfair prejudice

- Explanation of the position regarding arrears of undeclared dividend

Suggested answer

This problem raises the issue of the interpretation of class rights as set out in the company's articles and whether there has been a variation of those rights in breach of the requirements of **CA 2006**. It also concerns the date at which the right to a dividend vests and becomes an actionable right against the company.

The legal presumption in respect of the interpretation of class rights is that all shares have equal rights unless otherwise stated. The rights referred to are the right to a dividend, the right to attend and to vote at the general meetings of the company and the right to the return of capital in the event of the winding up of the company. In contradiction of this statement of equality, however, it has been held that where a particular class of share has been given a preferential right in any one of these areas, this is an exhaustive statement of the shareholder's right in that respect.

This was first decided in respect of the right of preference shareholders to a preferential, fixed dividend paid in priority to the ordinary shareholders. Thus, in *Will v United Lankat Plantations Ltd* [1914] **AC 11** the House of Lords affirmed a Court of Appeal decision that where shareholders were entitled to a fixed dividend of 10 per cent in preference to the payment of a dividend to the ordinary shareholders, they had no further right to participate when a higher dividend was paid to the ordinary shareholders. The decision was of great importance to the holders of preference shares which, previous to this decision, had been presumed to be participating preferential, or preferred ordinary, shares. This meant that, in addition to receiving their fixed dividend in priority to a payment of dividend to the ordinary shareholders, they could share in any payment of dividend in excess of their fixed dividend when the distribution was made to the ordinary shareholders.

This decision was later extended to cover the preferential right to a return of capital on winding up. In *Scottish Insurance Corporation Ltd v Wilsons & Clyde Coal Co Ltd* [1949] 1 All ER 1068 it was held that where preference shareholders enjoyed a preferential right to return of their capital on winding up, they had no further rights to share in the distribution of surplus assets. This meant that the rights in respect of any surplus assets were the sole preserve of the ordinary shareholders. In this case, the defendant company's business had been nationalized and the company proposed to pay off the preference capital in anticipation of liquidation. Once the company had paid off the preference shareholders, it intended to distribute as surplus assets to the ordinary shareholders, the compensation received by the company for the transfer of the company's business and assets to the National Coal Board.

This scheme was opposed by the holders of the preference shares who believed that this would rob them of their right to participate in surplus assets in the liquidation. The shareholders also claimed that the proposed selective reduction was unfair since it deprived them of the right to continue to receive a favourable return (7 per cent) on their investment. The court equated the position of preference shareholders to that of a creditor stating: 'Whether a man lends money to a company at 7% or subscribes for its shares carrying a cumulative preferential dividend at that rate, I do not think that he can complain of unfairness if the company, being in a position lawfully to do so, proposes to pay him off.' The consequence of this decision was to allow companies to engage in a selective reduction of capital under **s. 641** by reducing their capital to repay the preference shares and to cancel them.

In another decision arising out of the nationalization of the coal industry, *Re Chatterley-Whitfield Collieries Ltd* [1948] 2 All ER 593, the company proposed to continue its mining activities in Northern Ireland but the loss of its principal business activity meant that it had capital surplus to its requirements. The company proposed to repay out of its reserves the whole of the preference capital at par and to cancel them. The articles entitled the preference shareholders to the return of their capital on a winding up in priority to the ordinary shareholders. The Court of Appeal held that a company that reached a decision that it could no longer support the dividend payments on its preferential capital would be guilty of financial ineptitude if it did not take steps to reduce its capital by paying off the preferential shares. It also stated that, in confirming a reduction of capital, the court will require the reduction to be effected by the repayment of capital in the first instance to those shareholders entitled to priority in a winding up. This decision was confirmed by the House of Lords in *Prudential Assurance Co Ltd v Chatterley-Whitfield Collieries Ltd* [1949] AC 512.

In a more recent case, the court approved of the statement by Lord Greene MR in the *Chatterley-Whitfield* case that the risk of prior repayment on a reduction of capital 'is a liability that anyone has only himself to blame if he does not know it': *Re Saltdean Estate Co Ltd* [1968] 1 WLR 1844. The court also stated that such prior payment was not a variation or abrogation of any right attached to such a share. This was approved by the House of Lords in *House of Fraser plc v ACGE Investment Ltd* [1987] AC 387 where, faced with the cancellation of preference shares, it approved the statement in the Court of Appeal: 'the proposed cancellation of the preference shares would involve fulfilment or satisfaction of the contractual rights of the shareholders, and would not involve any variation of their rights'.

This means that it is impossible, therefore, for shareholders in such a situation to claim that they are the victims of a variation of their class rights in breach of **s. 630(2)**, unless the articles expressly provided that the rights attached to a class of share shall be deemed to be varied by a reduction of the capital paid up on the shares, when a separate class meeting would be required. In *Re Northern Engineering Industries plc* [1994] 2 BCLC 704, the preference shareholders had sought to protect themselves by the insertion into the company's articles of a provision that a reduction of capital paid up on their shares was deemed to be a variation of their rights requiring approval in a separate class meeting. The company argued that the variation only covered a reduction in the paid up value not the extinction of the capital by repayment of the total amount. The Court held that 'reduction' included 'extinction'.

The company can therefore pass a resolution (voted by the holders of ordinary shares) to reduce the company's capital by cancelling the preference shares and repaying them (possibly at their nominal value) without the preference shareholders having a say in the matter. It is also clear that the court will confirm the decision under **s. 645**.

It would not be possible, either, for the preference shareholders to claim unfair prejudice under **CA 2006, s. 994**.

We are also asked to advise the preference shareholders as to whether they are entitled to their arrears of unpaid dividend before they can be bought in and cancelled. Claims in respect of arrears of undeclared cumulative preference dividend are not provable in a winding up. Arrears of declared cumulative dividend are a deferred debt in a winding up and only payable out of surplus assets remaining after repayment of other debts. It would therefore not be possible for the preference shareholders to claim payment of arrears of undeclared dividend.

In conclusion, Utopia plc can proceed with its scheme without fear of any intervention in favour of the rights of the preference shareholders as long as they comply with the statutory rules relating to reduction of capital.

Question 5

To what extent can it be claimed that the law adequately protects shareholders against a variation of their class rights? Analyse the strengths and weaknesses of the current system with particular regard to preference shareholders.

Commentary

This question requires you to discuss the law relating to the protection of shareholders against a variation of their rights by the company. The position is that variation of class rights can only be achieved in accordance with express variation of class rights terms contained in the company's articles and, in the absence of such a provision, in compliance with the statutory provisions under **CA 2006**. An analysis of the effectiveness of the protection cannot be complete without discussion of the judicial interpretation of a variation or abrogation of class rights. This severely reduces the potential protection offered by the statute.

 Answer plan

- Statement of the statutory protection of class rights
- Judicial interpretation of class rights: positive and negative aspects
- Possibility of shareholders claiming that a variation could be successfully contested by a petition against unfair prejudice: **s. 994**
- Possible breach of directors' duty to act fairly between members of the company

Suggested answer

In an attempt to increase the protection of shareholders against a variation of their class rights, the **Companies Act 1985** introduced statutory regulation of variation of class rights where the company's articles were silent on the matter. As a result, class rights could not be varied under the normal statutory provision relating to the alteration of the company's articles in general (**CA 1985, s. 9(1)—CA 2006, s. 21**), but only in accordance with a variation procedure in the company's constitution or in accordance with **CA 1985, ss. 125–127**. The position is now covered by **Chapter 9, Part 17, ss. 630–640** which distinguish between companies with and without a share capital. In this respect, this answer deals only with the case of companies with a share capital.

Rights attached to a class of a company's shares can only be varied in accordance with a variation provision in the company's articles or with the consent of the holders of shares of that class in accordance with the section: **s. 630(2)**. The consent required for these purposes is consent in writing from the holders of at least three-quarters in nominal value of the issued shares of that class, or a special resolution passed at a separate class meeting: **s. 630(4)**. The section further provides that any amendment of a provision in the company's articles for the variation of class rights, or the insertion of such a provision into the articles, is itself to be treated as a variation of those rights: **s. 630(5)**. It further provides that any reference in the section and in a provision in the articles to variation of rights shall include a reference to their abrogation: **s. 630(6)**.

This is without prejudice to any other restrictions on the variation of the rights (**s. 630(3)**) which allows for the possibility that variation may be restricted by entrenched provisions of the articles under **s. 22**.

Nothing in **s. 630** affects the power of the court under **s. 98** (application to cancel resolutions for a public company to be re-registered as private), **Part 26** (arrangements and reconstructions—**ss. 895–901**), or **Part 30** (protection of members against unfair prejudice—**ss. 994–996, s. 632**).

As added protection, where rights attached to any class of share are varied under **s. 630**, the Act provides for the holders of not less in the aggregate than 15 per cent of the issued shares of the class in question (being persons who did not consent to or vote in favour of the resolution for the variation) to apply to the court to have the variation cancelled: **s. 633(2)**. In this case, the variation has no effect unless and until it is confirmed by the court: **s. 633(3)**. The application must be within 21 days of the giving of the consent or the passing of the resolution.

There would appear, therefore, to be adequate statutory protection of shareholders against variation of their class rights. To have a complete picture, however, it is necessary to look at the judicial interpretation of class rights and to analyse the protection that the courts have been willing to recognize.

On the positive side, the court has held that a vote on a resolution to modify class rights must be exercised for the purpose, or dominant purpose, of benefiting the class as a whole: *British America Nickel Corpn Ltd v O'Brien* [1927] AC 369. In this case, the company had issued mortgage bonds secured by a trust deed that provided that a majority of bondholders, representing not less than three-quarters in value, could sanction a modification of the bondholders' rights. A scheme for reconstruction of the company was approved by the requisite majority, but it was held that one of the bondholders, without whose vote the proposal would have failed, had been induced to support the proposal by the promise of a large block of ordinary shares. The Privy Council held that the vote was invalid.

In the same way, it has been held that shareholders voting in a class meeting in connection with a reduction of capital must have regard to the interests of the class as a whole: *Re Holders Investment Trust Ltd* [1971] 1 WLR 583. In this case, the company sought confirmation from the court of a reduction of capital by which it proposed to cancel the redeemable preference shares and to allot the holders an equivalent amount of unsecured loan stock. The proposal was approved by an extraordinary class meeting of the preference shareholders at which 90 per cent of the votes cast were held by trustees who also held about 52 per cent of the ordinary shares and who, as such, stood to gain substantially from the reduction. The court held that the vote was ineffective because the majority preference shareholders had voted in their own interests without regard to what was best for the preference shareholders as a class.

A further positive step was to increase the scope of the definition of what constituted class rights, over and above the traditional notion of rights attached to particular shares concerning the right to vote, to participate in dividends and to return of capital on winding up.

In a number of more recent decisions, the range of class rights has been judicially extended offering greater protection to shareholders. In *Cumbrian Newspapers Group Ltd v Cumberland & Westmorland Herald Newspaper & Printing Co Ltd* [1986] **BCLC 286** the plaintiff had acquired 10.67 per cent of the ordinary shares in the defendant company as part of an arrangement to concentrate the local newspaper business and make it difficult for outsiders to acquire control of the paper. In line with this, the articles of the defendant were altered to give the plaintiff: (a) rights of pre-emption over the company's other ordinary shares (articles 7 and 9); (b) rights in respect of unissued shares (article 5); and (c) the right to appoint a director for as long as the plaintiff continued to hold at least 10 per cent of the defendant's shares (article 12). The court held that these were rights or benefits conferred on the beneficiary in the capacity of member or shareholder of the company and thereby rights attached to a class of shares which could not be altered or removed by a special resolution under **CA 1985, s. 9(1)** (now **CA 2006, s. 21(1)**) but which could only be varied under **CA 1985, s. 125** (now **CA 2006, s. 630**).

In *Harman v BML Group Ltd* [1994] 1 WLR 893, a company had 190,000 B shares held by B and 310,000 A shares, 260,000 of which were held by H and M. Under a shareholders' agreement the two classes of shares ranked equally except for certain specified pre-emption rights, and a shareholders' meeting could not be quorate unless a B shareholder was present or represented by a proxy. The Court of Appeal held that B's right to be present in a quorum was a class right.

The courts have, however, equally operated to weaken the protection offered to holders of a particular class of shares by making a distinction between direct and indirect variation of shareholders' rights. While a direct variation of class rights is protected by the law, the court has held that the rights of a class of shareholders are not altered, or even 'affected', by a change in the company's structure or in the rights attached to other shares which affects merely the enjoyment of such rights. In *White v Bristol Aeroplane Co* [1953] Ch 65, the company's articles provided that the rights attached to any class of shares might be 'affected, modified, varied, dealt with, or abrogated in any manner' with the sanction of an extraordinary resolution at a class meeting. The company, which had an issued capital of £600,000 preference and £3.3m ordinary shares, proposed to issue to the existing ordinary shareholders 660,000 preference shares of £1 each and 2.64m ordinary shares at 50p each, financed from the company's reserves. This was help not to affect the rights of the existing holders of preference shares so as to require their approval. Their rights were as before although effectively swamped by the enlargement of the class of persons entitled to exercise them. This decision also applied in *Re John Smith's Tadcaster Brewery* [1953] Ch 308.

In *Greenhalgh v Arderne Cinemas Ltd* [1946] 1 All ER 512 the company had two classes of share: one with a nominal value of 10p and the other with a nominal value of 50p; both shares had the right to one vote per share. The holder of the 10p shares was able to dominate the company's decisions. To destroy the power of this class of share, the company passed a resolution splitting the 50p shares into five 10p shares, each with a right to one vote per share. The court held that this was not a variation of the rights of the holder of the 10p shares. In an extraordinary decision, the court also held that a rateable reduction of all shares, including preference shares, was not a variation of the class rights of the preference shares, although it resulted in a reduction of the preference dividend while it did not affect the ordinary dividend: *Re Mackenzie & Co Ltd* [1916] 2 Ch 450.

In respect of these decisions, it is clear that the disadvantaged shareholders would now be able to bring a claim in respect of unfair prejudice under **s. 994**. It is also clear that, if it could be established that the directors were not acting fairly as between members of the company in accordance with **s. 172(1)(f)**, they would be in breach of their duty to the company which would give rise to civil penalties under **s. 178**.

Further reading

Milne, E., 'Joint venture shareholders: protecting your position' (2010) PLC, 21(4): 45.

Pennington, R., 'Can shares in companies be defined?' [1989] Comp. Law., 10(7): 140–144.

7

Directors and their duties

Introduction

This is a very important chapter and a major source of examination questions in all company law programmes. The first thing that needs to be understood is the significance of the extended nature of the definition of directors. The **Companies Act 2006** (**CA 2006**) continues with the functional definition of a director as including any person occupying the position of director, by whatever name called (**s. 250**), which extends to de jure and de facto directors. In addition the statute also identifies the 'shadow director' as 'a person in accordance with whose directions or instructions the directors of the company are accustomed to act' (**s. 251(1)**) excluding persons giving advice in a professional capacity: **s. 251(2)**.

It is also important to realize that similar—but not always identical—definitions occur in the **Company Directors Disqualification Act 1986** (**CDDA 1986**) and the **Insolvency Act 1986** (**IA 1986**). It is important that you refer to the correct definition depending on the context. There has been much judicial agonizing about the legal distinction—if any—between de facto and shadow directors. You need to be able to analyse the points established in these decisions.

The **Companies Act 2006** sets out the statutory duties of directors in **ss. 170–177** and the civil consequences of a breach of any duty are detailed in **s. 178**. The sections are a codification of the existing common law rules and equitable principles and the civil consequences of their breach, and it is important to be familiar with the judicial decisions establishing those duties and to relate them to the appropriate section.

The statute radically changes the general duty of care, skill, and diligence which mirrors that established in respect of wrongful trading in **IA 1986, s. 214**.

Other topics of importance in this area of the syllabus are:

(a) the newly established age qualification for appointment as a director: **s. 157–159**

(b) the removal of directors by ordinary resolution of the general meeting with special notice: **s. 168–169**

(c) statutory disqualification of directors under **CDDA 1986**

(d) regulation of loans to directors and connected persons: **s. 197–214**

(e) transactions with directors requiring consent of the members, and

(f) insider dealing under the **Criminal Justice Act 1993 (CJA 1993)**

Question 1

Section 250 of the **Companies Act 2006** gives an extended definition of 'director' to include not only 'de jure' directors but also 'de facto' directors. In respect of 'de facto' and 'shadow directors' consider the ways in which the courts have attempted to distinguish between the two and whether there is a meaningful distinction between them.

 Commentary

This is a relatively straightforward question that nevertheless requires appreciation of the different statutory definitions of shadow director in the statutes and the significance of the difference. It also calls for discussion and analysis of a number of judicial decisions to trace the evolution of the concepts of de facto and shadow directors. Since other common law jurisdictions make the same or similar distinctions, many of the relevant judicial decisions derive from Australia and New Zealand. Until the recent creation of the New Zealand Supreme Court the Judicial Committee of the Privy Council was the final court of appeal for New Zealand.

 Answer plan

- Statement of the definitions of 'director' in UK legislation and analysis of the differences arising from those definitions
- Identification of the vulnerable parties
- Analysis of judicial decisions concerning attempts to define and distinguish between de facto and shadow directors
- Flexible approach of the UK Court of Appeal stressing similarities

Suggested answer

A director is defined as including 'any person occupying the position of a director, by whatever name called': CA 2006, s. 250. There are three categories of director: de jure directors, de facto directors, and shadow directors. The last is defined as persons 'in accordance with whose directions or instructions the directors of the company are accustomed to act', but excluding persons giving advice in a professional capacity: CA 2006, s. 251. There is a proviso that 'a body corporate is not to be treated as a shadow director of any of its subsidiary companies by reason only that the directors of the subsidiary are accustomed to act in accordance with its directions or instructions'.

The **Company Directors Disqualification Act 1986** contains a similar definition of a director (**s. 22(4)**) and shadow director (**s. 22(5)**), as does **IA 1986** (**s. 251**). The proviso excluding parent companies in respect of their subsidiaries is missing, however, and parent companies can be shadow directors of subsidiaries for the purposes of **s. 214** (wrongful trading) and are subject to statutory disqualification. The parties most vulnerable to claims of being de facto or shadow directors are major shareholders, creditors (including banks), and consultants, and they are the subject of most of the legal decisions considered below.

UK decisions have attempted to define and distinguish between de facto and shadow directors. In *Re Lo-Line Electric Motors Ltd* [1988] Ch 477, Sir Nicolas Browne Wilkinson VC likened a shadow director to an *éminence grise*. And Harman J in *Re Unisoft Group Ltd* [1994] 1 BCLC 609 referred to the shadow director as 'the puppet master' and the board as the 'cat's paw' of the shadow director.

In *Re a Company (No 005009 of 1987), ex p Copp* [1989] BCLC 13 it was claimed that a bank which imposed terms on a technically insolvent company allowing it to continue to trade was a shadow director. In *Kuwait Asia Bank EC v National Mutual Life Nominees Ltd* [1991] 1 AC 187, the Kuwait Bank and another company held 80 per cent of the shares in AIC Securities Ltd (AICS). By agreement, AICS was to have five directors, two nominated by the bank and three by the other company. The bank's nominees were bank employees. Rejecting a claim that the bank was a shadow director of ACIS, Lord Lowry stated: '[the bank's nominees] were two out of five directors ... And there is no allegation ... that the directors ... were accustomed to act on the direction and instruction of the bank'. This is authority that a person could only be a shadow director if the board as a whole was accustomed to act on their directions or instructions.

In *Re Hydrodam (Corby) Ltd* [1994] 2 BCLC 180, the liquidator of Hydrodam, a wholly owned subsidiary of Eagle Trust plc, applied for orders against 14 defendants under **IA 1986, s. 214** including Eagle Trust plc and all of its directors maintaining that they were shadow or de facto directors of Hydrodam, which only had two corporate directors. Millett J held there was an essential difference between the two, seeing them as alternatives and even 'in most ... cases ... mutually exclusive'.

According to Millett J, a de facto director is held out as a director, and claims to be a director although never actually appointed as such. He held that it was necessary to prove that they undertook functions which only a director could properly discharge, and not sufficient to be involved in the company's management or undertaking tasks performable by a manager. In contrast, a shadow director does not claim to be a director and is not held out as such. To be a shadow director, it was necessary to prove: (a) who are the directors of the company—de facto or de jure; (b) that the alleged shadow director directed them how to act; (c) that they acted in accordance with such directions; and (d) that they were accustomed to do so.

The main issue was whether the directors of a corporate director of another company were automatically shadow or de facto directors of that other company. Millett J held that something more would be required in order for this to arise such as active participation of the board member in making board decisions by the corporate director in relation to the actions of the subject company. This position has been endorsed by the majority of the Supreme Court in *Re Paycheck Services 3 Ltd* [2010] UKSC 51.

This distinction was not made in *Re Tasbian Ltd (No 3)* [1991] BCLC 792 where the Court of Appeal referred to a 'company doctor' as either a de facto or a shadow director for the purposes of disqualification proceedings.

The Australian decision *Standard Chartered Bank of Australia Ltd v Antico* [1995] 18 ACSR 1 concerned the insolvent liquidation of Giant Resources Ltd (Giant) of which Pioneer International Ltd (Pioneer) held 42 per cent of the shares and appointed three officers as non-executive directors. The claimant had advanced loans to Giant and received nothing from the liquidation whereas Pioneer, a major unsecured lender, had taken charges over Giant's assets in June 1989 before suspending further financial support triggering Giant's liquidation. Hodgson J held that the mere fact that Pioneer had 42 per cent of Giant's shares and three nominees on its board did not make it a shadow director, but that it was a shadow director since the three nominee directors made decisions only in their capacity as directors of Pioneer in respect of Giant's funding and the granting of security.

Another Australian decision, *Australian Securities Commission v AS Nominees* [1995] 13 ACLC 1822, held that the issue was simply to identify the locus of effective decision-making. If the power lay with a third party not claiming adviser protection, the court could find that person a shadow director.

In respect of de facto directors, Robert Walker J in *Re Kaytech* [1999] 2 BCLC 351, CA, stated that the court should take account of all external and internal factors as a question of fact rather than a single test. Shadow and de facto directors had in common the fact that they exercised real influence (otherwise than as professional advisers) in the governance of a company, and that this could be concealed or open and even a combination of both.

The UK Court of Appeal considered the definition of shadow director in *Secretary of State for Trade and Industry v Deverell* [2000] 2 WLR 907 in respect of disqualification orders against two men who claimed to be 'consultants'. It was established that both men regularly gave advice, which the board followed as a matter of course. Morritt LJ, finding that the two defendants were shadow directors, stated that the issue was who had real influence in the company regardless of labels and forms of communication and that 'shadow director' was to be broadly construed to give effect to the parliamentary intention of the protection of the public rather than strictly construed because of its quasi-penal consequences. The aim was to identify those, apart from professional advisers, with real influence in the company. He agreed with Finn J in *Australia Securities Commission* and Robert Walker J in *Re Kaytech* that this did not have to be over the whole field of its corporate activities, but must cover essential matters of corporate governance including financial affairs. Whether a communication was a direction or instruction was to be objectively ascertained from all available evidence. The label attached to the communication by either or both parties was only one factor to consider and that non-professional advice was sufficient since the concept of 'advice' is not excluded by the terms 'direction' and 'instruction'. It was not a necessary requirement to prove that some or all of the directors placed themselves in a subservient role or surrender their discretion to the shadow director. Describing the board as the cat's paw, puppet, or dancer to the shadow director's tune was a degree of control in excess of the statutory requirement. Neither was it necessary for a shadow director to lurk in the shadows.

Later decisions have continued this debate and the distinction between shadow and de facto directors is increasingly blurred. In *Re Mea Corpn Ltd, Secretary of State for Trade and Industry v Aviss* [2006] **EWHC 1846** the court held that the role of the shadow director did not have to extend over the whole range of the company's activities and that there was no conceptual difficulty in reaching the conclusion that a person could be a de facto and shadow director at the same time. In *Gemma Ltd v Davies* [2008] **EWHC 546**, the court held that in order to be a de facto or shadow director, it had to be shown that the person had 'real influence' on the corporate decision making. In *Re Mumtaz Properties Ltd* [2011] **EWCA Civ 610** it was held that a person was a de facto director even though he had held not held himself out to be a director.

In conclusion, while recognizing the value of the extended definition of directors, it is arguably counter-productive to attempt to distinguish between shadow and de facto directors.

Question 2

Datacon plc specializes in IT installations for the retail trade. Tariq, a director of Datacon plc, was approached in a private capacity as a well-known expert in the field and invited to join the board of Input Ltd, whose business mirrors to a certain extent Datacon plc's business. Tariq accepted an invitation to be a director while remaining on the board of Datacon plc, and acted as a consultant and adviser.

Having developed a rival system to Datacon plc, Input Ltd organized a public launch of the new product. For the launch, Tariq contacted a number of Datacon plc's clients. The launch led to the signing up of a number of major clients, including some clients of Datacon plc.

(a) Advise the board of Datacon plc of any breaches of duty committed by Tariq, and any remedies available against him

(b) Would your answer be different if he had resigned his directorship of Datacon plc when he joined the board of Input Ltd?

Commentary

This problem question raises two related issues: whether a director of one company can become a director of a competing company; and the duty of confidentiality. These are related since early decisions on the issue of overlapping directorships accept the possibility, and only envisage a problem where the director breaches his duty of confidentiality in carrying information from one company into the other. Since the 1970s the problem of overlapping directorships has been frequently discussed but the matter is still largely unresolved.

 Answer plan

- Identification of legal problems raised by the questions
- Discussion of legality of interlocking/overlapping directorships
- Breach of confidentiality during directorship and after leaving

Suggested answer

The legal issues raised by this question concern whether a person can hold directorships in competing companies and the issue of the duty of confidentiality in the situation of interlocking directorships.

The first issue to examine is whether by merely joining the board of Input Ltd, Tariq had acted in breach of his fiduciary duties to the company. The legal issue of overlapping directorships was raised initially in *London and Mashonaland Exploration Company Ltd v New Mashonaland Exploration Co Ltd* [1891] WN 165 where the plaintiff company sought to restrain its chairman and director from acting as director of a rival company. The judgment of Chitty J initially approached the issue by looking for any contractual restraint and concluded that there was nothing in the articles which required him to give any part of his time, much less the whole of his time, to the business of the company, or which prohibited him from acting as a director of another company. He then identified the problem as one of confidentiality stating that no case was made out that the chairman was about to disclose to the defendant company any confidential information gained from his position. This decision was cited with approval by Lord Blanesborough in *Bell v Lever Bros* [1932] AC 161, 195.

The issue was raised again in the light of the decision in *Hivac Ltd v Park Royal Scientific Instruments Ltd* [1946] Ch 169 which held that employees could be restrained from working for a business competing with that of their employer. Following this decision, doubts were expressed as to whether *Bell v Lever Bros* still accurately reflected the law: per McDonald J in *Abbey Glen Property Corpn v Stumborg* (1975) 65 DLR (3d) 235, 278.

The issue was dealt with in *Plus Group Ltd v Pyke* [2002] EWCA Civ 370, [2002] 2 BCLC 201 where the Court of Appeal approved the trial judge's statement that: 'it is not a breach of fiduciary duty for a director to work for a competing company in circumstances where he has been excluded effectively from the company of which he is a director'.

The court, however, seemed to indicate that, in general, the holding of competing directorships would require the approval of the companies in question; but that there was no rigid rule that a director could not be involved in the business of another company which was in competition with the company of which he was a director, and stressed that the situation was 'fact specific'. In this case the court referred to *Scottish Co-operative Wholesale Society Ltd v Meyer* [1959] AC 324 which, while not entirely relevant to the situation, shows the problems that can arise regarding owing fiduciary duties to more than one company, although the situation in that case concerned the problem of the nominee director.

The fiduciary and common law duties of directors have now been codified in **CA 2006**. Since this is a codification, however, and because it is expressly stated that the general duties are based on the common law rules and equitable principles and should be interpreted and applied in the same way (**s. 170(3) and (4)**), it is difficult to argue that the legislation will have changed the situation.

In conclusion, there would not appear to be a breach of duties by merely joining the board of Input Ltd. The problem arises in that Tariq clearly acts in breach of his duty of confidentiality in publicizing the launch of Input Ltd's competing software to clients of Datacon plc, while remaining on the board of Datacon plc. In this case, Datacon plc would be entitled to claim damages against Tariq. This would clearly be a breach of the general duty to avoid situations in which a director has, or can have, a direct or indirect interest that conflicts, or possibly may conflict, with the interests of the company (**s. 175(1)**), which applies to exploitation of any property, information, or opportunity: **s. 175(2)**. In addition, the decision in *Item Software (UK) Ltd v Fassihi* [2004] EWCA Civ 1244 suggests that the director would also have a duty to disclose to the company his own wrongdoing.

The position would be different, however, had Tariq resigned from the board of Datacon plc as soon as he joined the board of Input Ltd. Once he had resigned from his directorship, and in the absence of any restraint of trade clause prohibiting him from contacting clients of Datacon plc during a reasonable period of time, Tariq would be able to escape claims of breach of confidentiality in contacting Datacon plc's clients.

The situation would be analogous to the decision in *Island Export Finance Ltd v Umunna* [1986] BCLC 460 where the plaintiff company was unsuccessful in an action regarding breach of confidentiality against the defendant, the ex-managing director of the company. The issue in this case concerned Umunna's knowledge of the Cameroon postal authorities' need for postal boxes, previously supplied by IEF Ltd. The court held that, once Umunna had resigned from the company, this knowledge ceased to be confidential and could be used by him in the absence of any restraint of trade clause to bring in business to the business that he had since established. The court applied the classification of confidential information that had been established in *Faccenda*

Chicken Ltd v Fowler [1987] Ch 117. In this case, the court held that there were three types of confidential information and that knowledge of a former employer's client list was category 2 information which an employee (and by analogy a director) was able to use once leaving their employment or the board.

Thus, in conclusion, by merely joining the board of a competing company, Tariq is not in breach of any duty to Datacon plc. Once however, he communicates confidential information belonging to Datacon plc to the board of Input Ltd he is breach of his duty to avoid conflicts of interest: **CA 2006, s. 175**. Once he has resigned from the board of Datacon plc, however, he is free to use this information in his new position as director of Input Ltd.

Question 3

Analyse the development of the director's duty of care, skill, and diligence from the common law position of *Re City Equitable Fire Assurance Co Ltd* [1925] Ch 407 up to and including CA 2006.

 Commentary

This essay question requires you to analyse the influences that have changed the law from the old laissez-faire attitude typified by the decision in *Re City Equitable Fire* into something more suited to the modern, regulated world of business. The standard textbook notion that the common law duty of care, skill, and diligence continued unchanged until the **CA 2006** ignores the enormous influence of late twentieth-century legislation in the form of **the IA 1986** and **CDDA 1986**. The influence of **IA 1986** fed into the common law in the early 1990s as can be seen in the judgments of Hoffmann J when he was influenced by the dual test established for the offence of wrongful trading in **IA 1986, s. 214(4)**. The influence of **CDDA 1986** is seen in decisions as to whether directors should be disqualified because they were unfit. The influence of both of these sources had resulted in a radical rethink of the standards required of directors by the end of the twentieth century. These have directly influenced the statutory duty to exercise reasonable care, skill, and diligence under **CA 2006, s. 174**.

 Answer plan

- The three propositions of *Re City Equitable Fire Assurance*
- Influence of **IA 1986, s. 214** and relevant decisions
- Influence of **CDDA 1986** and relevant decisions

- Evidence of change to the understanding of the duties of care, skill, and diligence of directors
- The current position in **CA 2006, s. 174**

Suggested answer

The area of directors' duties where there were the most calls for a rethink was in respect of the duties of care, skill, and diligence which reflected the nineteenth-century approach to the role of the director and were no longer compatible with current perceptions of the standards to which directors should aspire.

The accepted seminal decision in this field was the judgment of Romer J in *Re City Equitable Fire Assurance Co Ltd* [1925] Ch 407 which established three propositions:

(i) 'A director need not exhibit in the performance of his duties a greater degree of skill than may reasonably be expected from a person of his knowledge and experience.'

(ii) 'A director is not bound to give continuous attention to the affairs of his company. His duties are of an intermittent nature to be performed at periodical board meetings, and at meetings of any committee of the board ...'

(iii) 'In respect of all duties that ... may properly be left to some other official, a director is, in the absence of grounds for suspicion, justified in trusting that official to perform such duties honestly.'

The main problem with *City Equitable* is that the judgment was influenced by earlier decisions which reflected contemporary values and culture. Decisions like the *Marquis of Bute's Case* [1892] 2 Ch 100 where the Marquis became chairman of the Cardiff Savings Bank at the age of six months and who attended only one board meeting in 38 years and was not guilty of breach of a duty of care, and *Re Brazilian Rubber Plantations and Estates Ltd* [1911] 1 Ch 425 where one of the directors was described as being absolutely ignorant of business and who had consented to become a director because he was told that the office would 'give a little pleasant employment without his incurring any responsibility'. In that decision Neville J stated that 'directors were not bound to bring any special qualifications to their business'; and could 'undertake the management of a rubber company in complete ignorance of anything connected with rubber'.

Taking each of these *City Equitable* propositions, it is clear that the law had evolved away from the common law position by the end of the twentieth century. Thus the subjective nature of the duty owed by directors was influenced by the dual test of care and skill imposed in respect of the offence of wrongful trading in **IA 1986, s. 214(4)** which judged directors against: (a) the general knowledge, skill, and experience that may reasonably be expected of a person carrying out the same functions as are carried out by that director in relation to the company; and (b) the general knowledge, skill, and experience that that director has. In *Norman v Theodore Goddard (A Firm)* [1991] BCLC 1028, Hoffmann J stated that he was willing to assume that the test of the director's duty of care should be on the knowledge, skill, and experience that he actually had in addition to that which a person carrying out his functions should be expected to have. This was restated as a proposition of the law in *Re D'Jan of London Ltd* [1994] 1 BCLC 561.

Another major influence came from decisions relating to the disqualification of directors under **CDDA 1986**. **Sections 6–9 CDDA 1986** require a court to disqualify a director if satisfied that he has been a director of a company which has at any time become insolvent and that his 'conduct as a director of that company … makes him unfit to be concerned in the management of a company': **CDDA 1986, s. 6**. The court may disqualify a director following a statutory investigation of the company even where it has not become insolvent: **CDDA 1986, s. 8**. In determining whether the director is unfit, **s. 9** requires the court to have regard in particular to the matters in **Part I** of **Schedule 1**. Where the company is insolvent the court must also have regard to **Part II** of **Schedule 1**, which includes: 'Any misfeasance or breach of any fiduciary or other duty by the director in relation to the company.'

The courts have explicitly acknowledged that the major purpose of CDDA disqualification is to raise standards of conduct among directors generally. Thus in *Re Westmid Packing Services Ltd, Secretary of State for Trade and Industry v Griffiths* [1998] 2 All ER 124 Lord Woolf MR stated that the purpose of disqualification was not simply to keep 'bad' directors 'off the road' but to protect the public in a wider sense by encouraging other directors to behave well. And in *Re Grayan Building Services Ltd, Secretary of State for Trade and Industry v Gray* [1995] 1 BCLC 896, Henry LJ stated: 'The statutory corporate climate is stricter than it has ever been, and those enforcing it should reflect the fact that Parliament has seen the need for higher standards.'

The influence of this legislation can be seen in the statement by Hoffmann LJ in *Bishopsgate Investment Management Ltd v Maxwell (No 2)* [1994] 1 All ER 261: 'In the older cases the duty of a director to participate in the management of a company is stated in very undemanding terms. The law may be evolving in response to changes in public attitudes to corporate governance as shown by the enactment of the provisions … in the Company Directors Disqualification Act 1986.'

The second and third propositions that directors are not bound to give continuous attention to the company's affairs, and can delegate responsibility to others were also qualified by subsequent decisions. Thus in *Re Barings plc (No 5)* [1999] 1 BCLC 523, in formulating the scope and extent of directors' duties of care, skill, and diligence Jonathan Parker J drew widely on Australian and US authorities and derived three general propositions:

(a) Directors have, both collectively and individually, a continuing duty to acquire and maintain a sufficient knowledge and understanding of the company's business to enable them properly to discharge their duties as directors

(b) While directors are entitled to delegate particular functions to those below them … and to trust their competence and integrity to a reasonable extent … the power of delegation does not absolve a director from the duty to supervise the discharge of delegated functions. This reiterated the statement by Lord Woolf MR in *Re Westmid Packing Services Ltd, Secretary of State for Trade and Industry v Griffiths* [1998] 2 All ER 124, at 130:

'Each individual director owes duties to the company to inform himself about its affairs and to join with his co-directors in supervising and controlling them. A proper degree of delegation is of course permissible, and often necessary, but total abrogating of responsibility is not ...'

and:

'any individual who undertakes the statutory and fiduciary obligations of being a company director should realize that these are inescapable personal responsibilities'.

(c) The extent of the duty [in Proposition 2], and the question whether it has been discharged, must depend on the facts of each particular case, including the director's role in the management of the company.

In a disqualification application in *Landhurst Leasing plc* [1999] 1 BCLC 286 Hart J was required to determine the scope of the duty of the defendants under **Schedule 1, Part I, para. 1**. The judge appeared to have equated the standard of the duty at common law, for the purposes of the **CDDA 1986** and the *D'Jan* test based on **IA 1986, s. 214**. In *Cohen v Selby* [2001] 1 BCLC 176, a company in which father and son were directors but where the son—a student—took no part in the company's affairs, the son escaped personal liability for negligence for failure to insure the company's property since it was regarded as reasonable for him to trust his father. He was, however, disqualified from acting as a director for three years.

From this discussion, it should be apparent that, in spite of the continued tendency to regard the *City Equitable* decision as the seminal statement regarding the duties of care, skill, and diligence, the basic standard had already been raised by reference to the **CDDA 1986** and the **IA 1986**. The legal account of a director's functions had already developed towards the recognition of an objective standard with an emphasis on monitoring and supervision.

The **Companies Act 2006** has consolidated this perception of the director's role. The position has been reinforced by recent decisions. Thus in *Lexi Holdings (in administration) v Luqman and Others* [2009] EWCA Civ 117 the claimant company had been the victim of a major fraud. The first four defendants were directors. The fraud was committed by the first defendant and it was held that the second defendant was aware of the first defendant's misconduct. In respect of the third and fourth defendants, there was a claim that their failure to perform their duties as directors had prevented the misconduct from being discovered and either prevented or terminated. As a result of their inactivity, the two defendants were held liable for the full amounts claimed against them: £41,968,294 and £39,968,988 respectively. It was further held that directors who do nothing cannot rely on **CA 1985, s. 727** (now **CA 2006, s. 1157**) which allows the court to give relief where a director has acted 'honestly and reasonably'.

Question 4

Paradise plc, a quoted company, produces fresh organic fruit. There are three executive directors, Adam, Eve, and Barry as well as three other non-executive directors. Three years ago, Utopia Ltd approached the board of Paradise plc and offered to sell the company a plot of land adjoining one of its principal market gardens.

Because of current uncertainties and a large debt burden, the board rejected the proposal. Subsequently, Adam and Barry, acting through AB Properties Ltd, of which they are the only shareholders and directors, acquired the land in the name of their company for the original asking price of £250,000.

Owing to the recent fall in interest rates and optimistic forecasts by the CBI, the board of Paradise plc regretted its initial failure to acquire the property, which is back on the market at £350,000, and the board contracts on behalf of Paradise plc to acquire the property from AB Properties Ltd. The board was not informed about the identity of the controllers of AB Properties Ltd. Adam and Barry attended the board meeting at which the decision was taken.

Consider the criminal and civil liabilities of Adam and Barry.

 Commentary

This problem question raises the following legal issues: the potential liability of Adam and Barry in taking up a corporate opportunity of Paradise plc and, in the resale of the asset to the company at a profit to a company controlled by them, of their statutory obligation to declare an interest in the transaction and, in view of the size of the transaction, the statutory obligation to obtain the approval by a resolution of the members of the company. This involves you in a discussion of a number of contradictory common law decisions and the application of the statutory provisions of **CA 2006**.

 Answer plan

- Identification of the legal issues raised by the question
- Discussion of the potential conflict of interest of Adam and Barry in the acquisition of a corporate opportunity of Paradise plc
- Statutory controls regarding the resale of the asset owned by AB Ltd to Paradise plc

Suggested answer

The legal issues raised by this question concern conflict of interests (**s. 175**) and the application of **s. 177** concerning the duty of directors to declare their interest in any proposed transaction or arrangement and the need to obtain members' approval for substantial property transactions between the company and directors under **s. 190**.

Paradise plc's rejection of the offer of a plot of land adjoining one of its principal market gardens resulted in two of Paradise plc's directors, Adam and Barry, taking up the offer personally and purchasing the property in the name of their company, AB Properties Ltd. Subsequently, once Paradise plc reconsidered the matter, the property was sold to Paradise plc by AB Properties Ltd at a profit.

This raises two legal issues. In the first place, it is necessary to consider whether Adam and Barry were in breach of their duty to the company in taking up the offer personally. Directors must avoid situations in which they have, or can have, a direct or indirect interest that conflicts, or possibly may conflict, with the interests of the company: **CA 2006, s. 175(1)**. This is stated to apply to the exploitation of any property, information, or opportunity (and it is immaterial whether the company could take advantage of the property, information, or opportunity): **CA 2006, s. 175(2)**.

Applying the 'no conflict/no profit' rule established in *Regal (Hastings) Ltd v Gulliver* **[1942] 1 All ER 378** they would appear to have acted in breach of the duty since they learned of the opportunity in their position as fiduciaries. The issue is complicated by the fact that it would appear that the offer to Paradise plc was rejected bona fide by the company's board. In *Peso Silver Mines Ltd v Cropper* **[1966] SCR 673** the defendant, one of the directors of the claimant, was not liable to account when he formed a syndicate with others to take up an offer of mining claims that had bona fide been rejected by the company.

In reaching its decision, the court was influenced by a statement by the Master of the Rolls in *Regal Hastings* before the Court of Appeal. In this case the court was also influenced by the fact that the offer to the company was not accompanied by any confidential information that was unavailable to any prospective purchaser. It is important to note that this decision is by a Canadian court and is probably influenced by the adoption in Canada of the corporate opportunity doctrine which signals a move away from the rigidity of *Regal Hastings*. The UK decision in *Boardman v Phipps* **[1966] 3 All ER 721**, while not a company law case, is nevertheless an example of the application of *Regal Hastings* and reveals a much stricter approach. Unless the court agrees to adopt a more flexible approach than it has so far, this could clearly be a breach of duty and Adam and Barry could be liable to account for their profits from the subsequent sale.

A further problem arises in connection with the sale of the property by AB Properties Ltd to Paradise plc. Directors who are in any way, directly or indirectly, interested in a proposed transaction or arrangement with the company, must declare the nature and extent of that interest to the other directors: **CA 2006, s. 177(1)**.

This declaration need not be made at a meeting of the directors and can be in writing or in the form of a general notice but it must be made before the company enters into the transaction: **s. 177(2) and (3)**. There are statutory exceptions to this duty to disclose. One does not require a declaration of an interest of which the director is not aware or where a director is not aware of the transaction or arrangement in question: **s. 177(5)**. Since, for this purpose, a director is treated as being aware of matters of which he ought reasonably to be aware, this defence is unavailable. The other cases where a director does not need to declare an interest relate to situations where the transaction cannot be regarded as likely to give rise to a conflict of interest, or to the extent that the other directors are aware of it: **s. 177(6)(a)** and **(b)**. Once again, these are not available for Adam and Barry. As a result of this failure to declare an interest, the company can avoid the contract as in *Aberdeen Rly Co v Blaikie Bros* (1854) 2 Eq Rep 1281 since the civil consequences of a breach of the statutory general duties are stated to be the same as if the corresponding equitable principle applied: **CA 2006, s. 178(1)**. In the alternative, the company could also claim damages against the pair.

Since the transaction is for the sum of £350,000, the transaction also falls within the statutory regulations relating to substantial property transactions. Under these regulations, a company may not enter into an arrangement under which a director of the company or of its holding company, or a person connected with such a director, acquires from the company a substantial non-cash asset, or the company acquires a substantial non-cash asset from such a director or person so connected unless the transaction is approved by a resolution of the members or is conditional on their approval: **s. 190(1)**. An asset is substantial if its value exceeds 10 per cent of the company's asset value and is more than £5,000, or exceeds £100,000: **s. 191(1)**. The civil consequences of a failure to comply with this requirement is that the contract is voidable: **s. 195(2)**. Adam and Barry would also be liable to account to the company for any gain and indemnify the company for any loss: **CA 2006, s. 195(3)**.

In conclusion, Barry and Adam will probably be in breach of their fiduciary duties in respect of the purchase by their company of the property offered to Paradise plc unless the court is prepared to follow the decision in *Peso Silver Mines*. They will also be in breach of their statutory obligation under **s. 177** and **s. 190**. As a result, Paradise plc can avoid the contract. Should the company decide to continue with the purchase, Adam and Barry will be liable to account for the profits derived from the sale and indemnify the company for any loss.

Question 5

Vernon is a director of Infocon plc, an information technology consultancy whose securities are quoted on the Alternative Investment Market (AIM).

At a party on 5 April 2008, Vernon was tipped off by the managing director of Softcell plc that his company was contemplating a takeover bid for Infocon plc, whose shares were currently trading at £1.05p.

On 9 April 2008, Gwen, a shareholder in Infocon plc contacted Vernon and said that she wished to dispose of her holding of 10,000 shares. Vernon acquired the shares directly from Gwen for £1.05p per share.

On 10 April 2008, Vernon instructed his stockbroker to acquire 10,000 shares in Infocon plc at the current market price. Vernon also phoned Bob, a friend, and advised him to acquire some shares in Infocon plc. On 11 April 2008, Bob purchased 5,000 shares at the current market price.

On 15 May 2008, Softcell plc made a cash offer to the shareholders of Infocon plc of £1.60 per share. Vernon sold his shares to Softcell plc who subsequently acquired control of Infocon plc.

(a) Advise Gwen of any rights she may have against Vernon

(b) Consider any civil and criminal liability of Vernon

(c) Consider any criminal liability of Bob

 ## Commentary

This is fairly standard problem question on the topic of duties owed to shareholders individually and the issue of insider dealing as regards directors and tippees. Nevertheless, these are important legal issues and, in respect of any civil liability of Vernon, a situation that is completely undeveloped.

 ## Answer plan

- Identification of the legal problems raised by the question
- Discussion of liability of directors to shareholders individually
- Discussion of the two offences of insider dealing in connection with Vernon and Bob
- Discussion of any potential civil liability of Vernon to Infocon plc

Suggested answer

The question concerns legal problems relating to situations where directors owe a fiduciary duty to shareholders individually and a discussion of the offence of insider dealing under **CJA 1993**. It is also necessary to identify whether Vernon has in any way breached one or more of the general duties that he owes to Infocon plc as a director.

The directors of a company generally owe their duty to the company and not to individual shareholders. This position was initially stated in the decision in *Percival v Wright* [1902] 2 Ch 421, where the claimants offered to sell shares to the directors at a specific price. After the sale they discovered that the directors had been negotiating for the sale of the company at that time, and that they had placed a higher value on the shares than had been received by Percival. The court rejected the claim to set aside the contract on the grounds of non-disclosure and held that there was no fiduciary relationship between directors and the shareholders individually.

This position is now covered by statute and **CA 2006** states that the general duties specified in **ss. 171–177** are owed by a director to the company: **s. 170(1)**. The section further provides, however, that the general duties are based on common law rules and equitable principles, and that the general duties shall be interpreted and applied in the same way as common law rules or equitable principles, and regard shall be had to the corresponding common law rules and equitable principles in interpreting and applying the general duties: **s. 170(3) and (4)**.

In respect of the statement that directors' general duties are owed exclusively to the company and not to shareholders individually, the court has identified exceptional situations where directors have been held to owe a duty to shareholders individually. An early exception was identified in *Allen v Hyatt* **(1914) 30 TLR 444** in which the directors of a company entered into negotiations with the directors of another company to merge the two companies. During these negotiations, they induced the other shareholders to give them options to buy their shares at par, representing that it was necessary to have the consent of the majority in order to effect the merger. The shareholders were not informed that the directors were buying the shares on their own account. The directors exercised the options and made a large personal profit. In an action brought by the shareholders, the Judicial Committee of the Privy Council (JCPC) affirmed the decision of the Ontario Court of Appeal, that the directors must be taken to have held themselves out to the individual shareholders as acting for them as agents, and were bound to account to their principals for the profit.

In *Coleman v Myers* **[1977] 2 NZLR 225** the defendants were directors of a family company. The first defendant made a takeover offer to the other shareholders and succeeded in acquiring total control of the company. The plaintiff minority shareholders had reluctantly agreed to sell only when the first defendant invoked statutory compulsory purchase powers equivalent to **CA 2006, ss. 979–982**. They alleged breach of a fiduciary duty owed to themselves as shareholders. The New Zealand Court of Appeal held that the defendants were liable to compensate the plaintiff but merely because the minority shareholders had habitually looked to the defendants for business advice, and information regarding the true value of the shares had been withheld from them by the defendants.

This was approved in *Re Chez Nico (Restaurants) Ltd* **[1992] BCLC 192** where Browne-Wilkinson VC said: 'Like the Court of Appeal in New Zealand, I consider the law to be that in general directors do not owe fiduciary duties to shareholders but owe them to the company: however, in certain special circumstances fiduciary duties, carrying with them a duty of disclosure, can arise which place directors in a fiduciary duty vis-à-vis the shareholders.' *Coleman* was also followed in *Platt v Platt* **[1999] 2 BCLC 745** where the shareholders of a BMW dealership were three brothers. All the ordinary shares were held by one brother who was the only one involved in running the business. When the company's financial position was weak, this brother persuaded the other two to sell their entire preference shareholdings to him for £1, representing that this was necessary to enable the business to be sold at the insistence of BMW. The finances subsequently improved and BMW did not require the business to be sold. The brothers successfully claimed on the basis of misrepresentation and on the basis of breach of fiduciary duty. The basic principle of *Percival* was also upheld by the Court of Appeal in *Peskin v Anderson* [2001] 1 BCLC 372.

Applying the above principles to the facts of the case, since there are no special circumstances applicable to the situation involving Gwen, she would fail in her claim against Vernon for breach of fiduciary duty. She would have an alternative right to bring an action in misrepresentation if the price of £1.05p per share was suggested as a fair price by Vernon. If she had suggested the price, there would be no possibility of such a claim.

In respect of instructing his solicitor to purchase 10,000 shares in Infocon plc and encouraging Bob to purchase shares in the company, these actions by Vernon could constitute the criminal offence of insider dealing under **CJA 1993, Part V**.

The Act creates two separate offences under **CJA 1993, s. 52**. Thus an individual who has information as an insider is guilty of insider dealing if he deals in securities that are price affected in relation to the information: **CJA 1993, s. 52(1)**. An individual with information as an insider is also guilty of insider dealing if he encourages another person to deal in securities that are price-affected securities in relation to the information: **CJA 1993, s. 52(2)(a)**. Both offences are subject to the proviso that the acquisition or disposal occurs on a regulated market, or that the person dealing relies on a professional intermediary or is himself acting as such: **CJA 1993, s. 52(3)**. Shares are classified as securities for the purposes of the Act (**CJA 1993, Schedule 2, para. 1**) and the AIM is a regulated market. Thus, in purchasing the shares from Gwen, there is no criminal liability since the purchase was off-market.

Inside information means information which relates to particular securities or to a particular issuer of securities; is specific or precise; has not been made public; and if it were made public would be likely to have a significant effect on the price of any securities: **s. 56(1)**.

It is clearly likely that the proposed takeover bid would have a significant effect on the price and therefore in instructing his stockbroker to purchase shares in Infocon plc, and advising his friend, Bob, to purchase shares, Vernon is clearly guilty of offences under **s. 52** since none of the statutory defences (**s. 53**) would seem available to Vernon.

As regards Bob, a person is an insider for the purposes of the Act if and only if it is, and he knows that it is, inside information, and he has it, and knows that he has it, from an inside source: **s. 57(1)**. The concept of an inside source is explained in the following sub-section and Bob would qualify as having information from an inside source since thedirect source of his information is through a director of an issuer of the securities: **s. 57(2)**. As a result of this, Bob is also guilty of the offence of insider dealing under **s. 52(1)**.

Both Vernon and Bob are liable on summary conviction to a fine not exceeding the statutory maximum or imprisonment for a term not exceeding six months or both; or on conviction on indictment to a fine or imprisonment for a term not exceeding seven years or both: **CJA 1993, s. 61.**

As a director of Infocon plc, Vernon owes general duties to the company under **CA 2006.** There is a statutory duty for a director to avoid a situation in which he has, or can have, a direct or indirect interest that conflicts, or possibly may conflict, with the interests of the company (**s. 175(1)**). This applies in particular to the exploitation of any property, information, or opportunity: **s. 175(2)**. In this respect, having been informed about the possible takeover of Infocon plc, Vernon has used the information for his own personal profit. It seems that decisions like *Regal (Hastings) Ltd v Gulliver* [1942] 1 All ER 378 and *Boardman v Phipps* [1966] 3 All ER 721 could be used to make directors liable to account to their company for any profit they made. Against this it could be argued that the company is not really a victim from this situation and is unlikely to pursue the matter.

Question 6

'If English law is to strike the optimum balance between protection and directorial freedom it should survey judicial developments abroad. Most notable are those jurisdictions ... which have preferred to shift fiduciary liability in the corporate arena from the stringent standards applied to trustees onto a different axis. This has seen the emergence of a corporate opportunity doctrine which has gained currency throughout much of North America, and attracted differing measures of academic and judicial support within the Anglo-Commonwealth legal world.'

('The no-conflict-no-profit rules and the corporate fiduciary: challenging the orthodoxy of absolutism' John Lowry and Rod Edmunds [2000] JBL, March: 122–42)

Discuss.

 Commentary

This question requires you to consider whether the UK courts should abandon the absolute 'no-conflict/no-profit' rule of **Regal Hastings**, based as it is in the eighteenth-century equitable principles applicable to trusts, in favour of the adoption of the more flexible corporate opportunity doctrine. This doctrine developed from decisions in the courts of Delaware in the USA and has now been adopted by the courts in Australia, Canada, and New Zealand. This involves an analysis of the different judicial approach required by the doctrine and an assessment as to whether relaxing the absolute rule would result in more widespread abuse of corporate opportunity than at present. The evidence that emerges from jurisdictions where the doctrine has been adopted suggest that this is not the case.

 Answer plan

- Statement of the absolute 'no-conflict/no-profit' rule and cases illustrating the doctrine
- Introduction to the corporate opportunity doctrine as introduced in Delaware
- Examples of commonwealth and UK decisions espousing the doctrine
- Restatement of the traditional UK approach and related decisions
- Concluding remarks concerning evidence of the effect of the corporate opportunity doctrine on corporate morality

Suggested answer

This contrasts the UK approach to fiduciary duties of directors with that developed in the USA. The UK position is based on the equitable principles that regulate trustees and beneficiaries. The central principle is that the fiduciary's duty and interest must not conflict and that they cannot make a personal profit from their position. This 'no-conflict/no-profit' prohibition is absolute. In America—and increasingly throughout the Anglo-Commonwealth legal world—the regulation of directors' duties is a specialist, tailor-made doctrine: the 'corporate opportunity doctrine'.

The classic example of the UK approach is in *Regal (Hastings) Ltd v Gulliver* [1942] **1 All ER 378** where the claimant decided to form a wholly owned subsidiary to acquire the leases of two further cinemas and to sell the cinema business as a going concern. The company could not raise the required capital of £5,000 so the directors invested in person. When the group was sold to new owners, the directors made a personal, undisclosed profit on their investment. The company's claim for an account of these profits was rejected by the High Court and the Court of Appeal on the grounds that the directors had acted in good faith and in the absence of fraud and that the profits had not been made at the company's expense. In the House of Lords, Lord Russell of Killowen held: 'The liability arises from the mere fact of a profit having … been made. The profiteer, however honest and well-intentioned, cannot escape the risk of being called upon to account.' In reaching this decision, Lord Russell drew on the decision in *Keech v Sandford* (1726) **Sel Cas Ch 61** concerning the duty owed by a trustee to a beneficiary.

This approach can be seen at its most absolute in *Industrial Development Consultants Ltd v Cooley* [1972] **2 All ER 162** where the defendant managing director of IDC, having failed to obtain a contract for IDC with the Eastern Gas Board who would not deal with a limited company, was awarded the contract in person and fraudulently obtained a release from his service contract. Roskill J held that he was accountable for the whole of his benefits under the contract.

The corporate opportunity doctrine began with the Delaware Supreme Court decision in *Guth v Loft* **Del Supr 5 A2d 503 (1939)** and can be stated in the following terms: when a corporate officer is presented with a business opportunity which the corporation is financially able to undertake, and which falls within the line of its business and is of practical advantage to it, or is an opportunity in which the corporation has an actual or expectant interest, the officer is prohibited from allowing his self-interest to conflict with the corporation's interest and he or she may not take up the opportunity for himself. The director or officer may, however, take a corporate opportunity if: (a) the opportunity is presented to the director or officer in his individual capacity; (b) the opportunity is not essential to the corporation; (c) the corporation holds no interest or expectancy in the opportunity; and (d) the director or officer has not wrongfully employed the resources of the corporation in pursuing or exploiting the opportunity.

In contrast to the UK, Delaware decisions base liability upon a fact-intensive investigation into the fiduciary's conduct and their ability to establish their good faith. From an analysis of the cases, the doctrine does not weaken the fiduciary duty of loyalty or foster judicial toleration of corporate abuse.

The corporate opportunity doctrine has found favour in Canadian and New Zealand courts. In *Canadian Aero Services Ltd v O'Malley* **(1973) 40 DLR (3d) 371** the president and executive vice-president of the claimant had been negotiating a contract on the claimant's behalf but they resigned and formed their own company to which they diverted the contract. In awarding damages against the individuals and their company, key factors were that: (a) the defendants had diverted a maturing business opportunity to themselves which the claimant was actively pursuing; (b) they participated in the negotiations on behalf of the claimant; (c) their resignation was prompted or influenced by a desire to acquire the opportunity personally; and (d) that they obtained the contract by their position with the claimant rather than by a fresh initiative. In his judgment Laskin J stressed that the general standards of loyalty, good faith, and the avoidance of conflict of duty and self-interest must be tested by many factors.

In three English decisions, the philosophy and judicial language is in line with the corporate opportunity doctrine. In *Island Export Finance Ltd v Umunna* **[1986] BCLC 460**, the defendant, who was the managing director of the claimant company, resigned and subsequently obtained for his own company contracts with one of IEF's customers. In an action for an account of profits, the court held that the defendant was not in breach of his fiduciary duties. The evidence showed that IEF was not actively seeking further contracts with the client either at the time of Umunna's resignation or when he secured the contracts for himself. In doing so, he had not misused any confidential information and that he had secured the contract as a result of his own fresh initiative. In reaching this decision, Hutchinson J relied on passages in *O'Malley*.

In *Balston Ltd v Headline Filters Ltd* **[1990] FSR 385**, Head, an employee and director of the claimant, resigned to set up his own business. He was later informed by one of the claimant's customers that Balston were discontinuing manufacture of filter tubes and subsequently commenced manufacturing and supplying them. The court held that it was not a breach of duty for a director to start up a business in competition with his former company. It was also influenced by the fact that Head's decision only crystallized when approached by Balston's former customer.

In *Framlington Group plc v Anderson* [1995] 1 BCLC 475 the claimant sold its business knowing that three of its employee-directors had been offered employment by the purchaser. The three directors did not inform the claimant that they were offered shares in the company because the claimant had stated that it was not interested in their remuneration. The court dismissed a claim that they were accountable for these shares as secret profits.

The traditional approach was, however, restated by Lord Browne-Wilkinson in *Target Holdings Ltd v Redfern* [1995] 3 All ER 785, at p. 799 when holding that the amount recoverable in respect of secret profits depended upon the profit made by the fiduciary, not the loss suffered by the company. In addition, in *Re Bhullar Bros Ltd* [2003] EWCA Civ 424 where two directors of BB Ltd, a property development company, acquired in their own name an adjacent property to one held by BB Ltd. At the time, it had been agreed that BB Ltd should acquire no further property. The Court of Appeal held, however, that the two directors had acted in breach of their fiduciary duties and that the property should be held on trust for BB Ltd. The fact that the acquisition had not been a maturing business opportunity of BB Ltd did not rule out liability. In *Re Allied Business & Financial Consultants Ltd* [2009] EWCA Civ 751 the Court of Appeal overruled the trial judge who had relied on *Aas v Benham* [1891] 2 Ch 244. It held that the fact that the benefit acquired by a director was completely unconnected with the company's business was nevertheless a breach of the 'no conflict' rule since knowledge of the business opportunity was through a company client.

The courts seem to adopt a more flexible approach for retiring directors. In *Foster Bryant Surveying Ltd v Bryant and Savernake Property Consultants Ltd* [2007] EWCA Civ 200, B resigned as director of FBS Ltd but during the notice period was approached by Alliance, FBS Ltd's major client, with a view to sharing its work between FBS Ltd and B. B agreed to the proposal and formed SPC Ltd a few days before his resignation took place. F, the remaining director of FBS Ltd, refused to share Alliance's work and claimed for breach of fiduciary duties against B. The Court of Appeal held that B had not breached his fiduciary duties to FBS Ltd identifying three main reasons: (a) B had no ulterior motive in resigning which was forced on him by F's hostile manner; (b) Alliance had approached B and not the other way round; and (c) there was complete transparency throughout in that F was aware of Alliance's proposal to share its work between the two parties. In his judgment, Rix LJ doubted that the no-profit/no-conflict rules were 'inflexible' principles to be applied 'inflexibly', and favoured a 'common-sense and merits based approach', particularly in the context of retiring directors where 'the critical line between a defendant being or not being a director becomes hard to police'. This is an endorsement for Laskin J's approach in the *Canadian Aero Service* case. The critical line can be hard to establish and where the preparations occur prior to the resignation, they can be a breach of fiduciary duty: *Shepherd Investments Ltd v Walters* [2006] EWHC 836 (Ch).

Since the corporate opportunity doctrine appears to deter and punish directors who wrongly exploit a company's business opportunities whilst allowing for greater entrepreneurial freedom, the no-conflict/no-profit rule is not essential to ensure boardroom fidelity. The failure to adopt the doctrine is seen in the statutory duty to avoid conflicts of interest which covers the exploitation of any property, information, or opportunity (and it is immaterial whether the company could take advantage of the property, information, or opportunity): **CA 2006, s. 175(2)**. It is to be hoped that the approach taken in *Foster Bryant* survives the coming into force of the **Companies Act 2006** which provides that regard is to be had to the existing law when interpreting and applying the new statutory duties: **s. 170(4)**.

Further reading

Breakey, P., 'Difficulties with Re Grayan Building Services Ltd.: does the interpretation of the CDDA 1986 s.6(1) need to be reconsidered?' [2010] Comp. Law., 31(12): 409.

Copp, S.F., 'S.172 of the Companies Act 2006 fails people and planet' [2010] Comp. Law., 31(12): 406.

Hemraj, M. B., 'Duty of loyalty: company directors' positive obligation to disclose their own misconduct' [2006] Comp. Law., 27(6): 183.

Keay, A., 'Directors taking into account creditors' interests' [2003] Comp. Law., 24(10): 300.

Keay, A., 'Section 172(1) of the Companies Act 2006: an interpretation and assessment' [2007] Comp. Law., 28(4): 106.

Keay, A., 'The duty of directors to exercise independent judgement' [2008] Comp. Law., 29(10): 290.

Keay, A., 'Good faith and directors' duty to promote the success of their company' [2011] Comp. Law., 32(5): 138.

Li, J., 'The Peso Solver Case: an opportunity to soften the rigid approach of the English courts on the problem of corporate opportunity' [2011] Comp. Law., 32(3): 68.

Reed, R., 'Company directors—collective or functional responsibility' [2006] Comp. Law., 27(6): 170.

Scanlan, G., 'Offences concerning directors and officers of the company—fraud and corruption in the United Kingdom—the future' [2008] Comp. Law., 29(9): 264.

Shaw, P., 'Bribes, secret commissions and profits earned by fiduciaries' Corp. Brief. (2011) May: 10.

8

Corporate governance in the UK

Introduction

Recent financial scandals have led to questions about corporate governance mechanisms resulting in a series of reports seeking to strengthen the self-regulatory codes applicable to publicly quoted companies. These reports were:

- The Cadbury Report 1992
- The Greenbury Report 1995
- The Hampel Report 1998
- Higgs Report 2003
- The report of the committee chaired by Sir Robert Smith 2003
- The Turner Report 2009
- The Walker Review of Corporate Governance of the UK Banking Industry 2009

The Cadbury Report led to the Cadbury Code of Best Practice and the London Stock Exchange amended the Listing Rules to require listed companies to make a compliance statement in respect of the Code and state their reasons for non-compliance.

The Cadbury Report contained a recommendation—endorsed by the Greenbury Committee—that a new committee should be appointed to examine compliance and to update the Cadbury Code. This led to the establishment in November 1995 of the Committee on Corporate Governance chaired by Sir Ronald Hampel on the initiative of the Chairman of the Financial Reporting Council (FRC).

Their role was to review the role of executive and non-executive directors, to consider matters relating to directors' remuneration and the roles of shareholders and auditors in respect of corporate governance issues. The Committee produced a draft set of principles and a code embracing its own work and that of the two previous committees.

The London Stock Exchange issued the Combined Code on 25 June 1998, which became mandatory for all listed companies for financial years ending on or after 31 December 1998.

The Higgs Report followed on from the Enron scandal in the USA. The committee chaired by Sir Robert Smith reported at around the same time and these led to a revision of the Combined Code.

Changes from 2007 removed the restriction on individuals chairing more than one FTSE 100 company, and for listed companies outside the FTSE 350, allowed the company chairman to sit on the audit committee where he or she was considered independent on appointment. This took effect at the same time as the new Financial Services Authority (FSA) Corporate Governance Rules implementing EU requirements. The FSA Rules can be found on the FSA website. Readers should be aware that the FSA is to be dismantled by 2012, to be replaced by two new regulators: the Prudential Regulation Authority (PRA) to regulate banks and other financial institutions and the Consumer Protection and Markets Authority (CPMA) to regulate wholesale financial services firms, exchanges and other trading platforms.

Following the Turner Report of 18 March 2009 and the Walker Review of Corporate Governance of UK Banking Industry of 18 July 2009, the FRC engaged in a review of the Combined Code. The FRC introduced changes in the Corporate Governance Code—formerly known as the Combined Code—on 28 May 2010. The new edition of the Code applies to financial years beginning on or after 29 June 2010.

On a related matter, the **Companies (Shareholders' Rights) Regulations 2009 (SI 2009 No 1632)** implement **Directive 2007/36/EC** and aims to improve shareholder rights and corporate governance in particular.

Question 1

In respect of corporate governance, what abuses were highlighted by the various reports, how were they to be addressed and how effective were the proposed remedies?

 Commentary

This question requires you to consider the events and the concerns that led to the issue of corporate governance becoming a predominant topic from the 1990s. You need to recognize the choice of self-regulation as the chosen means for effecting reforms and the importance placed on the role of non-executive directors. The Cadbury Report established a code of best practice that was refined by subsequent committees and the result is the Combined Code 2003, enforced by way of the requirement of statement of compliance by listed companies. You are also required to assess whether self-regulation has been successful in addressing the situation.

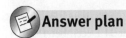
Answer plan

- The abuses leading to the establishment of the Cadbury Committee
- The approach adopted by the committee and the emphasis on the role of the non-executive director
- The Code of Best Practice
- Refinement of the Code by subsequent committees
- Assessment of effectiveness of self-regulation

Suggested answer

Corporate governance as an issue arose from a number of corporate scandals from the 1980s relating to the excessive power wielded by despotic bosses and the failure of the board to control them. Other issues were the length of directors' service contracts and their excessive remuneration. In addition, a series of corporate insolvencies indicated a failure of the regulatory system, particularly in respect of auditors. This led to huge damages claims against the large accountancy firms.

The large accountancy firms along with the Financial Reporting Council and the London Stock Exchange were instrumental in setting up the Committee on the Financial Aspects of Corporate Governance in 1991 under Sir Adrian Cadbury.

The Cadbury Report relied mainly on self-regulation in corporate governance through a Code of Best Practice for listed companies, compliance with which was to be a condition of continued listing. Important recommendations were shortening the length of directors' contract of employment; and a significant role in regulating companies through independent non-executive directors. In that respect the Report recommended that boards should comprise one-third non-executive directors. The code was monitored by the Stock Exchange and a sub-committee of the Cadbury Committee. Among the only changes proposed to the law was to require shareholder approval for directors' service contracts exceeding three years.

The Cadbury Report set out three approaches: structural and functional alterations to spread balance of power; increased assumption of responsibility; and enhanced disclosure.

The structural and functional alterations addressed the board's tendency to fall in with the chief executive's wishes and the proposed solution was the enhanced status and function for non-executive directors, of whom there had to be at least three. The function assigned to these non-executives was to bring 'an independent judgment to bear on issues of strategy, performance, resources, including key appointments, and standards of conduct'. They were to form an independent element within the board, playing a directorial role but also exercising a supervisory function.

They were to be an important part of board sub-committees. In particular, the Report recommended a nomination committee appointed largely from the company's non-executive directors to vet appointment of executive directors. A further recommendation was that the role of chairman of the board should be separate from that of the chief executive. The combination of the two roles in one person was seen as stifling board discussion.

The Report also recommended the creation of an audit committee, to which the board would delegate the task of a thorough review of audit matters and on which the non-executive directors were to play a positive role. Another recommendation was the appointment of remuneration committees consisting wholly or mainly of non-executives which would make recommendations on the level of board remuneration. Non-executive directors were to have no part in fixing their own level of remuneration.

A further recommendation was to enhance the status of the company secretary who would have responsibilities for seeing that board procedures are not only followed but regularly reviewed and that all directors should have access to the advice and services of the company secretary.

As regards increased responsibility, the report aimed to ensure that company directors should know their responsibilities and discharge them effectively and in full. The Report recommended a statement of directors' responsibilities in respect of the company's accounts, and a statement of the auditors' auditing responsibilities. Directors were to make a statement in the report and accounts regarding the establishment of a proper system of control over the company's financial management. Institutional investors were also required to make a policy statement about the use of their voting power and take more responsibility for monitoring the board's performance.

As regards the enhanced disclosure, accurate disclosure of financial information was linked with the market's ability to accurately assess the value of the company's securities. Recommendations aimed at ensuring the effective working of financial reporting and the audit function, and proposed measures to increase the effectiveness and objectivity of the audit with the annual audit as one of the cornerstones of corporate governance. The London Stock Exchange amended the Listing Rules to require listed companies to make a compliance statement in respect of the Code and state their reasons for non-compliance.

The Confederation of British Industries (CBI) set up the Study Group on Directors' Remuneration chaired by Sir Richard Greenbury in January 1995. The Report in July of 1995 contained a Code of Best Practice for Directors' Remuneration which reinforced the Cadbury Report in relation to remuneration committees and required the audit committee to report annually to shareholders on remuneration policy and provide more detail about directors' remuneration packages. It recommended that directors' service contracts should be restricted to one-year rolling contracts with the proviso that two-year rolling contracts might sometimes be acceptable, but were not to be encouraged; however, the two-year contract became the norm.

The Greenbury Report recommended the compilation by the remuneration committee of an annual report forming part of the annual accounts to include a statement that full consideration had been given to the best practice provisions of the Report and, in the event of non-compliance, an explanation of the reasons for non-compliance.

The Cadbury Report contained a recommendation—endorsed by the Greenbury Committee—that a new committee should be appointed by the end of June 1995 to examine compliance and update the Cadbury Code. The resulting Committee on Corporate Governance under Sir Ronald Hampel was tasked to review the role of both executive and non-executive directors, to consider matters relating to directors' remuneration and the roles of shareholders and auditors in respect of corporate governance. It produced a final report in January 1998.

The Hampel Report held that executive and non-executive directors should be subject to the same corporate duties and should be given more information concerning those duties. Executive directors should have sufficient experience to understand the nature and extent of the company's interests, while non-executive directors should be independent and comprise at least one-third of the board. One individual should not generally occupy the position of chairman and chief executive. Companies should have nomination committees to recommend board appointments and directors should seek re-election at least every three years. Remuneration of executive directors should not be excessive and be based on recommendations from remuneration committees comprised of non-executive directors. A general statement of remuneration policy should be included in the annual report. Directors' service contracts should not exceed one year.

The Hampel Committee produced a draft set of principles and a code embracing the work of the two previous committees and its own work. In March 1998 the London Stock Exchange published a consultation document concerning the draft Combined Code and revisions to the Listing Rules. It then issued the Combined Code, subtitled 'Principles of Good Governance and Code of Best Practice' on 25 June 1998. The Combined Code became mandatory for all listed companies for financial years ending on or after 31 December 1998.

The Higgs Report of 20 January 2003 rejected the adoption of two-tier boards and stressed the chairman's pivotal role in ensuring an effective board. It supported the separation of the roles of chairman and chief executive to the extent that a person stepping down as chief executive should not then become chairman. To strengthen the board's independence it recommended that at least half of the board should be independent, non-executive directors and that the procedures for recruitment of non-executives should be formalized, that nomination committees should be made up of a majority of independent non-executives, and that new non-executives needed an induction process. It approved the recommendation of the committee chaired by Sir Robert Smith that there should be at least three members of audit committee who should all be independent non-executives.

Following the FRC review in 2009, the Combined Code became the Corporate Governance Code aimed at making company boards more effective and accountable. Changes aim to improve risk management, setting out new principles on the composition and selection of the board with members being appointed on merit judged by objective criteria with respect for diversity including gender diversity. All directors of FTSE 350 companies should be put forward for annual re-election with externally facilitated board effectiveness reviews at least every three years. Enforcement is by the Listing Rules requirement of a compliance statement.

As regards directors' remuneration, self-regulation has been overtaken by the **Directors' Remuneration Report Regulations 2002 (SI 2002/1986)** which added **CA 1985, Schedule 7A**. This required quoted companies to publish an annual report approved by the board on directors' remuneration with copies to the Registrar. Shareholders must vote on the report at each Annual General Meeting (AGM) although their decision is not binding. As a result, some of the UK's biggest companies are facing shareholder pressure to scale back directors' pay deals and set more challenging targets for bonus payouts. The provisions are now contained in **CA 2006, Part 15**. The new Code stresses that performance-related pay should be aligned to the long-term interests of the company and its risk policy and systems.

A threat to corporate governance is private equity buyouts taking public companies into the less regulated world of private companies. The chairman of financial brokers, Collins Stewart, has criticized the whole regulatory framework and claimed that many companies will go private to avoid this 'tosh'. In response, the head of the Association of British Insurers (ABI)—the voice of shareholder interest—has argued that this must be met with increased regulation of private companies.

Question 2

It has been claimed that two important and complementary aspects of any corporate governance regime are a statutory business judgement rule and a statutory derivative action. Following consultation, however, the Law Commission ruled out the need for a statutory business judgement rule in the UK.

Explain the nature of the business judgement rule and how, in relation to the statutory derivative claim, it can play a role in promoting corporate governance.

 Commentary

This question considers a topic that is considered of vital importance in the USA, where it originated in Delaware, and which has been adopted in Australia, Canada, and elsewhere but which it has not been found necessary to be incorporated into UK company law despite many claims in favour of it being so. You are required to explain the nature of the business judgement rule and its operation in a number of contexts and to consider how, in combination with the statutory derivative claim it can be claimed to contribute to the enhancement of corporate governance.

Answer plan

- Definition of the business judgement rule
- Burden of proof required of shareholders contesting actions by corporate officers
- Examples of operation of the rule in respect of negligence, takeovers and derivative claims
- Justification for the adoption of the business judgement rule in the **Corporations Law 2001** in Australia and its importance in conjunction with the statutory derivative action towards enhancing corporate governance
- Consideration of the UK rejection of the need to adopt the business judgement rule and claimed advantages of its adoption

Suggested answer

While the **Companies Act 2006 (CA 2006)** has introduced a statutory derivative claim, the Act does not include a statutory business judgement rule, and indeed, the concept is almost unknown in the UK. This answer will explain the concept of the business judgement rule and its origins and explain why, in combination with the statutory derivative claim, it could be seen as contributing to improved corporate governance.

The business judgement rule (BJR) was initially developed in Delaware (USA) and operates to reduce the severity of the standard of care demanded of directors. The rule presumes that officers and directors have made all their business decisions on an informed basis, in good faith and in the honest belief that the action taken was in the best interests of the corporation, and places the burden of rebutting this presumption upon shareholders challenging the board. In order to overcome the presumption of the BJR, a plaintiff must prove that officers or directors have engaged in fraud, acted in bad faith, or made business decisions for their profit or betterment. The justification is that corporate matters are to be settled by the sound business judgement of the directors, and not be exposed to second-guessing by courts.

The BJR protects directors from liability for actions that turn out badly for the corporation. The most controversial case was *Smith v Van Gorkom* (**Del 1985**). Van Gorkom (VG) was the Chief Executive Officer (CEO) of a publicly held corporation. During a review of its future, the possibility was discussed of selling it outright. VG contacted a corporate takeover specialist and social acquaintance, who offered to buy the corporation at $55 per share, the deal to be agreed in three days. VG presented the deal to the board as a matter of urgency and urged approval. The board approved without asking questions or extended discussion. VG then obtained shareholder approval without considering alternatives and the transaction was completed. VG signed the sale documents without reviewing them. The Delaware Supreme Court held that the directors had not adequately informed themselves about the company's value and were not entitled to protection of the BJR.

Following this decision, lawyers warned director/clients of the risk of liability in the absence of a careful investigation and recommended a 'paper trail' to show that adequate investigation had been made to comply with the BJR.

The BJR is important in respect of defensive steps taken to defeat takeover bids. In *Panter v Marshall Field & Co* (**7th Cir 1981**) Marshall Field, a department store, fought off a takeover bid by acquiring or opening additional stores creating an anti-trust problem for the suitor who then withdrew, and the shares in Marshall Field collapsed in value. Minority shareholders sued the directors for damages but the court applied the BJR. Another defence to takeover is the 'poison pill' which usually provides that if an outsider acquires a specified percentage of voting shares, the corporation will issue debt or equity securities to the remaining shareholders at a bargain price making it impractical for the suitor to gain control by market purchases. In *Moran v Household International Inc* (**Del 1985**) the court upheld the basic concept of the 'poison pill' in advance of a specific takeover attempt.

It is always possible for the court to find that the decision to take defensive measures involves a conflict of interest and is therefore not entitled to the protection of the BJR. Defensive tactics approved by the independent directors are more favourably regarded by the court.

The BJR also operates in respect of derivative claims by shareholders. Most states require plaintiffs to serve a written demand upon the corporation to take suitable action followed by a period of ninety days, unless the shareholder has been notified earlier that the demand has been rejected or unless irreparable injury to the corporation would result by waiting. The Delaware Supreme Court developed a set of rules allowing the independent litigation committees to dismiss derivative litigation on the basis of a business judgement that it was not in the best interests of the corporation. The scope of the power depends on whether the case is classified as 'demand required' or 'demand futile' (or 'demand excused'). The latter arises where the specific facts alleged establish a reasonable doubt that the directors' action was entitled to the protection of the BJR.

In 'demand futile' cases, if a litigation committee recommends that the litigation is not continued, a court review should establish: (a) the committee's independence and absence of conflict of interest; (b) whether the decision meets the BJR requirements; and (c) whether in the court's own 'independent business judgement' the dismissal should be accepted. In a 'demand required' situation, the case will be dismissed if no demand is made and a decision by the litigation committee that the action should not be pursued is protected by the BJR and the court has no reviewing role. A judicial review of the rejection can only be obtained by the shareholder establishing that the decision was not protected by the BJR and is not entitled to discovery.

Under the BJR, a court presumes that directors act in good faith and there is divergence as to whether good faith is purely subjective or whether there is an objective element. In effect, most courts have employed a standard that involves some element of objective review. Where there is a conflict of interest between their personal interests and those of the corporation and its shareholders, directors are denied the protection of the BJR and must prove the 'entire fairness' of their business decision in any litigation.

The linking of the two statutory rights is seen most clearly in the Corporate Law Economic Reform Programme—Proposals for Reform (CLERPS) that led to the **Australian Corporations Law 2001** in which they were both introduced. CLERPS states that 'any reform ... should provide an appropriate incentive for directors to behave properly without unduly fettering the exercise of their judgment or their enterprise' and that 'proposals for the introduction of a statutory business judgment "safe harbour" for directors and a statutory form of derivative action for shareholders are particularly relevant to the wider debate on corporate governance'.

The combination of the two is seen as the means by which efficient and effective corporate government may be achieved. On the one hand, directors and corporate officers want greater certainty in relation to their potential liabilities and on the other the investors want directors to be more accountable. The Australian legislators saw the combination statutory business judgement rule and derivative action as the answer. The statutory business judgement rule offers directors some protection from personal liability if they make honest, informed and rational business judgements while the statutory derivative action allows a shareholder or a director to bring an action on behalf of the company for a wrong done to the company, where the company is unable or unwilling to do so itself.

In deciding whether or not to have a statutory business judgement rule, an important consideration was the weight of judicial uncertainty about directors' liability and accountability. It was decided that this was a factor which contributed most to directors' conservative and risk-averse behaviour when carrying out their duties, and that such behaviour could only harm shareholders and the economy. Considering accounting and economic factors as well as legal ones, it was found that costs are increased because of directors' uncertainty about liability, and that from an economic point of view 'a statutory business judgement rule would provide an incentive for boards to adopt effective corporate governance practices that promote transparency, accountability and investor confidence'. From a legal perspective, the statutory business judgement rule 'would clarify and confirm the position reached at common law that courts will rarely review bona fide business decisions' and 'would create more certainty for directors'.

In the discussion leading to **CA 2006**, the Law Commissions rejected the adoption of a statutory business judgement rule in the UK, arguing that the court has never interfered in business decisions. This view is often based on the statement in *Re City Equitable Fire Insurance Co Ltd* [1925] Ch 407 where Romer J stated: 'directors are not liable for mere errors of judgment'. In addition, the dual standard for the statutory duty of care can be argued to allow a degree of mitigation from the objective duty of care which in any event excludes consideration of 'any special qualification that a director has'.

In view, however, of the wide areas over which directors are required to exercise their duty of care, skill and diligence where the standards are infinitely variable, it could be argued that this is an opportunity missed. Claimed advantages of the business judgement rule are an enhancement and clarification of the process of decision-making; an increased awareness of the duties owed to the company; encouraging responsible risk taking with the comfort of knowing that decisions will not be second-guessed by the court if the requirements of the rule are met; and attracting a high calibre of directors and officers in the knowledge of the limits on their duty of care.

Question 3

The need for quoted companies to have independent, non-executive directors is a major requirement of the corporate governance regime.

Analyse the role of the non-executive directors, the skills required, and their independence. In addition, consider possible reasons for refusal to act as non-executives.

Commentary

The role of the non-executive director has increased in scope for listed companies and there is a distinction made between non-executives and independent non-executives which is now of great importance. In this question you are required to identify the role of the non-executive in a company and to identify the skills required of such a person. The question also requires you to consider the criteria for assessing whether non-executives are independent, a point that is important in respect of their appointment to the audit committee. The last part of the question requires you to consider the duty of care imposed on non-executives and consider whether this can discourage people from accepting appointment as non-executives.

Answer plan

- The role of the non-executive director
- The skills and knowledge required of a non-executive director
- The criteria for judging independence of non-executive directors
- The liability of non-executive directors and its possible effect on recruitment

Suggested answer

The non-executive director is often described as having two roles: monitoring executive activity and contributing to strategic development. In both the Cadbury Report and the Hampel Report it was felt that there was some tension between these two elements. However, research referred to in the Higgs Report based on a number of in-depth interviews with directors, found that, in spite of some tension there was no essential contradiction between the two roles. The research identified, however, dangers in non-executives concentrating too much on one aspect of their role. Thus an overemphasis on monitoring and control carried the risk of non-executives seeing themselves—and being seen—as alien policing influences detached from the rest of the board. On the other hand, overemphasis on the strategic development aspect carried the risk of non-executives becoming too close to the executive, and therefore undermining shareholder confidence in the effectiveness of board governance.

From the research, it emerged that it was necessary for non-executives to work in a spirit of partnership and mutual respect to gain recognition by the executives of their contribution. The Report highlighted the fact that the 1998 Code offered no guidance on the role of the non-executive director and that lack of clarity of their role had been a recurrent theme in submissions and interviews. As a result, the Code now states that non-executive directors should constructively challenge and help develop proposals on strategy; should scrutinize the performance of management in meeting agreed goals and objectives; and monitor the reporting of performance. In addition, they should satisfy themselves on the integrity of financial information and that financial control and systems of risk management are robust and defensible. They are also responsible for determining the appropriate levels of remuneration of executive directors and have a prime role in appointing, and where necessary removing, executive directors. They are also involved in succession planning.

In respect of financial control, the significance of the requirement that the audit committee should be composed of at least three non-executives, all of whom should be independents is important; as is the requirement for the remuneration committee to be comprised of non-executive directors.

Non-executives must acquire the expertise and knowledge to discharge their duties effectively. They must be well-informed about the business, the environment in which it operates and the issues it faces. This requires knowledge, not only of the company itself, but of the markets in which it operates. In this respect the requirements of non-executives are integrity and high ethical standards in common with all persons acting as directors. They also need to have sound judgement and must be willing to enquire and probe in order to obtain satisfactory answers within the board. They also require strong interpersonal skills since their effectiveness depends on the influence they exert and not on their power to give orders.

The Code also establishes the role of the senior independent non-executive director (senior independent director). The senior independent director should be identified in the annual report and the chairman of the company should hold meetings with the senior independent director and the non-executives in the absence of the executive directors. And, in the absence of the chairman and led by the independent senior directors, the non-executive directors should meet at least annually to appraise the chairman's performance.

While accepting that it is not possible for all non-executive directors to be independent—particularly in smaller listed companies—at least a proportion of the non-executive directors should be independent. The requirement for a greater degree of independence on boards was a theme in US corporate governance reform and the **Sarbanes–Oxley Act (USA)** requires all members of the audit committee to be independent. In addition under NASDAQ and the NYSE listing rules, there is a requirement that the majority of the board should be independent. The Bouton report on corporate governance in France also recommended that half the board should be independent. Following the Higgs Report, the Combined Code gives a definition of independence (A.3.1).

Under this provision, the board is required to identify in the annual report each non-executive director it considers to be independent. The board should state its reasons if it decides that a director is independent in spite of the existence of relationships or circumstances which may appear relevant to this including:

(a) if the person has been an employee of the company or group within the last five years

(b) has or had with the last three years a material business relationship—directly or indirectly—with the company

(c) has received or receives additional remuneration from the company apart from director's fee, participates in the company's share option or a performance-related pay scheme, or is a member of the company's pension scheme

(d) has close family ties with any of the company's advisers, directors, or senior employees

(e) holds cross-directorships or has significant links with other directors through involvement in other companies or bodies

(f) represents a significant shareholder, or

(g) has served on the board for more than nine years from the date of their first election

Except for smaller companies, defined as one below the FTSE 350 in the prior financial year, at least half the board, excluding the chairman, should be independent non-executive directors and a smaller company should have at least two independent non-executives.

An important issue for persons considering acting as non-executive directors is the question of their liability to the company. In the UK the duty of care, skill, and diligence owed by directors, executive, and non-executive, is the same. This was established in *Dorchester Finance Co Ltd v Stebbing* **[1989] BCLC 498**. The Higgs Review set out a new schedule 'Guidance on liability of non-executive directors: care, skill, and diligence' to be annexed to the Combined Code. This accepts that executive directors and non-executives have the same legal duties and objectives as board members but indicates that different levels of expectation in respect of time devoted to company affairs and the detailed knowledge and experience that could reasonably be expected of a non-executive will generally be less than for an executive director and that: 'These matters may be relevant in assessing the knowledge, skill and experience which may reasonably be expected of a non-executive director.'

The same position is adopted in Australia as seen in *Daniels v Anderson* (1995) 13 ACLC 614 where the appeal court overruled the high court's finding that non-executive directors should be judged by a lower standard of care. This decision was instrumental in causing the inclusion of a statutory business judgement rule into the **Corporations Law 2001** to mitigate the objective duty of care imposed on directors of all types. The rule presumes that directors have made all their business decisions on an informed basis, in good faith and in the honest belief that the action taken was in the company's best interest and places the burden of rebutting this on shareholders challenging the board.

It is clear that the possibility of liability for breach of the duty of care is a factor that can make people think twice about becoming a director, executive or non-executive, of a company. The executive and non-executive directors of Equitable Life faced a negligence claim for more than £1bn over the company's near collapse. Although the case was later dropped, it made many people less ready to accept non-executive positions. This was also seen in the USA following the decision by the Delaware Supreme Court in *Smith v Van Gorkom* (**Del 1985**) that there was no distinction between the liability of executive and independent, non-executive directors. This resulted in many people refusing to accept to be independent directors.

In conclusion, non-executive directors have an important role to play in the corporate governance of listed companies and are required to be strong enough to stand up to the executive directors but in a sensitive way so as to maintain a mutual sense of trust. Following the finding of the Higgs Report that almost 50 per cent of non-executives were recruited though personal contacts, and that only 4 per cent had been formally interviewed, the position is now more formalized. In addition, although most non-executives still come from the business world, there is a move to encourage candidates from other walks of life: the armed forces, charities, and the public sector.

Further reading

Adeyeye, A., 'The limitations of corporate governance in the CSR agenda' [2010] Comp. Law., 31(6): 172.

Arora, A., 'The corporate governance failings in financial institutions and directors' legal liability' [2011] Comp. Law., 32(1): 18.

Du Plessis, J. J., 'Corporate law and corporate governance lessons from the past: ebbs and flows, but far from "the end of history…".": parts 1 & 2' [2009] Comp. Law., 30(2): 43 and 30(3): 81.

Hemraj, M. B., 'Good corporate governance: the recipe for corporate survival' [2005] Comp. Law., 26(4): 122.

Ho, J.K.S., 'Is s. 172 of the Companies Act 2006 the guidance for CSR?' [2010] Comp. Law., 31(7): 207.

Pedamon, C., 'Corporate Social Responsibility: a new approach to promoting integrity and responsibility' [2010] Comp. Law., 31(6): 172.

Sammon, A., 'Increasing boardroom diversity' (2011) Emp. LJ, 120: 15

Sweeney-Baird, M., 'The role of the non-executive director in modern corporate governance' [2006] Comp. Law., 27(3): 67.

Tomasic, R., 'Corporate rescue, governance and risk taking in Northern Rock: parts 1 & 2' [2008] Comp. Law., 29(10): 297 and 29(11): 330.

Young, A., 'Frameworks in regulating company directors: re thinking the philosophical foundations to enhance accountability' [2009] Comp. Law., 30(12): 355.

9

Minority protection

Introduction

The basic rule in company law is that of majority control. Thus the will of the majority controls the destiny of the company. Where minority shareholders disagree with the will of the majority, the basic rule is that—unless they can drum up overwhelming support for their own view—they must either accept the expression of that will or, if they cannot, sell their shares and leave the company. There are, however, occasions when the law will intervene to protect the minority shareholder against abuse by the majority of its dominant position.

For a long time, the protection was left to the common law and was severely restricted by the decision in *Foss v Harbottle* (1843) 2 Hare 461 which prevented minorities from bringing actions in respect of wrongs done to the company by its controllers by way of a derivative claim except in exceptional circumstances. The **Companies Act 2006 (CA 2006)** has introduced a statutory right for members to bring derivative claims on behalf of companies in place of the common law derivative claim, which had been shown to be inadequate over many years.

The statutory right to petition on the grounds of oppression was introduced in the **Companies Act 1948** to circumvent the inadequacies of the common law derivative claim. This was replaced in 1970 by what became the right of members to petition against unfair prejudice in **CA 1985, s. 459**. The right to petition on the grounds of unfair prejudice is now largely unchanged in **CA 2006, s. 994**.

In addition, there has always existed the possibility of members petitioning the court for a winding-up order on the just and equitable ground (**Insolvency Act 1986 (IA 1986), s. 122(1)(g)**). Following the decision in *Ebrahimi v Westbourne Galleries Ltd* [1973] AC 360, this developed into an alternative to **CA 1985, s. 459** (now **CA 2006, s. 994**). The court has, however, ruled that petitioners should not petition under both sections in the alternative.

The major topics of importance in the area are:

(a) The scope of the statutory derivative claim

(b) The scope of the petition for unfair prejudice with particular reference to:

   (i) what constitutes unfairly prejudicial behaviour

(ii) the importance of the petitioner's behaviour in determining the success of a petition, and

(iii) the overlap between the petition for unfair prejudice and the petition for the just and equitable winding up of the company

Question 1

To what extent does the statutory right of members to bring a derivative claim in respect of a company mirror the derivative claim evolved at common law as an exception to the rule in *Foss v Harbottle*?

 Commentary

This question requires you to show your familiarity with the law relating to the old common law derivative claim and to compare and contrast this with the new statutory derivative claim introduced in the **CA 2006**. It is important to be aware of the old law since the situations when the new statutory right apply will, to a certain extent, mirror the situations that gave rise to a derivative claim previously. Obviously, the new provisions have widened the scope of the claim and the circumstances relating to the court giving permission for an action to continue are now statutorily defined and thus render the law more definite and predictable.

 Answer plan

- Majority control and the rule in *Foss v Harbottle*
- Exceptions to *Foss v Harbottle*
- Abuse of majority power against the company
- Restriction on the bringing of a derivative claim at common law
- The statutory derivative claim and the details of permission to proceed
- Analysis of the common law derivative claim and the statutory claim: similarities and differences

Suggested answer

The basic principle of majority control and the restriction of actions by minorities was established in *Foss v Harbottle* (1843) 2 Hare 461 and restated in *Edwards v Halliwell* [1950] 2 All ER 1064 in two propositions: (a) the proper claimant in an action in respect of a wrong to a company is prima facie the company; and (b) where the alleged wrong may be made binding on the company by a simple majority of the members, no individual member is allowed to maintain an action in respect of it.

To claim in respect of a wrong to the company, the minority had to establish that they fell within an exception to the rule. The major exception involved abuse of majority power against the company: the expropriation of corporate opportunities or assets as in *Cook v Deeks* [1916] 1 AC 554 where three directors sought to take over a contract for their own benefit. In such a situation, the shareholders brought a derivative claim on the company's behalf. For this they had to obtain the court's permission by establishing prima facie that: (a) the company was the victim of a 'fraud', defined as an abuse of power as director or shareholder, *Estmanco (Kilner House) Ltd v GLC* [1982] 1 All ER 437; and (b) the wrongdoers were in control of the company and preventing it from bringing an action itself. The claim was equitable and discretionary.

The term 'fraud' did not cover 'mere negligence', *Pavlides v Jensen* [1956] 2 All ER 518, unless the alleged negligent action resulted in profit to a director, *Daniels v Daniels* [1978] Ch 406.

To establish that the wrongdoers were 'in control', the claimant had to establish actual voting control not mere de facto control through dominance of shareholding and management position: *Prudential Assurance Co Ltd v Newman Industries Ltd (No 2)* [1982] Ch 204.

The court could order the company to indemnify minority shareholders where it was reasonable and prudent to bring an action and where it was brought in good faith: *Wallersteiner v Moir* (No 2) [1975] 1 QB 373. In *Smith v Croft (Nos 2 and 3)* [1987] BCLC 206 and [1987] BCLC 355, however, the minority shareholder's claim for indemnity was rejected as his claim regarding excessive remuneration of directors was in contradiction of an independent report and against the wishes of the independent majority shareholder.

Derivative claims could not be brought if the shareholder had a right to a personal action, which is difficult to establish. In *Stein v Blake* [1998] 1 All ER 724, the Court of Appeal ruled that a shareholder could not bring a personal action for an alleged misappropriation of corporate assets by the other shareholder because his loss was a mere reflection of the company's loss which would be redressed by the company recovering damages from the wrongdoer. The House of Lords endorsed the principle of reflective loss in *Johnson v Gore Wood & Co* [2002] 2 AC 1, HL.

Shareholders could, however, sue where the wrong prevented the company from suing. In *Giles v Rhind* [2002] 4 All ER 977 a company formed by G and R went into receivership after R diverted a major contract to his new business, and the company was forced to abandon its claim against R. The Court of Appeal allowed G to sue for the fall in value of his shares, even though this was reflective of the company's loss.

Members now have a statutory right to bring derivative claims in respect of a cause of action vested in the company, and seeking relief on behalf of the company: **s. 260(1)**. These actions can only be brought under **Chapter 1, Part 11** or proceedings for unfair prejudice: **s. 994**.

A derivative claim may be brought in respect of a cause of action arising from an actual or proposed act or omission involving negligence, default, breach of duty, or breach of trust by a director: **s. 260(3)**. It is immaterial whether the cause of action arose before or after the person seeking to bring or continue the derivative claim became a member of the company: **s. 260(4)**.

Members bringing a derivative claim must apply to the court for permission to continue it (**s. 261(1)**), and if the application and evidence filed do not disclose a prima facie case for permission, the court must dismiss the application: **s. 261(2)**. In *Iesini v Westrip Holdings Ltd* [2009] EWHC 2526 (Ch) the court held that in this respect it was wrong to engage in a mini-trial of any action but the court had to form a provisional view on the strength of the claim which must involve an allegation of default or breach of duty under **s. 260(3)**. If the application is not dismissed, the court may give directions as to the evidence to be produced by the company and adjourn the proceedings to enable evidence to be obtained: **s. 261(3)**.

Permission must be refused if the court is satisfied that a person acting in accordance with **s. 172** (duty to promote the company's success) would not seek to continue the claim: **s. 263(2)(a)**. In the *Iesini* case, the court held that the section only applied where the court was satisfied that not director acting in accordance with **s. 172** would seek to continue the claim. If some would and others would not, **s. 263(3)(b)** should be applied which concerns the importance that such a person would put on continuing it: **s. 263(3) (b)**. This test of the 'hypothetical director' has been considered in a number of cases. In *Mission Capital plc v Sinclair* [2008] EWHC 1339 (Ch), the court refused permission despite the fact that it could not be satisfied that the notional director would not continue the claim, but that it could not be said he would attach that much importance to it. In this case and in *Franbar Holdings Ltd v Patel* [2008] EWHC 1534 (Ch) the court was also influenced by the fact that the applicants could achieve all that they could possibly want through a petition under **s. 994 CA 2006**. This was also endorsed in *Stimpson and Others v Southern Landlords Association and Others* [2009] All ER (D) 193 (May). On the other hand, in *Kiani v Cooper* [2010] EWHC 577 (Ch) in granting permission to continue a derivative action, the court held that the existence of an alternative remedy under **s. 994** was only one factor to consider.

In addition, the court refuses permission where the action arises from a prospective act or omission that has been authorized by the company or, where is arises from an existing act or omission, that it was previously authorized by the company or subsequently ratified: **s. 263(2)**. In considering whether to give permission, the court must take into account in particular: whether the member is acting in good faith in seeking to continue the claim; whether in the case of a proposed act or omission it would be likely to be authorized or ratified and where it is an existing act or omission whether it could be, and would be likely to be, ratified; whether the company has decided not to pursue the claim; and whether the act or omission gives rise to a personal cause of action for the member: **s. 263(3)**.

Where permission is granted to continue a derivative claim, the court will also grant a right of indemnity to the claimant for his reasonable costs subject to limits: *Stainer v Lee* [2010] EWHC 1539 (Ch) and *Kiani v Cooper* [2010] EWHC 577 (Ch).

The Act also covers applications from a member to continue a claim as a derivative claim where the company has brought the claim but has failed to prosecute the claim diligently: **s. 262**. The Act also provides for a member to take over a derivative claim initiated by another member, or from a member who has continued as a derivative claim one initiated by the company, or from a member who has abandoned a derivative claim that was taken over from another member under this section: **s. 264**.

In conclusion, the statutory remedy is wider in that it encompasses negligence. The fact that claims can also be brought in respect of wrongs committed prior to a person becoming a shareholder merely reiterates the common law position. The need for permission to continue the claim also reflects the common law, as do the circumstances when permission must be refused as well as the criteria to be taken into account in giving permission.

The requirement that the claimant acts in good faith reflects the equitable nature of the common law derivative claim and the provisions relating to adopting claims commenced by the company or another member are also merely clearly spelled out as opposed to radically new.

The one area of radical change is in respect of the court ordering the company to produce evidence and adjourning the proceedings while the evidence is acquired: **s. 261(3)**. This is a major improvement on the common law where obtaining evidence of wrongdoing was always a problem for the claimant. This should facilitate derivative claims in the future.

Finally, the emphasis on whether the act or omission has been, is likely to be, or can be ratified, reflects the principle of majority control that gave birth to the rule in *Foss v Harbottle*.

Question 2

Brenda, Charles, and Diana set up a catering business called 'Just Desserts'. They each held one-third of the shares and were directors of the company.

Charles became involved in a new venture and neglected his duties. Brenda and Diana decided to remove Charles from the company. The articles provide that 'in the event of a resolution to remove a person from the board, the shares held by that director shall on a poll have three votes per share instead of the usual one'. It is known that Charles has overreached himself financially due to his involvement in the new venture.

Advise Brenda and Diana how they might go about removing Charles from the board and of the statutory remedies available to Charles.

 Commentary

This problem question requires you to recognize the steps that Brenda and Diana would have to take in order to remove Charles from the board and also to recognize that taking such steps in the context of a quasi-partnership company would give Charles statutory rights of action against Brenda and Diana. You are required to advise Charles as to whether he would be able to succeed in a petition for unfair prejudice under **CA 2006, s. 994**, and of the remedies available to him under **s. 996**. You are also required to recognize that, because of his own behaviour, he may not succeed in his petition. At this point you must consider an alternative claim by way of a petition for the just and equitable winding up of the company under **IA 1986, s. 122(1)(g)**.

 ## Answer plan

- Need for Brenda and Diana to alter the company's articles by special resolution to remove the weighted voting provision
- Need to make a rights issue to enable them to acquire necessary voting control for a special resolution
- Recognition that this scheme could be regarded as a ground for a petition for unfair prejudice by Charles and discussion of possible remedies
- Problems of Charles succeeding in his petition because of his behaviour
- Alternative petition for just and equitable winding up of the company

Suggested answer

Brenda, Charles, and Diana are director/shareholders in Just Desserts Ltd, which is a quasi-partnership company in the sense that the shareholders have equal shareholdings and are all directors of the company.

Brenda and Diana have become discontented with Charles because of his neglect of the company's business since his involvement in a new and unconnected venture. Having decided to remove Charles from the board, they are faced with the problem that the articles contain a weighted voting provision as in *Bushell v Faith* [1970] AC 1099 whereby, on a resolution to remove a director from the board, the shares held by that director will have multiple votes and enable the director to defeat the resolution. In *Bushell v Faith* the articles provided that on a resolution to remove a director, shares held by the director should have three votes per share as opposed to the normal one vote per share.

It is possible, however, for the articles to be altered to remove this weighted voting procedure, unless it is an entrenched provision in the articles as permitted by **CA 2006, s. 22**. Failing this, the articles can always be altered by special resolution of the members: **CA 2006, s. 21**. In order to secure the passing of a special resolution, Brenda and Diana must command 75 per cent of the votes in favour of the change at the company's general meeting. Since at present they only have between them two-thirds of the issued shares, this is impossible.

A possible course of action open to Brenda and Diana is to increase the share capital of the company by way of a rights issue. Since it is a private company with one class of shares, the directors can allot shares in the company: **s. 550**. Since it would be an allotment of ordinary shares, there would have to be a rights issue whereby existing shareholders have a right of pre-emption in respect of the new issue in proportion to their current shareholding: **s. 561**. Since, however, it is known that Charles is currently financially embarrassed, and unable to take up his entitlement, the result will be that his shareholding will be reduced to below 25 per cent, making it impossible for him to block special resolutions.

Having taken up their entitlement and that rejected by Charles, Brenda and Diana would be able to proceed with the removal of the weighted voting provision and ultimately propose an ordinary resolution with special notice to remove Charles as a director: **CA 2006, s. 168**. Charles would have a statutory right to protest against his removal under **CA 2006, s. 169**, but this would not prevent his removal.

On the other hand, Charles would be able to intervene at all stages in the implementation of this scheme: the rights issue, the alteration of the articles, and the resolution to remove him as a director on the grounds that individually and collectively these constitute an act which is unfairly prejudicial to him.

Thus, at any stage in the implementation of the scheme, Charles could petition the court under **s. 994**. In respect of the predecessor of this section, **CA 1985, s. 459**, the court has held that a rights issue in the knowledge that the minority could not afford to take it up constituted unfair prejudice: *Re Cumana Ltd* [1986] BCLC 430. In respect of the alteration of the articles, whereas previously Charles might have based a claim on the grounds that the proposed alteration was not in good faith for the benefit of the company as a whole, it would now be possible to petition under **s. 994** and ask for the court to make an order requiring the company not to make any, or any specified, alterations in its articles without leave of the court: **s. 996(2)(d)**. In addition, in a quasi-partnership company where there is an understanding that members shall be entitled to participate in the management of the company, removal from the board has also been recognized as unfair prejudice: *Re OC (Transport) Services Ltd* [1984] BCLC 251.

In the event of Charles petitioning on the grounds of unfair prejudice, he would be likely to seek an order that the company (and/or Brenda and Diana) should purchase his shares at a value to be determined by the court under **s. 996(2)(e)**. In this case, his shareholding would be valued pro rata according to the value of the business as a whole (*Re Bird Precision Bellows Ltd* [1984] Ch 419), unless the conduct of the parties justified their value being discounted to reflect the fact that it was a minority holding.

In order to succeed in his petition, he must establish that he is the victim of unfairly prejudicial behaviour on the part of Brenda and Diana. The problem in this is that it could be argued that he has no grounds on which to base a petition since Brenda and Diana are justified in commencing proceedings to remove him from the board, since his removal is due to his neglect of his duties as a director: the treatment is prejudicial but not unfair.

In *Re RA Noble & Sons (Clothing) Ltd* [1983] BCLC 273, the court held that since the petitioner had been excluded from the management of the company because of his neglect of his duties as a director, his exclusion, although prejudicial, was not unfair. As a result he failed in his **s. 459** petition. Thus, where the petitioner's behaviour totally justifies the action complained of as prejudicial, the petitioner will not succeed in a petition under **s. 994**: *Kelly v Hussain* [2008] **EWHC 1117 (Ch)**. In *Re London School of Electronics Ltd* [1986] Ch 211, however, the court held that the petitioner's misconduct in trying to attract students away from the school did not disqualify him from petitioning. His misconduct was a reaction to the unfairly prejudicial behaviour suffered at the hands of the other shareholder (who had earlier tried to attract students away to another establishment). The court held that a petitioner's misconduct could, however, influence the remedies accorded to him.

If, as a result of his behaviour, Charles fails in his petition for unfair prejudice under **s. 994**, he could, nevertheless, petition for the just and equitable winding up of the company under **IA 1986, s. 122(1)(g)**. The decision in *Ebrahimi v Westbourne Galleries Ltd* [1973] AC 360 established that the removal of a director of a quasi-partnership company from the board constituted grounds to petition for the just and equitable winding up of the company. Subsequent decisions in *Re RA Noble & Sons (Clothing) Ltd* [1983] BCLC 273 and *Jesner Ltd v Jarrad Properties Ltd* [1993] BCLC 1032 have shown that, even if a person cannot petition successfully under **s. 994** against his removal from the management of the company of a quasi-partnership company, that person would succeed in a petition to wind up the company on the just and equitable ground. This would enable Charles to recover his investment from the company in the same way as a petition under **s. 994** asking for the purchase of his shares under **s. 996(2)(e)**.

The practice of petitioning for these remedies as alternatives is now discouraged. It would, therefore, be in his interest to petition under **s. 122(1)(g)** at the outset.

Question 3

Mark became a shareholder in Landsite plc, a commercial property company, in January 2009. He subsequently learnt that during 2008 the board sold a major site scheduled for development for the Olympic Games to New World Properties plc. The property was sold for £20m but it is now valued at £50m in documents issued by New World Properties plc in connection with their flotation on the Alternative Investment Market (AIM).

He raised the issue at the AGM of Landsite plc but the managing director claimed that the property was sold at its market value on the basis of an independent valuation. He stated that the value had been affected by the need to decontaminate the site.

No reports to this effect were produced and the meeting became quite rowdy with angry shareholders demanding an inquiry.

The share price of Landsite plc fell by 10 per cent when it was reported in the financial press that the managing director of Landsite plc had a significant, financial stake in New World Properties plc.

Advise Mark of any action he may take faced with inactivity by the company.

Commentary

In this question you are required to apply to the problem the law relating to the statutory derivative claim. This involves explaining the conditions on which Mark can bring the claim and the grounds on which the court will refuse or grant permission for the bringing of the derivative claim. Of particular importance here is the question of whether Mark has the alternative of a right to bring a personal action in place of a derivative claim. This involves a discussion on the concept of reflective loss.

 Answer plan

- Legal justification for the bringing of a derivative claim by Mark
- Need to establish prima facie case and role of court in organizing the production of evidence
- Grounds on which the court must either refuse or may grant permission to continue the action
- Discussion of Mark's right to bring a personal action
- Concluding advice as to the likely success of the claim

Suggested answer

Following the sale of the company's property at an apparent undervalue, it is possible for the company to bring an action against the controllers for damages for the loss suffered by the company. The basis of the claim could be in negligence if it is established that the price at which the property was sold was significantly below its market value. There is also the possibility of a claim based on fraud if any degree of dishonest collusion could be established between the managing director of Landsite plc and the controllers of New World Properties plc.

If this were to be the case, the managing director of Landsite plc would be in breach of his statutory duty to promote the success of the company by acting in the interests of the company: **s. 172(1)**. It has been held that the failure of the director to declare his own wrongdoing in his relations with the controllers of New World Properties plc would also constitute a breach of his duty to act in the best interests of the company *Item Software (UK) Ltd v Fassihi* [2004] EWCA Civ 1244.

Faced with a refusal by the company to take action, Mark could commence an action on the company's behalf by way of a derivative claim under **s. 260(1)**. Unlike the common law derivative claim, it is no longer necessary to establish a 'fraud' against the company. Neither is there a need to establish that the wrongdoers are in control of the company. The statutory derivative claim can be brought in respect of a cause of action arising from an actual or proposed act or omission involving negligence, default, breach of duty or breach of trust by a director of the company: **s. 260(3)**. The term 'director' extends to former and shadow directors: **s. 260(5)**.

Mark is able to bring the derivative claim even though the cause of action arose before he became a member of the company: **s. 260(4)**. Landsite plc would be the claimant and the board of directors would be named as defendants.

Mark would be required to apply to the court for permission to continue this claim (**s. 261(1)**) and the court must dismiss the claim if the application and the evidence filed in support of it do not disclose a prima facie case for giving permission: **s. 261(2)**.

This could be a potential problem for Mark since he can only point to documents establishing the price at which the property was sold in 2008 and its current valuation in the documents lodged by New World Properties plc. Although the managing director of Landsite plc referred to an independent valuation prior to the sale and indicated that the value of the site was affected by the need for it to be decontaminated, there are no documents to that effect apart from the fact that the statement that such an independent valuation existed is in the public domain through the minutes of the AGM and the reports in the financial press.

In this case, Mark would have to request the court to give directions requiring Landsite plc to produce the documents in question and the court could adjourn the proceedings to allow the evidence to be obtained: **s. 261(3)**. Once this documentary evidence had been produced, the court could then at a reconvened hearing give permission to continue the claim on such terms as it thinks fit if the evidence produced supports Mark's claim: **s. 261(4)**. If the company is unable to produce the documents that it claims to have, this would also constitute evidence of negligence or breach of trust sufficient to enable the court to give permission to continue the claim.

In deciding whether to refuse or give permission, the court must have regard to the provisions of **s. 263**. If the court holds that a person acting to promote the interest of the company in accordance with **s. 172** (duty to promote the success of the company) would not seek to continue the claim (**s. 263(2)(b)**), or that the sale was authorized or has since been ratified by the company, it must refuse permission: **s. 263(2)(a)** and **(c)**.

In considering whether to give permission the court must in particular take into consideration whether Mark is acting in good faith in seeking to bring his claim or whether his claim is an abuse of the legal process: **s. 263(3)(a)** and the importance that a person acting in accordance with **s. 172** would attach to continuing it: **s. 263(3)(b)**. It must also consider whether the act gives rise to a cause of action that the member could pursue in his own right as a personal action rather than on behalf of the company: **s. 263(3)(f)**.

The reference in **s. 263(2)(a)** and **s. 263(3)(b)** to the person acting in accordance with **s. 172**, is a reference to the hypothetical or notional director of the company. In deciding whether to refuse permission to continue the action, this has been an important consideration and the court has been loath to grant permission, particularly when the applicant has an adequate remedy in respect of a petition for unfair prejudice under CA 2006, **s. 994** where the applicant has brought an action under both heads: *Franbar Holdings Ltd v Patel* [2008] EWHC 1534 (Ch). This would not appear to be an issue in this case. The other matters required to be considered under **s. 263(3)** do not appear to be a problem: the sale has clearly not been ratified by the company in general meeting and the company has not decided not to pursue the claim, it has merely failed to act.

As regards the possibility that Mark could pursue the action personally, he has clearly suffered a loss in the immediate due to the collapse in the value of the shares which might suggest that he could sue personally. In *Prudential Assurance Co Ltd v Newman Industries Ltd (No 2)* [1982] Ch 204, however, it was held that a shareholder could not bring a personal action in respect of a fall in the value of his shares caused by the wrongdoing of the company controllers who had disposed of a corporate asset at an undervalue. In *Johnson v Gore Wood and Co* [2002] 2 AC 1, HL, a member claimed unsuccessfully for contributions to his pension fund among other things when the company did not have enough money due to losses allegedly caused by the defendants' negligence. This is because the loss suffered is merely a reflection of the loss suffered by the company which could be remedied by an action for damages by the company against the directors. As a result, Mark will not be able to bring a personal action in respect of the loss in value of his shares.

Since there is no possibility of Mark bringing a personal action against the directors of Landsite plc, there would appear to be no barrier to his bringing a derivative claim on behalf of the company. If he does so, he should be able to anticipate being given permission by the court to do so.

Question 4

'A member of a company may apply to the court by petition for an order … on the ground—

(a) that the company's affairs are being or have been conducted in a manner that is unfairly prejudicial to the interests of its members generally or of some part of its members (including at least himself), or

(b) that an actual or proposed act or omission of the company … is or would be so prejudicial'

(CA 2006, s. 994(1))

Discuss.

Commentary

In respect of this question you are required to analyse the wording of the sub-section paying specific attention to the critical terms: 'unfairly prejudicial to the interests of its members generally or of some part of its members'. This involves tracing the history of the development of this so-called alternative remedy from the original formulation in **CA 1948, s. 210** up to the current definition and the judicial interpretation of this provision from its original appearance as **CA 1980, s. 75** through to **CA 1985, s. 459**.

This is one of the most vital areas of company law and it can be guaranteed to feature as a discussion or problem in any company law examination.

 ## Answer plan

- Discussion of limitations of petition against oppression under the **Companies Act 1948, s. 210** and changed situation with the **Companies Act 1980, s. 75** (later **CA 1985, s. 459**, now **CA 2006, s. 994**)
- Members for the purposes of petitioning
- Meaning of unfairly prejudicial 'to the interest of members'
- Criteria for unfairly prejudicial conduct and whether restricted by notion of concept of 'legitimate expectations'
- Examples of unfairly prejudicial conduct

Suggested answer

Section 994 derives from the right to petition against 'oppression' in **CA 1948, s. 210** which was an alternative to a petition for the compulsory liquidation of the company and members could only succeed if the oppression would justify a winding-up petition on just and equitable grounds. 'Oppression' was a course of conduct which was 'burdensome, harsh and wrongful' and limited to situations where the member was oppressed in his capacity as a member.

The right to petition was most famously rejected in *Ebrahimi v Westbourne Galleries Ltd* [1973] AC 360 where E was removed as a director from a quasi-partnership company which had previously been a partnership. The court rejected E's claim since his removal from the board was oppression as a director not as a member.

The section was replaced by **CA 1980, s. 75** (later **CA 1985, s. 459**) and covered any actual or proposed act or omission. An isolated act or the threat of an isolated act was sufficient to found a petition. Furthermore, the new right was no longer restricted by being linked to just and equitable winding up.

The petition can be brought by a member that includes a person to whom the shares have been transferred or transmitted by operation of law: s. 994(2). A proper instrument of transfer must have been executed and delivered to the transferee or the company; an agreement to transfer is not sufficient: *Re Quickdome Ltd* [1988] BCLC 370. A person with one share registered in his name is, however, qualified to petition: *Re Garage Door Associates Ltd* [1984] 1 WLR 35. A petition may also be presented by a person who acquired shares knowing that its affairs were being conducted in the unfairly prejudicial manner complained of: *Bermuda Cablevision Ltd v Colica Trust Co Ltd* [1998] AC 198.

The statutory formula still referred to something unfairly prejudicial 'to the interests of its members' and the first reported decision on **s. 459**, *Re A Company* [1983] 2 All ER 36, limited the right to cases where the unfair prejudice affected the petitioner as a shareholder. However, in *Re A Company* [1983] 2 All ER 854, Vinelott J stated obiter: 'It seems to me unlikely that the legislature could have intended to exclude from the scope of **s. 459** a shareholder in the position of Mr Ebrahimi ...'. And in *Re A Company* [1986] BCLC 376 Hoffmann J said: 'In the case of a small private company in which two or three members have ventured their capital ... on the footing that each will earn his living by working for the company as a director ... [the] member's interests ... may include a legitimate expectation that he will continue to be employed as a director and his dismissal ... and exclusion from the management ... may therefore be unfairly prejudicial to his interests as a member.'

Since then, relief has been given where members have been removed from office: *Re Bird Precision Bellows Ltd* [1986] 2 WLR 158; *Re Cumana Ltd* [1986] BCLC 430; *Re London School of Electronics Ltd* [1986] Ch 211 and *Croly v Good* [2010] EWHC 1 (Ch). In *Re Ghyll Beck Driving Range Ltd* [1993] BCLC 1126 a father and son set up a company with two others to run a golf range. Each was an equal shareholder and director. Following a scuffle between the petitioner and his father, the business was run without reference to him. The court held that he had been unjustifiably excluded from a joint venture where it was contemplated that the business would be managed by all four for their mutual benefit.

In *Re A Company* [1986] BCLC 376, the court refused to strike out a petition on the grounds that it related only to the petitioners' interests as vendors and employees. Hoffmann J stated 'the interests of a member are not necessarily limited to his strict legal rights under the constitution of the company'. And in *Re Sam Weller & Sons Ltd* [1990] Ch 682 the court held that a company that had followed the same dividend policy for 37 years was unfairly prejudicial to members who relied on the dividend for their income, as opposed to those remunerated as directors: holders of the same class of share could have different interests.

In *Re Bovey Hotel Ventures Ltd* (1981) (**unreported**), Slade J suggested that a member might bring himself within the scope of the section if his shareholding has been seriously diminished or jeopardized. He added that the test of unfairness is objective and not subjective: whether a reasonable bystander would regard the actions as unfairly prejudicial to the petitioner.

Following *Re Saul D Harrison & Sons plc* [1995] 1 BCLC 14, there were claims of attempts to impose a restrictive interpretation on **s. 459**. The case concerned a family company in which the petitioner held 'C' shares which carried a right to dividends and return of capital on liquidation but no right to vote. The company had substantial assets but had been running at a loss. The petitioner claimed the directors had unreasonably continued to run the business instead of closing it down.

The High Court and the Court of Appeal rejected her claim on the ground that she had no 'legitimate expectations' over and above the expectation that the board would run the company in accordance with their fiduciary obligations, the terms of the articles and the Companies Act. Hoffmann LJ rejected the notion of the reasonable bystander, except to emphasize the objective standard of fairness, but that 'fairness' was in the context of a commercial relationship essentially determined by the articles of association.

The issue was raised once again by Lord Hoffmann in the House of Lords in *O'Neill v Phillips* [1999] 2 All ER 961. In this case, Phillips gave a 25 per cent shareholding in his company to O'Neill, the foreman and chief employee, and appointed him director in the hope that O'Neill would take over the management of the business and draw 50 per cent of the profits. Phillips later retired, leaving O'Neill as sole director. The company prospered and the possibility of increasing O'Neill's shareholding to 50 per cent was discussed. During a subsequent recession, however, Phillips took back control, reduced O'Neill's status to branch manager and took away his share of the profits, although he remained a director. O'Neill resigned and petitioned under **CA 1985, s. 459.**

Lord Hoffmann held that there was no basis to his claim that Phillips had acted unfairly, that 'fairness' depended on the context, and that 'a member of a company will not ordinarily be entitled to complain of unfairness unless there has been some breach of the terms on which he agreed that the affairs of the company should be conducted' while accepting that 'there will be cases in which equitable considerations make it unfair for those conducting the affairs of the company to rely upon their strict legal powers'.

Following this decision, the Law Commission thought that the remedy would be less readily available whereas the DTI Company Law Review Steering Group believed it remained substantially unchanged but agreed with *O'Neill v Phillips*, saying 'the basis for a claim ... should be a departure from an agreement, broadly defined, between those concerned, to be identified by their words or conduct ... in the interests of certainty and the containment of the scope of s. 459 actions' (Modern Company Law for a Competitive Economy: Final Report, vol. 1).

Certainly for public companies—especially quoted companies—the court is unlikely to consider alleged understandings and agreements not recorded in documents available to outside investors: *Re Blue Arrow plc* [1987] BCLC 585 (rejection of the petitioner's claim that there was an agreement that she should remain in office as chairman); and *Re Tottenham Hotspur plc* [1994] 1 BCLC 655 (rejection of an alleged understanding that the petitioner would continue to have a say in the company's management even after he had ceased to hold 50 per cent of the shares). The court was reluctant to use the section for resolving private disputes between shareholders in publicly quoted companies. This approach was affirmed in *Re Astec (BSR) plc* [1999] BCC 59.

Successful actions have been brought in respect of breaches of fiduciary duties including conflict of interests, excessive remuneration of directors, and a rights issue found to dilute the interest of a shareholder: *Re A Company* (No 002612 of 1984) [1985] BCLC 80; and *Re Cumana Ltd* [1986] BCLC 430. In *Re Elgindata Ltd* [1991] BCLC 959, the court rejected a petition alleging mismanagement. However, in *Re Macro (Ipswich) Ltd* **[1994] 2 BCLC 354**, the court stated that where the mismanagement was sufficiently significant so as to cause loss to the company then it could constitute the basis for finding unfair prejudice. In *Oak Investment Partners XII Ltd Partnership v Boughtwood* **[2009] EWHC 176 (Ch)** the court stated that there was no reason in principle why the conduct of a senior manager should not be relevant to relief under **s. 994**. A complaint could be made under **s. 994** even if the mismanagement was not the product of business decisions taken by the board, but by individual directors or others (decision affirmed **[2010] EWCA Civ 23**).

Further reading

Almadani, M., 'Derivative action: does the Companies Act 2006 offer a way forward?' [2009] Comp. Law., 30(5): 131.

Arsalidou, D., 'Litigation culture and the new statutory derivative claim' [2009] Comp. Law., 30(7): 205.

Davies, B., 'Fulham Football Club (1987) Ltd v Richards [2010] EWHC 3111 (Ch)' (2011) Bus. LR, 32(3): 54.

Cheung, R., 'Corporate wrongs litigated in the context of unfair prejudice claims: reforming the unfair prejudice remedy for the redress of corporate wrongs' [2008] Comp. Law., 29(4): 98.

Gibbs, D., 'Has the statutory derivative claim fulfilled its objectives?' Parts 1 and 2 [2011] Comp. Law., 32(2): 41; 32(3): 76.

Hemraj, M. B., 'Maximising shareholders' wealth: legitimate expectation and minority oppression' [2006] Comp. Law., 27(4): 125.

Paterson, P., 'A criticism of the contractual approach to unfair prejudice' [2006] Comp. Law., 27(7): 204.

Quigxiu, B., 'The indemnity order in a derivative action' [2006] Comp. Law., 27(1): 2.

Singla, T., 'Procedural aspects of unfair prejudice and the re-use of company names' [2008] Comp. Law., 29(7): 214.

Yap, T.L., 'Authorising derivative actions on unfair prejudice petitions' [2011] Comp. Law., 32(5): 150.

10

Corporate insolvency

Introduction

This chapter deals with the very important and complex matter of corporate insolvency. This is often taught as a separate subject but it cannot be ignored as an aspect of a general programme of studies on a company law course since it impinges on so many aspects of the other topics in the syllabus.

Important examples of topics where this is the case are:

(a) Separate legal personality of the company and exceptions to *Salomon v Salomon* with particular regard to liability of directors and shadow directors for fraudulent and wrongful trading

(b) Duties owed by directors to creditors of the company when the company is insolvent or on the brink of insolvency

(c) Validity of fixed and floating charges created by a company within the period running up to the onset of insolvency

(d) Remedies of secured creditors in the event of default by the company under a debenture secured on the assets of the company

It is important to be aware of the formal procedures which aim to deal with failing companies and the emphasis on providing alternatives to liquidation resulting in the death of the business and economic loss to employees and society in general.

Inspired by the Chapter 11 bankruptcy procedure in the USA, the Cork Report 1982 recommended the introduction of new as well as improved mechanisms which form part of the current 'rescue culture' designed to salvage the business. The mechanisms included: the Administrative Receiver with statutory powers to take over and run a failing business with the aim of selling it on as a going concern; the Administration procedure with an administrator with similar powers and the stated aim of saving as much of the business as possible; the Company Voluntary Arrangement (CVA) to enable companies in financial difficulties to enter into formal agreements with their creditors with the aim of rescuing a business as an alternative to the existing complex and expensive composition and arrangement procedure under the Companies Act 1985 (now **Companies Act 2006, ss. 895–901**).

Liquidation and the dissolution of the company would be reserved for extreme cases only, where any possibility of saving the business was out of the question.

The system was initially established in the **Insolvency Act 1986 (IA 1986)**. However, a major reform by the **Enterprise Act 2002** simplified the administration procedure, avoiding the need for an application to the court. In addition, the administrative receivership procedure was limited to exceptional cases. Administration is now the automatic legal remedy for creditors with floating charges over the company's assets.

The insolvency procedures extend to general partnerships and Limited Liability Partnerships (LLPs) as well as companies incorporated in states outside the European Economic Area (EEA). The administration procedure is not, however, available for an insolvent members' club: *Keith Panter v Rowellian Football Social Club & Ors* [2011] EWHC 1301 (Ch).

The major aspects of this topic that are the subject of examination questions are:

(a) The role of the administration procedure and the CVA in saving sick businesses

(b) The different forms of liquidation: members' and creditors' voluntary liquidation and compulsory liquidation by order of the court

(c) The priority of creditors in an insolvent liquidation

(d) The distributable assets that pass to the liquidator, the liquidator's powers to recover previously disposed of assets and to disclaim assets which are burdensome

(e) Civil remedies against directors: summary remedy against delinquent directors, fraudulent, and wrongful trading

(f) Disqualification of directors under the **Company Directors Disqualification Act 1986 (CDDA 1986)**

Question 1

Top Drawer plc, a catering company, runs a successful hospitality operation for the principal sporting and social functions—Ascot, Henley, Wimbledon etc. The company established a wholly owned subsidiary, Toppers Ltd to operate an exclusive range of retail outlets. The directors of Toppers Ltd were nominees of Top Drawer plc.

The business, although initially successful, quickly became unprofitable and its bank and main suppliers only continued to extend credit on the basis of statements by Top Drawer plc promising its continued financial support including 'letters of comfort' agreeing to financial support and referred to in the annual accounts of Toppers Ltd.

In October 2007, the accountants of Toppers Ltd recommended that the directors should consider placing the company in administration but, on the advice of the board of Top Drawer plc, they continued trading. HC Ltd, a main supplier to Toppers Ltd, seeks advice on how to petition for the compulsory winding up of Toppers Ltd on the grounds of the company's inability to pay its debts.

(a) Advise HC Ltd on how it may bring a winding-up petition against Toppers Ltd

(b) Is there any potential liability of the directors of Toppers Ltd, Top Drawer plc, and of its directors in respect of Toppers Ltd's debts?

Commentary

This problem raises two important issues in connection with the compulsory winding up of a company under the **Insolvency Act 1986**. In this connection you are required to give advice on the way in which creditors can establish that a company is unable to pay its debts for the purpose of a winding up petition, including discussion of the situation where the debt is disputed by the company. You are required to consider the liability of the directors of Toppers Ltd and of the parent company, Top Drawer plc and of its directors to contribute towards the assets of Toppers Ltd.

Answer plan

- Discussion of the alternative ways in which creditors can establish a company's inability to pay its debts for the purpose of petitioning for the company's compulsory winding up
- The legal problem where the debt is disputed by the company
- Potential liability of the directors of Toppers Ltd and Top Drawer plc under the Insolvency Act 1986

Suggested answer

Creditors may petition for the compulsory winding up of a company on the grounds of inability to pay its debts under **IA 1986, s. 123(1)(a), (e) and (2)**. The first of these is by way of a statutory demand which requires creditors to serve a written demand for payment at the company's registered office. If after three weeks the company has failed to pay the debt or to secure or compound for it to the creditor's satisfaction, it is deemed unable to pay its debts. The debt must be for at least the statutory minimum of £750. The problem with this procedure is the element of delay.

As a result, many creditors now prefer to use the procedure under **s. 123(1)(e)** where the creditors merely present a petition to the court declaring that the company owes them an amount exceeding the statutory minimum (£750), that the debtor has not disputed its liability in respect of the debt, and that the company is therefore unable to pay its debts and should be wound up. This approach was endorsed by the Court of Appeal in *Taylor's Industrial Flooring Ltd v M & H Plant Hire (Manchester) Ltd* [1990] BCLC 216 where it rejected a claim that the process was abusive.

It is also possible to establish the inability to pay its debts by proving that the value of the company's assets is less than the amount of its liabilities, including contingent and prospective liabilities: s. 123(2).

In order for a creditor to petition, the debt must be undisputed. There are several reasons for this, one of which is that a petitioner whose debt is justifiably disputed is simply not in a position to present a petition for a winding-up order. A second reason is that the court does not allow the companies' jurisdiction to be used for resolving disputes between the parties.

In order to secure the dismissal of a winding-up petition by a creditor whose claim is disputed it is necessary for the company to establish that there is a genuine and bona fide dispute that the company honestly believes this to be the case and there are reasonable or substantial grounds for this belief. If this is established it has been stated that the dismissal of the petition is not discretionary but compulsory: *Re Bayoil SA* [1999] BCLC 62, per Nourse LJ at p. 62. There are, however, cases where the court has allowed a petition to proceed even where there is a bona fide dispute as to the exact amount of the debt if the company clearly owes money to the petitioner in excess of the statutory minimum: *Re Tweeds Garages Ltd* [1962] 1 Ch 406.

Because of the decision in *Salomon v Salomon*, Top Drawer plc is a separate legal person from Toppers Ltd and is not liable for its debts as such. Liability could, however, arise under the letter of comfort and also under the IA 1986.

In respect of the letter of comfort issued by Top Drawer plc, it was established in *Kleinwort Benson Ltd v Malaysia Mining Corpn Bhd* [1989] 1 WLR 379 that such a letter does not give rise to any contractual liability and is merely a statement of present intention. There would, therefore, be no contractual liability for Top Drawer plc. The directors of Toppers Ltd, Top Drawer plc and its directors are, however, potentially liable to contribute to the assets of Toppers Ltd under IA 1986, s. 212 (summary remedy against delinquent directors, liquidators etc); IA 1986, s. 213 (fraudulent trading) and IA 1986, s. 214 (wrongful trading).

Section 212 applies if in the course of the winding up of a company it appears that a person who is or has been an officer of the company, or has been concerned, or has taken part, in the promotion, formation, or management of the company, has misapplied or retained, or become accountable for, any money or other property of the company, or been guilty of any misfeasance or breach of any fiduciary or other duty in the relation to the company: s. 212(1).

While there is no suggestion that the directors of Toppers Ltd have misapplied or retained or become accountable for money or other property of the company, they can be said to have acted in breach of their general duty to promote the success of the company: CA 2006, s. 172. This requires the directors to act in a way in which they consider, in good faith, to be most likely to promote the success of the company for the benefit of its members as a whole. The section then lists particular matters (a) to (f) that they must have regard to: s. 172(1). The most relevant aspect of the section is the proviso that the section has effect subject to any enactment or rule of law requiring directors, in certain circumstances, to consider or act in the interest of creditors of the company: s. 172(3).

In *Winkworth v Edward Baron Development Co Ltd* [1987] 1 All ER 114 it was stated: 'A duty is owed by the directors to the company and to the creditors of the company to ensure that the affairs of the company are properly administered and that its property is not dissipated or exploited for the benefit of the directors themselves to the prejudice of the creditors' (per Lord Templeman at p. 118). This was also addressed in *Brady v Brady* [1988] BCLC 20 where Nourse LJ stated: 'in a case where the assets are enormous and the debts minimal it is reasonable to suppose that the interests of the creditors ought not to count for very much. Conversely, where the company is insolvent or even doubtfully insolvent, the interests of the company are in reality the interests of existing creditors alone.'

Where there is an identifiable breach of duty to creditors, this may be the subject of misfeasance proceedings under IA 1986, s. 212. On the application of the official receiver, the liquidator, or any creditor or contributory, the court may look into the conduct of those potentially liable under the section and may compel them to contribute to the company's assets in respect of the breach of duty as the court thinks just: s. 212(3). While there is clearly potential liability against the directors of Toppers Ltd, it could also be argued that Top Drawer plc and possibly some of its directors may be regarded as de facto or shadow directors of Toppers Ltd for the purposes of liability. They could otherwise fall within the ambit of the section as being concerned in the promotion, formation, and management of the company.

In respect of fraudulent trading, persons who were knowingly parties to the carrying on of the business of a company now in insolvent liquidation with the intent to defraud the company's creditors or for any fraudulent purpose can be declared liable to contribute to the company's assets such sums as the court orders. Liability of the directors of Toppers Ltd would depend upon it being established that they carried on trading in the knowledge that the company would be unable to pay its suppliers and with the intent of defrauding them. In this respect, the proof of intent required is the criminal test of beyond reasonable doubt. This makes it difficult to establish.

The directors of the parent company and Top Drawer plc, could also potentially be liable under this section but subject to the decision in *Re Augustus Barnett & Son Ltd* [1986] BCLC 170. In this case, the parent company of Augustus Barnett had issued a letter of comfort in respect of the company, which it had later refused to honour. When the liquidator sought to claim a contribution against the parent company under s. 213, the parent successfully applied for the claim to be struck out on the ground that there had been no similar allegation of fraud against the actual directors of the subsidiary that they had been carrying on business with intent to defraud creditors. This established that passive participants cannot be liable unless fraudulent trading is alleged against those actually carrying on the business.

A claim under s. 214 for wrongful trading is much more likely to succeed. All that is required for this to be established, is for the company to be in insolvent liquidation and that, at some stage prior to the commencement of the insolvency proceedings, the directors knew or ought to have concluded that the company could not avoid insolvent liquidation but continued to trade instead of placing the company in liquidation or administration. There is no problem in respect of the actual directors of Toppers Ltd who clearly ignored the advice of the company's accountants.

Top Drawer plc could also be liable if it can be established that the company was a de facto or shadow director of the subsidiary. The same is true of any of the directors of Top Drawer plc in respect of whom it could be shown that they were directly involved in the decision that Toppers Ltd should continue to trade in spite of trading at a loss and the accountants' warning.

The directors found guilty of fraudulent or wrongful trading could also be automatically disqualified under the **CDDA 1986** for a maximum of 15 years. Moreover, the directors of a company that has gone into insolvent liquidation and whose behaviour makes them unfit to be directors of a company must also be disqualified for a minimum of two years under **CDDA 1986, s. 6.**

Question 2

On the liquidation of a company, all of the assets belonging to the company at the commencement of the liquidation are available for the creditors.
  Discuss.

 Commentary

This question requires you to distinguish between assets belonging to the company in liquidation which are available to the creditors and those which are unavailable. In addition, you are required to discuss the liquidator's right to disclaim onerous assets. As regards recovering assets which have already been disposed of, this requires you to consider the importance of the backdating of the commencement of liquidation for compulsory winding up and the significance of **IA 1986, s. 127.** In addition to this you are required to show familiarity with the statutory provision allowing liquidators (and also administrators) to set aside transactions at an undervalue and voidable preference. In addition the avoidance of floating charges, the setting aside of extortionate credit transactions and transactions with intent to defraud creditors must also be referred to.

These are important topics with which you need to be familiar.

 Answer plan

- The commencement of winding up
- Unavailable assets and disclaimer

- Recovery of assets disposed of between the presentation of the petition and the making of a winding-up order: **IA 1986, s. 127**
- Transactions at an undervalue: **IA 1986, s. 238**
- Voidable preferences: **IA 1986, s. 239**
- Avoidance of floating charges: **IA 1986, s. 245**
- Extortionate credit transactions: **IA 1986, s. 244**
- Transactions at an undervalue with the intent to defraud creditors: **IA 1986, s. 423**

Suggested answer

The commencement of a voluntary winding up is the date of the passing of the resolution to wind up (**s. 86**), and for a compulsory winding up, the date of the presentation of the petition (**s. 129(2)**) except where the company is already in voluntary winding up: **s. 129(1)**. In effect, not all of the property belonging to the company at the commencement of the winding up passes to the liquidators but, on the other hand, liquidators may be able to recover property previously disposed of.

Assets that do not pass to the liquidator include property held as agent, trustee or bailee for another. In *Re Kayford Ltd* [1975] 1 All ER 604, money sent in by customers of a mail-order company and paid into a special account pending delivery of the goods ordered was held on trust to be returned to the customers.

In addition, property in the company's possession under a contract containing a reservation of title clause does not pass if correctly stored and marked to indicate that they belong to the supplier. Where under the terms of the clause there is a valid term extending the suppliers claim into the proceeds of any sub-sale to be held in a separate account, these sums of money will not pass to the liquidator.

Liquidators may also reject property belonging to the company exercising their right of disclaimer in respect of unprofitable contracts, property that is unsaleable or not readily saleable, or property giving rise to liability to pay money or perform any other onerous act. Disclaimer terminates the rights, interests, and liabilities of the company and victims of disclaimer must prove as creditors. Liquidators can disclaim at any time unless served with written notice to elect whether to disclaim or not when the period is reduced to 28 days or such period fixed by the court: **ss. 178–182**. Special rules relate to disclaimer of leases. In *Hindcastle v Barbara Attenborough Associates Ltd* [1996] 2 WLR 262, the House of Lords held that the disclaimer of a lease does not release a director who had guaranteed payment of the rent.

There are several statutory provisions allowing the liquidator to recover previously disposed of property.

Backdating the commencement date of a compulsory liquidation is important since 'any disposition of the company's property ... after the commencement of the winding up is void unless the court otherwise orders': **s. 127**. The liquidator can recover the property disposed of unless the disposition is validated by the court. The court will approve bona fide transactions with third parties for companies not trading at a loss, but not payments to existing creditors since they may be preferential payments where the company prefers one creditor over others. This was a problem for the company's bank honouring cheques drawn payable to creditors before the decision in *Bank of Ireland v Hollicourt (Contracts) Ltd* [2001] 1 All ER 289 which held that the payments were not recoverable from the bank.

Liquidators may also avoid transactions at an undervalue within a relevant time: **s. 238**. This is within two years prior to the onset of insolvency and the company must at the time have been unable to pay its debts for the purposes of **s. 123**, but this is presumed for transactions with connected persons: **s. 240(2)**.

A company enters into a transaction at an undervalue if: (a) it makes a gift to a person, or enters into a transaction on terms whereby it receives no consideration; or (b) where the consideration is significantly less than the value of the consideration supplied by the company: **s. 238(4)**. An order to avoid the transaction will not be made if the company entered into the transaction in good faith and where there were reasonable grounds for believing that it would benefit the company: **s. 238(5)**. The burden of proof lies on the applicant and the consideration passing between the parties is to be valued as at the date of the transaction and, if unable to reach a precise valuation, the court could decide that it fell within a range; *Stanley v TMK Finance Ltd* [2010] EWHC 3349 (Ch).

The creation of a charge is not a transaction at an undervalue: *Re MC Bacon Ltd* [1990] BCLC 324. There is no territorial limit, however, and in *Re Paramount Airways Ltd* [1991] 3 WLR 318, an administrator succeeded in respect of funds paid into a bank account in Jersey.

Liquidators can set aside payments and charges made within the relevant time prior to the onset of insolvency to put creditors or their guarantors or sureties into a better position in the event of the company's insolvent liquidation. This is two years for connected persons and six months for outsiders (**s. 240(1)(a)** and **(b)**), and the company must have been unable to pay its debts within the meaning of **s. 123**. Preferences are only voidable where the company was motivated by a desire to confer a benefit on the person preferred. For connected persons, defined in **s. 249**, an intention to advantage the person is presumed: **s. 239(6)**. The onset of insolvency is as for transactions at an undervalue.

In *Re MC Bacon Ltd* [1990] BCLC 324, the company had an unsecured overdraft limit of £300,000. In 1986 it lost its major customer and two of the directors retired from active management. In May 1987, a bank report found the company technically insolvent. As a condition of continuing to operate the bank account, the bank demanded fixed and floating charges over the company's assets. In September 1987 the company went into liquidation and the liquidator sought to set aside the charge as a transaction at an undervalue or as a voidable preference. Regarding the latter, the court concluded that the company did not desire to confer a benefit and that the charge was not voidable.

In respect of transactions at an undervalue and voidable preferences, the court may order retransfer of property, release or discharge of security, repayments to administrator or liquidator, revival of guarantees, and so on: **s. 241**. Third parties who are bona fide purchasers for value are protected: **s. 241(2)** and **(2A)**. Proceeds of a successful claim are held for the unsecured creditors: *Re Yagerphone Ltd* [1935] **1 Ch 392**.

Floating charges created in favour of outsiders within one year before the onset of insolvency are invalid under **s. 245(3)(a)** unless the chargee can prove that the company was not unable to pay its debts at that time or became so as a consequence: **s. 245(4)**. For connected persons, the period is extended to two years and is not conditional upon the company being unable to pay its debts.

There is an exception as regards the aggregate of: (a) the value of money paid, or goods or services supplied to the company at the same time as, or after, the creation of the charge; (b) the value of the discharge or reduction, at the same time as or after, the creation of the charge of any debt of the company; and (c) any interest payable in pursuance of (a) or (b): **s. 245(2)(a)**. The exception in respect of cash, goods, and services paid or supplied to the company at the same time as, or after, the creation of the charge means that contemporaneous advances or supplies of goods and services can at least partially, if not entirely, validate the floating charge. Where the consideration consists of goods or services, the security will only be valid to the extent that the charge was reasonable: **s. 245(6)**.

In *Power v Sharp Investments Ltd* [1994] **1 BCLC 111**, the court decided that, on the basis of the ordinary meaning of the words used, loans made between April and early July in consideration of the proposed creation of a debenture secured by a floating charge were not made at the same time as the creation of a debenture executed on 24 July 1990. The floating charge was therefore invalid.

There are advantages for banks and suppliers under a current account due to the operation of the rule in *Clayton's Case* (1816) **1 Mer 572**, which provides that credits to a current account discharge debts in the order in which they were incurred in the absence of specific appropriation. In *Re Yeovil Glove Co Ltd* [1965] **Ch 148**, the bank honoured cheques totalling some £110,000 after the creation of a debenture. This was held to be a new advance made after the creation of the charge, even though the charge was created in respect of an existing debt and the overdraft remained virtually unchanged.

Liquidators may also apply to set aside extortionate credit transactions within the three years prior to the commencement of the liquidation: **s. 244**. Transactions are presumed to be extortionate, and the court can: (a) set aside the whole or part of the transaction; (b) vary the terms of the transaction or terms under which an security is held relating to the transaction; (c) require any person to refund sums paid by the company; (d) require the surrender of any security; or (e) provide for accounts to be taken between any persons.

Liquidators can also set aside transactions at an undervalue made at any time with the aim of putting assets beyond the creditors' reach or to prejudice their interests: **s. 423(3)**. Potential applicants include individual victims: **s. 424**. Possible court orders are similar to those in **s. 241: s. 425**. The test for intention under **s. 423(3)** is more difficult to satisfy than under **ss. 238 or 239**.

From this, it can be seen that liquidators have enormous scope for increasing the available assets of companies in liquidation for the benefit of creditors. It must also be remembered that there is the possibility of claiming contributions to the company's assets from company directors under **IA 1986, ss. 212–214**.

Question 3

Utopia plc is in insolvent liquidation and the following proofs have been lodged:

(a) A claim for £60,000 by Finance Ltd secured by a floating charge over the company's stocks in respect of wages and salary for the employees of Utopia plc. When the loan was made and the charge was created, Finance Ltd was aware of the presentation of the petition which resulted in the eventual winding-up order against Utopia plc.

(b) A claim for £80,000 by Dogger Bank plc, a secured creditor with a fixed charge over Utopia plc's freehold offices. On Utopia plc's liquidation, the company's total indebtedness to Dogger Bank plc was £300,000. Of this, £180,000 was in respect of the company's General Business Account and £120,000 in respect of the company's Wages and Salaries Account. Dogger Bank plc had earlier sold the freehold office property for £220,000 which had been appropriated first to discharging the amount outstanding on the Business Account and the balance towards discharging part of the Wages and Salaries Account.

(c) A claim for £50,000 by Grange Ltd who guaranteed Utopia plc's total indebtedness to West Bank plc subject to a limit of £50,000. Grange Ltd has discharged its liability to the bank.

(d) A claim for a total of £200,000 from Letters Ltd, the lessor of Utopia plc's factory premises. The claim is for: (i) £45,000 for pre-petition arrears; (ii) £15,000 for the period after the liquidator's appointment; and (iii) £140,000 for the remaining five years, taking into account annual rent increases.

(e) A claim for £35,000 by Eden Ltd in respect of goods supplied. The claim includes an amount in respect of interest of 5 per cent per annum from the date of supply but fails to take account of the usual trade discount of 2 per cent. Eden Ltd owes £10,000 to Utopia plc under a credit note issued for a previous delivery of faulty goods.

Advise the liquidator concerning the debts provable in a liquidation and the validity and priority of these claims.

Commentary

This question first requires you to explain the debts that can be proved in a liquidation and to explain the categorization of debts and their priority ranking in the liquidation. There then follow five claims of creditors for you to analyse and categorize according to whether their debts are provable and for how much and to identify their priority in the liquidation. This is a very significant area of the topic of corporate insolvency and a popular area for questions.

 Answer plan

- Proof of debts and priority of creditors including the expenses of the liquidation, preferential creditors and the options available to secured creditors with fixed charges
- Analysis of the individual cases

Suggested answer

The assets of a company in liquidation, including property and sums of money recovered by the liquidator under powers contained in the **IA 1986**, and any amounts collected from contributories in respect of unpaid share capital, are applied as a single fund in paying off the expenses of the liquidation, the debts of the company and, in the event of there being surplus funds remaining, in making distributions to the persons who were members of the company when it went into liquidation or those to whom they have since transferred their shares.

Creditors must prove the existence of their debt in order to share in the company's assets. Debts or claims can be proved in a winding up only if they could be maintained against the company before it went into liquidation. There are also non-provable debts which include debts or claims avoided by statute or the general law: illegal debts, oral guarantees, statute-barred debts. One category of valid debt or claim which is non-provable is for criminal or civil penalties or for taxes etc. by or on behalf of a foreign country or region (eg local taxes). All debts, apart from non-provable debts, can be proved: liquidated and unliquidated, certain and uncertain, contingent, present, and future. If the total amount of the debt is uncertain, the liquidator is required to assess the value of the debt for the purposes of its proof. If creditors disagree with the liquidator's valuation, there is a right of appeal to the court.

Secured creditors with fixed charges are in a rather anomalous position and they have four options in respect of proof of debts:

(a) realize the security and prove for any balance outstanding as an unsecured creditor

(b) value the asset held as security, declare the value to the liquidator and claim in respect of any balance outstanding as an unsecured creditor

(c) rely on the security as full satisfaction of the debt and lodge no proof, or

(d) surrender the security to the liquidator and prove for the whole debt as an unsecured creditor

Where the secured creditor values the asset, the liquidator can opt to buy in the asset at the valuation in the event that the asset would have an enhanced value in association with other assets of the company.

Debts are ranked in order of priority and satisfied in that order. If the assets are insufficient to satisfy all the debts within a category, the shortfall is borne equally between the creditors in that category who rank *pari passu* (on equal footing), except for deferred creditors. The order of priority is as follows:

(a) secured creditors with fixed charges

(b) expenses of the liquidation, including the liquidator's remuneration

(c) preferential creditors as defined in **IA 1986, s. 386** and **Schedule 6**

(d) secured creditors with a floating charge over the assets

(e) ordinary unsecured creditors

(f) deferred creditors, and

(g) return of capital to shareholders

If the assets available for payment of the general creditors are insufficient to meet the expenses, the expenses have priority over claims to property subject to any floating charge: **IA 1986, s. 176ZA**. This new provision was inserted into the Insolvency Act 1986 by **s. 1282 CA 2006** and reverses the decision in *Re Leyland Daf Ltd* **[2004] UKHL 9** which had overruled the decision in *Re Barleycorn Enterprises Ltd* [1970] Ch 465 (CA).

The preferential debts are paid in priority to all other debts (**s. 175(1)**) including secured creditors with a floating charge over the company's assets: **s. 175(2)**. The category of preferential debts was considerably reduced by the **Enterprise Act 2002** and restricted to employee benefits as follows:

(a) remuneration for up to four months prior to the liquidation subject to a maximum of £800 per employee

(b) accrued holiday remuneration

(c) sums loaned to the company and used for the specific purpose of the payment of employees' remuneration

As part of this cutting back of preferential claims, the law was also changed to improve the claims of unsecured creditors, insolvency practitioners have a duty to prescribe part of the company's net assets that would be available for claims by a chargee of the holders of floating charges, for the satisfaction of unsecured debts. In *Re Airbase (UK) Ltd* **[2008] EWHC 124** it was held that floating and fixed chargeholders were excluded from participating in respect of the prescribed assets in respect of any shortfall and in *Re Courts Plc (in liquidation)* [2008] EWHC 2339 (Ch) it was held that the court did not have the power to disapply the section in part for creditors owed less than a specified amount.

In respect of the specific aspects of the problem, the answers are as follows:

(a) The floating charge created by Utopia plc in favour of Finance Ltd was created in consideration of the advance of a contemporaneous loan to the company by Finance Ltd. In that respect, the validity of the charge cannot be questioned as a voidable preference (**s. 239**), neither can it be avoided under **s. 245**. Finance Ltd is entitled to prove as a secured creditor in respect of the loan and as a preferential creditor in respect of parts of the advance used to discharge debts which would, if still outstanding, rank as preferential debts, namely wages and salaries for the four months previous to the commencement of the liquidation, subject to a limit of £800 per employee.

(b) Dogger Bank plc as a secured creditor with a fixed charge has elected to sell the charged asset. The total debt owed to the bank by Utopia plc was £300,000 divided between two accounts: a general business account (£180,000) and a wages and salaries account (£120,000). Having realized the security for £220,000, the bank has elected to appropriate the proceeds towards discharging the total debt on the General Business Account and the balance of £40,000 to discharging part of the debt outstanding on the Wages and Salaries Account, leaving a balance outstanding of £80,000. Dogger Bank could therefore claim as a preferential creditor in respect of the Wages and Salaries Account to the extent that the loan was used to discharge debts which would, if still outstanding, rank as preferential. It will claim as an unsecured creditor for the balance. In *Re William Hall (Contractors) Ltd* [1967] 2 All ER 1150 it was held that the bank could appropriate the proceeds from the realization of a security in any way it chooses.

(c) The position of Grange Ltd depends on the terms of the guarantee signed in respect of Utopia plc's indebtedness to West Bank plc. At common law, Grange Ltd would be able to claim as a creditor in respect of the £50,000. If, however, the bank guarantee contained a 'Whole Debt Clause', Grange Ltd will not be able to claim against Utopia plc until such time as the bank recovers the whole debt. West Bank plc will place the £50,000 obtained from Grange Ltd into a suspense account and prove for the total debt owed by Utopia plc, including the £50,000 that it has already recovered from Grange Ltd.

(d) Letters Ltd would be able to claim in respect of the £45,000 pre-petition arrears as an unsecured creditor. For the arrears incurred after the liquidator's appointment, the claim would rank as a liquidation expense but only if the factory premises have been used by the liquidator to complete ongoing production to increase the assets available for the creditors. Failing this, the claim for £15,000 would rank as an unsecured debt. Although Utopia plc is notionally liable for the aggregate rent for the five remaining years, in practice the liquidator would disclaim the property under **IA 1986, ss. 178–182**. Letters Ltd could then lease the property to another tenant and so reduce any claim against Utopia plc. The practical advantages are that, in a property market where it is difficult to lease business properties, the actual rental value of the property may be less than under the current lease, and Letters Ltd's claim would therefore be reduced.

(e) If Eden Ltd's contract with Utopia plc expressly provided for the payment of interest, it would be entitled to claim in respect of the total amount of interest of 5 per cent from the date of supply to the date of the winding-up order. If the debt arose under a written agreement which did not provide for the payment of interest, Eden Ltd can only claim interest for the period when the debt became due until the date of the winding-up order at the rate payable in respect of judgment debts. If the debt was payable under an oral agreement with no express provision for interest, Eden Ltd can claim interest at the rate payable in respect of judgment debts, but only if Eden Ltd served a written demand for payment when the debt became due stating that interest would be claimed. In that event, interest could be claimed from the date of the written demand until the winding-up order.

Eden Ltd's claim would in any event be reduced by setting off against it the sum of the £10,000 owed by them to Utopia plc under a credit note. It would be further reduced to take into account the trade discount of 2 per cent on the invoice price.

Question 4

What kinds of liquidation or windings-up are there and what distinguishes them from each other?

Commentary

This essay requires you to identify and distinguish between the different forms of winding up: voluntary and compulsory. While this does not require a great deal of analysis, it does require clear thinking so that the different aspects of the procedures are set out.

Answer plan

- Voluntary and compulsory liquidation by the court
- Distinction between voluntary members' winding up and voluntary creditors' winding up
- Dissolution of company following procedure
- Compulsory winding up by the court: jurisdiction and grounds for petition
- Identification of petitioners
- Appointment of the liquidator and procedure leading to dissolution

Suggested answer

The winding up of a company may be either voluntary or by the court: **s. 73(1)**. Voluntary winding up is initiated by the passing of a resolution for the winding up of the company in general meeting. By contrast, winding up by the court is a legal process commenced by a petition resulting in a winding-up order. In both cases the company is placed in the hands of a licensed insolvency practitioner, a liquidator, whose task is to realize the assets of the company, to pay off the debts of the company and dissolve the company. The process of winding up by the court is usually referred to as compulsory winding up.

There are two types of voluntary winding up depending on whether the company is solvent or insolvent: a voluntary members' winding up for a solvent company and a voluntary creditors' winding up where it is insolvent. The significance of the name 'creditors' voluntary winding up' merely serves to indicate the dominant power of the creditors.

A voluntary members' winding up is initiated by a special resolution accompanied by a statutory declaration of solvency by the directors that the company will pay its debts in full within 12 months: **s. 90**. This is made five weeks before the resolution, or on the same day as (but before) the resolution, and registered within 15 days. Directors are liable to fines if the declaration is made without reasonable grounds.

The resolution is advertised in the *London Gazette* within 14 days: **s. 85**. The commencement of the winding-up dates from the time of the resolution (**s. 86**); and the company ceases to carry on business except so far as required for a beneficial winding up: **s. 87**.

The general meeting appoints one or more liquidators (**s. 91**) and, if the liquidation extends beyond a year, the liquidator calls annual general meetings from the commencement of the winding up and presents interim reports: **s. 93**. When the company's affairs are finally wound up, the liquidator calls a final meeting and presents a final report: **s. 94(1)**. The company is automatically dissolved three months after the registration of the return of the final meeting with the Registrar: **s. 201**.

If the liquidator decides that the company is insolvent, he calls a creditors' meeting within 28 days, giving the creditors seven days' notice (**s. 95**) by advertisement in the *London Gazette* and two local newspapers. The liquidator presides over the creditors' meeting, submits a statement of affairs, and the liquidation proceeds as a creditors' winding up.

A creditors' voluntary winding up is commenced by an extraordinary resolution to the effect that the company cannot continue its business by reason of its liabilities (**s. 84(2)(c)**) and there is no statutory declaration of solvency.

The company calls a creditors' meeting not later than 14 days after the resolution. Creditors must be given seven days' notice and the meeting is advertised in the *London Gazette* and in two local newspapers. Creditors must be given the name and address of an insolvency practitioner who will give free information to them, or a local address where, on the two business days before the meeting, a list of names and addresses of creditors is freely available for inspection: **s. 98**.

The directors present a statement of affairs to the meeting and appoint a director to preside: **s. 99**. At separate meetings, members and creditors may nominate a liquidator but, where different persons are nominated, the creditors' nominee will be the liquidator unless any director, member, or creditor applies to the court within seven days for the members' nominee to be liquidator instead of or jointly with the creditors' nominee, or for the appointment of some other person: **s. 100**.

Creditors may appoint a maximum of five creditors to a liquidation committee, in which case the members may also appoint a maximum of five representatives. The liquidation committee works with the liquidator and sanctions the liquidator's powers where required: **s. 101**. The directors' powers cease on the liquidator's appointment except in so far as the liquidation committee or the creditors authorize them: **s. 103**.

The winding up procedure and dissolution is as for the voluntary members' winding up except that there are annual and final meetings of creditors as well as members: **ss. 105 and 106**.

County courts have jurisdiction for the compulsory winding up of companies unless the paid up share capital exceeds £120,000, when jurisdiction passes to the Chancery Division of the High Court: **s. 117**. The process begins with the presentation of a petition by one of a group of recognized persons on one of the statutory grounds: **s. 122(1)(a)–(g)**. In effect the most usual grounds are: that the company is unable to pay its debts (**s. 122(1)(f)**), or that it is just and equitable that the company should be wound up: **s. 122(1)(g)**. There are also special grounds when a petition can be presented by the Secretary of State or the Financial Services Authority (FSA).

A winding-up petition can be presented by the company, the directors, the Secretary of State, the Department for Business Innovation & Skills (BIS), the receiver, contributory(ories) or creditor(s): **s. 124**. Contributory means every person liable to contribute to the company's assets in the event of its being wound up (**s. 79(1)**) but this apparent limitation to members holding partly-paid shares is not true and all members and past members can petition. Apart from the right to petition under **s. 122(1)(e)**, members can only petition in respect of shares held and registered in their name which: (a) were originally allotted to them; or (b) have been held by them for at least six months out of the previous 18; or (c) have devolved on them through the death of a former holder: **s. 124(2)**.

In spite of the provision that 'the court shall not refuse to make a winding-up order on the ground only that the company's assets have been mortgaged to an amount equal to or in excess of those assets, or that the company has no assets' (**s. 125(1)**), petitioners must have a financial interest in the winding up: *Re Chesterfield Catering Co Ltd* [1977] Ch 373. Petitions will also be rejected on just and equitable grounds if there is an alternative available remedy and the petition is unreasonable. The most usual alternative is a petition for unfair prejudice: **CA 2006, s. 994**.

Creditors can petition only in respect of claims for £750 and more, but joint petitions are possible. The debt must be undisputed, unless, despite the company disputing the total amount claimed, there is an undisputed debt of more than £750 owed: *Re Tweeds Garages* [1962] Ch 406. The court may reject the petition if it is opposed by more important creditors.

At any time after the presentation of the petition, the court may appoint a provisional liquidator to carry out the functions conferred by the court: **s. 135**. On the making of the winding-up order, the Official Receiver becomes the liquidator until another person is appointed: **s. 136(2)**. The Official Receiver is a civil servant attached to a court with responsibilities for personal and corporate insolvency.

Official Receivers may summon separate meetings of contributories and creditors for the purpose of choosing a person to be liquidator in their place: **s. 136(4)**. They have 12 weeks in which to decide whether to call the meeting (**s. 136(5)**), but one or more creditors, representing a quarter of the total debts, can request the convening of the meeting. Where the meetings are convened, the creditors' appointee will be the liquidator subject to the members' right of appeal as for the creditors' voluntary winding up: **s. 139**.

Where the winding-up order is made following the failure of an administration, the court may appoint the administrator as liquidator (**s. 140**), and where there is a supervisor of a failed CVA in place, the court may appoint the supervisor. In neither case will the Official Receiver become liquidator.

Creditors and contributories may also decide to establish a liquidation committee to work alongside the liquidator, who can exercise any of the powers in **Parts I** and **II** of **Schedule 4** with the sanction of the court or the liquidation committee (payment of debts, compromise of claims and so on; institution and defence of proceedings; carrying on of business of the company); and, with or without that sanction, to exercise any of the powers in **Part III** of that **Schedule: s. 167**.

When the company's affairs are wound up, the liquidator calls a final creditors' meeting, which receives the final report and decides whether to release the liquidator. The return of the meeting and notice of vacation of office is registered with the Companies' Registrar and the company is dissolved three months later: **s. 205**.

Question 5

Pineapple Press plc is a successful publisher with a string of bestselling authors. Due, however, to major problems not of their making in India and China, where their books are produced, the company lost its whole autumn production for the Christmas market. Unable to find alternative printers, the company found it difficult to continue meeting its salary bills and the rental for its warehouse in the UK.

The company had created a floating charge over the undertaking several years previously to Croesus Bank, and with the collapse in income is now unable to pay the interest payments on the loan.

Once the immediate production problems are over, the business should return to its normal profitable state.

Advise Pineapple Press plc and Croesus Bank of the legal possibilities to resolve the problems.

Commentary

This question requires you to consider the alternative solutions to liquidation bearing in mind that a return to profitability is assured once the immediate crisis is over. This involves looking at non-terminal insolvency and the possibility of the company entering into a company voluntary arrangement (CVA) with its creditors, either directly or by means of an administration. This procedure could be initiated by the directors of the company or by Croesus Bank as holder of a floating charge over the undertaking. In answering the question, you need to recognize the advantages offered by entering a CVA by way of administration.

The law relating to administration is very complex and you would only be required to have outline knowledge of it as an alternative to liquidation.

 Answer plan

- Emphasis of the Cork Report and the **IA 1986** on saving sick businesses: role of CVA and administration in this respect
- Consideration of company directors applying for a CVA
- Disadvantages of CVA
- Entering a CVA by means of administration: advantages of this

Suggested answer

The Report of the Insolvency Law Review Committee, *Insolvency Law and Practice* 1982 (Cmnd 8558, 1982), known as the 'Cork Report' was a critical development of modern insolvency law in the UK and the very limited options open to insolvent companies wishing to avoid the terminal procedure of winding up. The Cork Report, inspired by the USA Chapter 11 Bankruptcy procedure, recommended a move towards the creation of a 'rescue culture' whereby insolvency law would seek to save sick businesses. To this end, it recommended the introduction of the CVA and administration.

The CVA was introduced to provide a simple procedure to allow companies to enter into arrangements with their creditors. Companies can put forward a proposal to their creditors which becomes binding if approved by more than three-quarters in value of the unsecured creditors. Proposals include a moratorium in respect of debt repayment or a composition agreement whereby the creditor agrees to accept a smaller sum in total settlement of the debt: 75 pence in the pound.

Administration was inspired by the receiver-manager procedure, whereby the company would be placed in the hands of an administrator who would come up with a plan for saving the business in whole or in part, failing which the company's assets would be disposed of in a more beneficial way than liquidation.

The CVA procedure is regulated by IA 1986, ss. 1–7A and can be used before or after the commencement of administration or winding up. Where the proposal is by the directors, there is no need for the company to be insolvent. CVAs cannot be proposed by creditors or members. Where the company is already in administration or winding up, the proposal is by the administrator or liquidator.

The proposal provides for a supervisor—'the nominee'—who is a qualified insolvency practitioner and includes an explanation as to why a CVA is desirable. Within 28 days, the nominee submits a report to the court on whether the proposal should be put to meetings of the company and creditors: s. 2. If the company is already in administration or liquidation, the administrator or liquidator can summon meetings when and where they think fit: s. 3(2).

If both meetings accept the proposals—in whole or as modified—they are binding on all notified creditors and on the company: s. 4. There is no need for formal approval of the court: s. 4(6). Proposals affecting the rights of secured or preferential creditors can only be approved with their consent: s. 4(3) and (4). Acceptance by creditors is a majority representing 75 per cent in value of those present (in person or by proxy), and voting; acceptance at the members' meeting is by simple majority unless otherwise provided in the articles.

On approval, the CVA binds dissenting creditors and all creditors with notice of and entitled to vote at the meeting: s. 5(2)(b). Application can be made to the court for revocation or suspension of the approvals or for further meetings for reconsideration of the proposal on the grounds that the CVA unfairly prejudices the interests of a creditor, member or contributory; or for some irregularity in relation to the meetings: s. 6. In *Re Gatnom Capital & Finance Ltd* [2010] EWHC 3353 (Ch) a CVA was revoked where contracts creating liabilities for two creditors were shams and they were not entitled to vote at the creditors' meeting.

Once the arrangement is approved, the court can stay all winding-up proceedings, discharge any administration and give directions to facilitate the composition or scheme: s. 7. On completion of the CVA, the supervisor notifies all creditors and members of its full implementation, together with a financial report, with copies to the Registrar of Companies and the court.

The CVA as originally introduced was criticized for the absence of any moratorium after the proposal to prevent creditors from taking proceedings against the company pending approval. It is now possible to apply for a 28-day moratorium (the period can be extended) for companies that qualify as small private companies under CA 2006, s. 382: s. 1A. For larger companies, the only way of obtaining moratorium protection is by way of an administration.

The administration procedure as initially introduced was criticized as over complicated and expensive. The procedure was completely revised by the Enterprise Act 2002 and is now regulated by IA 1986, Schedule B1. The purpose is rescuing the company as a going concern, or achieving a better result for the company's creditors as a whole than if the company were wound up, or realising property to make a distribution to one or more secured or preferential creditors: **para. 3(1)**. Administrators act in the interests of all the company's creditors, are officers of the court, and must be licensed insolvency practitioners. They can be appointed by the court, by the holder of a qualifying floating charge, or by the company or its directors.

A qualifying floating charge is one that entitles the chargee to appoint an administrator: **para. 14(2)**. A person holds a qualifying floating charge if he holds one or more debentures secured by a qualifying floating charge or other forms of security on the whole or substantially the whole of the company's property: **para. 14(3)**. Notice of the intention to appoint (**para. 14**), followed by notice of appointment must be filed with the court and declarations of the creditor's right to appoint an administrator and the administrator's willingness to serve: **para. 18**. The appointment takes effect once these requirements are satisfied: **para. 19**.

The company and the directors can appoint an administrator subject to certain restrictions: **para. 22**. Notice of intention to appoint must be filed with the court (**para. 27**) and also notice of the appointment together with statutory declarations of their right to make the appointment and the administrator's statement of consent: **para. 29**. The appointment is effective once these requirements are satisfied: **para. 30**.

Where the appointment is by the holder of a floating charge, there is an interim moratorium from the time when a copy of a notice of intention to appoint an administrator is filed with the court until: (a) the appointment of the administrator takes effect; or (b) the period of five business days from the date of filing expires without an administrator being appointed. If appointed by the company or the directors it operates from the filing of notice of intention to appoint an administrator until the appointment of the administrator takes effect or the lapse of a specified period without an administrator having been appointed. Once the administration commences, there is a permanent moratorium against legal proceedings for the duration of the administration.

The administrator sets out proposals for achieving the purpose of the administration, which may include a proposal for a CVA. The proposal is sent to the Registrar of Companies, every creditor of whose claim and address he is aware, and every member of whose address he is aware, within eight weeks. Copies of the proposals to creditors include an invitation to a creditors' meeting unless the administrator thinks that: (a) the company has sufficient property for each creditor to be paid in full; (b) the company has insufficient property to pay unsecured creditors; or (c) neither of the specified objectives of the administration can be achieved.

The meeting must be held within ten weeks, proposals may be approved without modification, or with modifications to which the administrator consents. The administrator reports any decision to the court, the Registrar of Companies and other prescribed persons. Where at the initial or a subsequent creditors' meeting the administrator's proposals or revised proposals are not accepted, the court may order that the administrator's appointment shall cease.

On their appointment, administrators take custody or control of all the company's property and manage the company's affairs, business, and property in accordance with the approved proposals, subject to non-substantial revisions made by them and any approved substantial revisions. Their appointment terminates after one year subject to extension for a specified period by the court or for a maximum of six months by consent. It can be further extended in both cases by court order before expiry.

The administrator can apply to the court to end the administration (a) if its purpose cannot be achieved; (b) if the company should not have entered administration; or (c) where a creditors' meeting requires him to make an application. Administrators appointed by floating charge holders and the company or directors may notify the court and the Registrar of Companies that the administration's purpose has been sufficiently achieved and the appointment will then automatically cease: **para. 80.**

Applying this to Pineapple Press plc and Croesus Bank, it can be seen that, while the directors of the company can propose a CVA, this is at the risk of creditors bringing proceedings to enforce their rights or petition for the winding up of the company. As an alternative, the directors and Croesus Bank can exercise their right to appoint an administrator without the need for any application to the court. The notice of their intent to appoint an administrator will immediately trigger an interim moratorium on any actions against the company which will become permanent once the administration is commenced. The administrator could propose a CVA as a solution to the company's immediate crisis and, once the crisis is over, the company could resume normal trading.

Further reading

Ashwin, A., 'Tortious liability of company in winding up: an analysis' [2005] Comp. Law., 26(6): 163.

Crystal, M., Phillips, M., and Davis, G., *Butterworths Insolvency Law Handbook* (London: LexisNexis Butterworths, 8th edn, 2006).

Kastrinou, A., 'An analysis of the pre-pack technique and recent developments in the area' [2008] Comp. Law., 29(9): 259.

Kastrinou, A., Shah, N., and Gough, O., 'Corporate rescue in the UK and the effect of the TUPE' [2011] Comp. Law., 32(5): 131

Keay, A., and Walton, P., *Insolvency Law Corporate and Personal* (Harlow: Pearson Longman, 2003).

Markovic, M., 'New legal risks for banks in business workouts: corporate law, banks and liquidators' [2009] Comp. Law., 30(12): 377.

Moore, M. T., 'Directors' pay as a creditor concern: the lesson from MG Rover' [2006] Comp. Law., 27(8): 237.

Walton, P., 'Re Kayley Vending Ltd.: pre-pack administration—is its Achilles' heel showing?' [2010] Comp. Law., 31(3): 85.

Mixed topics

Introduction

This chapter includes a number of questions which — to a greater or lesser extent—
cross-topic frontiers and require you to answer questions bringing in more than one
aspect of company law.

Question 1

Sonia, Tariq, and Iqbal set up a business in 2006 selling rejects from chain stores in a shop
called 'Cheep & Cheerful'. On 1 February 2008 they bought an off-the-shelf company, Kora Ltd,
and transferred the business it. They valued the business at £300,000, and issued 100,000 £1
fully paid shares to each of them. They were each named as a director.

On 5 February 2008, the board applied to the Registrar of Companies to register the company
as 'British Chainstore Massacre Ltd'. In anticipation of the change, new stationery was ordered.
On 10 February 2008, Sonia ordered a stock of reject jumpers on one of the new order forms.
The new Certificate of Incorporation was issued on 12 February. The directors intend to
continue trading under the name 'Cheep & Cheerful'.

Sonia and Tariq have recently discovered that Iqbal is currently involved in setting up a rival
business and decide to remove him from the board.

(a) What problems could the company have in seeking to register its proposed new name?

(b) Subject to what conditions can the company continue to trade as 'Cheep & Cheerful'?

(c) What is the legal position concerning the order placed by Sonia on 10 February?

(d) How easy will it be for Sonia and Tariq to remove Iqbal from the board?

 Commentary

This mixed topic question brings in regulations controlling company names and the power
to change a company's name, the date at which the change becomes effective, and the

consequences of the use by company officers of the new name before a certificate of incorporation is issued validating the change. In addition it requires knowledge of the rules relating to business names. With regard to the right to remove Iqbal from the board of directors, you must recognize that, although this is legally possibly by way of an ordinary resolution with special notice, Iqbal may be able to petition against his removal as being unfairly prejudicial or as grounds for the just and equitable winding up of the company.

 ## Answer plan

- Rules regulating choice of name for registered companies and for change of name
- Date and effect of change and legal consequences where officers anticipate the change before it is validated
- Right to remove a director subject to right to protest
- Possible right to petition on grounds of unfair prejudice or for just and equitable winding up

Suggested answer

Statutory regulation of company names is covered by the **Companies Act 2006, Part 5**. In this respect, a company must not be registered by a name if, in the opinion of the Secretary of State, its use would constitute an offence, or it is offensive: **s. 53**. In respect of company names and the use of sensitive words and expressions, the approval of the Secretary of State is required for registration of a company by a name that would be likely to give the impression that the company is associated with Her Majesty's government (including Scotland and Northern Ireland), a local authority, or any public authority specified by regulations made by the Secretary of State: **s. 54(1)**. In addition, approval is required for a company to be registered by a name that includes a word or expression specified by the Secretary of State in regulations under the section: **s. 55**. In respect of both provisions, the Secretary of State may require the applicant to seek the view of a specified government department or other body: **s. 56**.

Further restrictions include the fact that the name must not be the same as another in the registrar's index of company names: **s. 66**. The Secretary of State can order the change of a name that is too similar to an existing name (**s. 67**), the order must be within twelve months of the company's registration and specify the period within which the change must be effected, failing which an offence is committed by the company and every officer in default: **s. 68**.

Further provisions enable a third party to object to a company's registered name on the grounds that it is the same as a name associated with the applicant in which he has goodwill, or that it is sufficiently similar to such a name that its use in the UK would be likely to mislead by suggesting a connection between the company and the applicant: **s. 69**. For such cases, the **Companies Act** authorizes the Secretary of State to appoint company names adjudicators (s. 70) who, within ninety days of an application under s. 69, must make their decisions and their reasons for it available to the public: s. 72. If an application for a name change under s. 69 is upheld, the adjudicator can make an order requiring the respondent company to change its name (s. 73) subject to a right of appeal to the court against their decisions: s. 74.

The Secretary of State also has powers to order a company to change its name on the grounds that misleading information has been given for the purpose of the company's registration by a particular name, or that an undertaking given for that purpose has not been fulfilled: s. 75(1). Directions must be within five years of registration by that name and must specify the period within which the company is to change its name: s. 75(2). If the company's name also gives a misleading indication of the nature of the company's activities, the Secretary of State may direct the company to change its name within six weeks of the direction or such longer period as allowed: s. 77.

As regards the change of name from Kora Ltd to British Chainstore Massacre Ltd, a company may change its name by special resolution or by other means provided for by the company's articles: s. 77(1). Where a change of the company's name is made by other means than a special resolution in accordance with its articles, the company must notify the Registrar, and the notice must be accompanied by a statement that the change of name has been made by means provided by the company's articles. The name of the company may also be changed by resolution of the directors under s. 64 (change to comply with the direction of the Secretary of State under that section); on the determination of a new name by a company names adjudicator under s. 73; on the determination of a new name under s. 74 (appeal against decision of company names adjudicator); and under s. 1033 (company's name on restoration to the register). Any change of name must comply with the requirements of **Part 5** of the Act.

The essential problems in this case would arise under **ss. 53** and **54** in that the Secretary of State could regard the proposed name as offensive or simply object to the inclusion of the words 'Great British' which could be regarded as implying a connection with HMG.

With regard to the continued use of the business name 'Cheep & Cheerful', business names are regulated under **Part 41** of the Act, **ss. 1192–1199** which contain similar provisions regarding names suggesting a connection with central or local government, sensitive words or expressions and misleading names. These provisions apply to all companies trading under a name other than that under which it is registered. It is unlikely that any objection could be made to this name.

Sonia has, in anticipation of the change of name of the company from Kora Ltd to British Chainstore Massacre Ltd, placed an order for some reject jumpers using order forms printed with the proposed company name as opposed to the current name of the company. Since a change of the company's name has effect from the date on which the new certificate of incorporation is issued (s. 81(1)), Sonia has no right to use this name. The legal position, however, is that the law relating to pre-incorporation contracts will not apply and therefore Sonia will not be personally liable under s. 51(1). This position was established by the decision in *Oshkosh B'Gosh Inc v Dan Marbell Inc Ltd* [1989] BCLC 507.

In respect of the desire to remove Iqbal from the board on the grounds that he is involved in setting up a rival company, a company may by ordinary resolution with special notice remove a director (**s. 168**) subject to the director's right to protest against removal: **s. 169**. The complication in this case, however, is that since this is a quasi-partnership company, the removal of Iqbal from the board may trigger a petition by Iqbal against unfair prejudice: **s. 994**. The court could, however, decide that since Iqbal is involved in setting up a rival company that this is in breach of his general duty to promote the success of the company (**s. 172**): *Item Software (UK) Ltd v Fassihi* [2004] EWCA Civ 1244. In this case, his removal, although prejudicial, is not unfair: *Re RA Noble & Sons (Clothing) Ltd* [1983] BCLC 273.

In this case, however, Iqbal could then petition for the just and equitable winding up of the company on the grounds of his exclusion from the management of the company by analogy with the decision in *Ebrahimi v Westbourne Galleries Ltd* [1973] AC 360.

Question 2

Cleanathon Ltd has three directors Andrew, Ben, and Claire, who each hold one third of the shares. The company was registered under the **Companies Act 1985** with the following objects:

(a) To carry on business as a provider of laundry and dry cleaning services to the general public.

(b) To carry on any other business which in the opinion of the Company may be capable of being conveniently or profitably carried on in connection with or subsidiary to any other business of the company.

(c) To sell or otherwise dispose of the whole or any part of the business or property of the company for any consideration as the Company may think fit.

(d) To do all such things as may be deemed incidental or conducive to the attainment of the Company's objects or any of them.

None of the objects in any sub-clause of this Clause shall be in any way limited or restricted by reference to any other object set forth in any such sub-clause of this Clause, or by reference to or inference from the name of the Company.

The articles are in the form of Table A in the **Companies (Tables A to F) Regulations 1985** subject to a restriction limiting the authority of individual directors to contracts up to £25,000, above which the prior approval of the board is required.

In November 2007, the laundry business suffered due to the opening of a nearby launderette. The board decided to give up the laundry business and to acquire and operate a 'Winkie' fast-food franchise from the same premises. The company advertised to sell the washing machines and dryers, which had been placed in storage, and in February 2008 Claire eventually contracted to sell them for £35,000 to Spin & Tonic Ltd, a wine bar/launderette business. Claire's son, Edward, was a shareholder and director of Spin & Tonic Ltd.

In December 2007, Andrew became seriously ill. His friend, Jane, took over his day-to-day duties: ordering supplies and engaging part-time employees. In January 2008, the profits collapsed after a food poisoning outbreak linked with fast foods. The company's accountant warned Ben and Claire to consider closing down but, having discussed the matter with Jane—whom they had come to rely upon for financial and management advice—they continued the business until it went into insolvent liquidation in May 2008.

Advise the liquidator of the liability of the company and the directors relating to:

(i)   The change of business from laundry to fast food outlet

(ii) The sale of the laundry's assets to Spin & Tonic Ltd

(iii) The potential liability of Andrew, Ben, Claire, and Jane

Commentary

This question picks up points relating to the interpretation of a company's objects post the implementation of the **Companies Act 2006 (CA 2006)**, contracts beyond the company's capacity, contracts beyond the director's authority and where the transaction involves directors and their associates. The case also raises the issue of liability for wrongful trading and de facto and shadow directors and the possibility of disqualification. Since the issue of contracts beyond the capacity of the company and the directors' authority only arise frequently in connection with the liquidation of the company, this is a frequently met combination of topics.

Answer plan

- Status of objects for companies incorporated prior to the **Companies Act 2006**
- Interpretation of the objects clause and analysis of legality of company's change of business
- Statement of the law concerning directors acting beyond their authority and the position where transactions involve directors or connected persons—and the interpretation of connected persons in this context
- Liability of directors under the **Insolvency Act 1986, s. 214**—position of Jane as de facto or shadow director
- Possibility of disqualification under **Company Directors Disqualification Act 1986 (CDDA 1986)**

Suggested answer

Under the **Companies Act 2006**, the company's constitution is now contained in the articles of association of the company together with any resolutions and agreements under **Chapter 3 (s. 17)** as set out in **s. 29**. The Act also provides that, for existing companies, provisions that were contained in the company's memorandum are to be treated as provisions of the company's articles: **s. 28**.

The objects clause of Cleanathon Ltd continues, therefore, to determine the contractual capacity of the company unless and until the company adopts the unrestricted objects that are now possible under **s. 31**. This means that the objects, as drafted, must be interpreted under the common law principles applicable to traditional objects clauses. In this case, although the company has a limited object stated in clause 'A', clause 'B' contains a subjective objects clause that allows the company to engage in any business that 'in the opinion of the Company, may be capable of being conveniently or profitably carried on in connection with or subsidiary to any other business of the company'. The validity of this type of clause was established in *Bell Houses Ltd v City Wall Properties Ltd* [1966] 1 QB 207.

In spite of the fact that the company appears to have abandoned the object it was formed to carry on, the objects clause also states in a final clause that the objects of the company shall in no way be restricted by reference 'to any other object set forth in any such sub-clause of this Clause, or by reference to or inference from the name of the Company'. The company cannot, therefore, be wound up by the court for failure of its main object.

In addition, the objects would seem to allow the company the possibility of changing their business unless the court interprets the clause so as to mean that any new business under sub-clause 'B' must be additional to the principal business of the company. If this is so, the position would nevertheless be protected in respect of third parties dealing with the company since the validity of an act done by a company cannot be called into question on the ground of lack of capacity: **CA 2006, s. 39**. If this is the position adopted by the court, however, the directors of the company, in agreeing to the change of business, can be said to have approved the change of the company's constitution by their unanimous agreement and, since the objects are now presumed to be articles of association which can be altered by special resolution (**s. 21**) and by informal, unanimous consent of the members: *Cane v Jones* [1981] 1 All ER 533, there is no case to argue that the change of business is beyond the capacity of the company.

In respect of the contract by Claire to sell the washing machines and dryers, she has clearly exceeded her powers under the articles of the company where she is restricted to contracts up to £25,000 unless she has previously obtained the prior approval of the board. In this respect, the contract is covered by **CA 2006, s. 40** and the contract would be enforceable against the company by Spin & Tonic Ltd as persons who have acted in good faith in respect of their dealing with Cleanathon Ltd. Whether the courts will interpret **s. 40** widely so as to respect the intentions of the **First Company Law Directive**

1968 is unclear. If not, Spin & Tonic Ltd would have to enforce the contract through the rule in *Turquand's Case*.

In this context, it is also relevant to realize that Claire's son Edward is a shareholder and director of Spin & Tonic Ltd. This could raise the issue of a director acting beyond the scope of his/her authority in respect of a contract with a person who is an associate of the director: **s. 41**. If this is the case, then Cleanathon Ltd would be able to avoid the contract and, even if the contract was not avoided, Claire and Spin & Tonic Ltd would have to account for any profit made directly or indirectly from the contract, and indemnify the company in respect of any loss or damage.

In order to establish the application of **s. 41**, it is first of all necessary to establish whether Edward is a person connected with the director and second the scale of his shareholding in Spin & Tonic Ltd. Under **s. 252**, the persons connected with a director include the members of the director's family: **s. 252(2)(a)**. This is further defined in **s. 253** where members of the director's family include the director's children or stepchildren: **s. 253(2)(c)**. Edward is clearly connected with Claire, even though he may be over 18 years of age. It must then be considered whether Claire is connected with Spin & Tonic Ltd. For this purpose, if Edward's shareholding in the company is equal to 20 per cent of the share capital of Spin & Tonic, or if he is entitled to exercise or control the exercise of more than 20 per cent of the voting power of Spin & Tonic Ltd, then Claire will be regarded as connected with Spin & Tonic Ltd. If his shareholding is less than the 20 per cent, however, Claire will not be connected with Spin & Tonic Ltd and the legal status of the contract will be dealt with under **s. 40** or, failing that, the rule in *Turquand's Case*.

Cleanathon Ltd has gone into insolvent liquidation but the directors, Ben and Claire had ignored the advice of the company's accountant to stop trading and, following the advice of Jane, who is replacing Andrew while he is ill, opted to continue to trade. It is clear that this could constitute wrongful trading under **IA 1986, s. 214**. As a result, they could be liable to contribute to the assets of the company in liquidation: *Re Produce Marketing Consortium Ltd (No 2)* [1989] BCLC 520.

It is important to consider Jane's position in this respect. By becoming involved in the management of the day-to-day business of the company and as a person whose financial and management advice has come to be relied on by Ben and Claire, Jane could be defined as a de facto or shadow director of Cleanathon Ltd. In *Gemma Ltd v Davies* [2008] EWHC 546 the court stated that in order to be a de facto or shadow director, it had to be shown that the person had 'real influence' on corporate decision making. As such, she could also be held liable to contribute to the assets of the company: *Secretary of State for Trade and Industry v Deverell* [2000] 2 WLR 907.

If Ben, Claire, and Jane are found guilty of wrongful trading, they can also be automatically disqualified from acting as directors for a maximum period of 15 years: **CDDA 1986, s. 10**. They could also be liable for compulsory disqualification as directors of a company that has gone into insolvent liquidation if it is shown that they are, by their conduct, unfit to be directors: **CDDA 1986, s. 6**. Evidence of unfitness requires consideration of matters set out in **CDDA 1986, Parts I** and **II, Schedule 1**. In respect of **Part I, para. 1**, unfitness could be established by any misfeasance or breach of any fiduciary or other duty by the directors in relation to the company. Directors have a duty to promote the success of the company (**CA 2006, s. 172**) which requires them to have regard to a number of matters including any enactment or rule of law requiring them to consider and act in the interests of the creditors of the company. In this respect, it has been held that directors of a company which is insolvent or on the borderline of insolvency owe a duty to the company's creditors: *Brady v Brady* [1988] BCLC 20. It could be argued that, by continuing to trade after a warning by the company's accountant, they are jeopardizing the position of the company's creditors in breach of this statutory duty.

Andrew, who has been away from the company during a period of sickness, will escape liability for wrongful trading and the risk of disqualification.

Question 3

Gwen and Vernon are sole shareholders of Goldie Locks Ltd which operates a retail business selling security locks and safes. Goldie Locks Ltd owed £300,000 to its main supplier, Fail Safe Ltd, which refused to deliver further supplies unless the company created a floating charge in its favour over the whole undertaking to cover the outstanding debts and as security for future supplies.

Fail Safe Ltd also insisted on a reservation of title clause in all contracts relating to future supplies in respect of the goods supplied under that contract. On 10 January 2008, it was agreed to create a floating charge over Goldie Locks Ltd's assets for a total of £500,000. The charge was executed on 31 January 2008 and registered within 21 days. On 21 January, Fail Safe Ltd made a delivery supplies worth £50,000 in reliance on the charge. On 30 April, Fail Safe Ltd made a further delivery worth £25,000.

Following warnings from their accountants, Gwen and Vernon placed Goldie Locks Ltd into administration on 1 June 2008.

In respect of this scenario, advise on the following points:

(a) The validity of the charge created in favour of Fail Safe Ltd

(b) If Goldie Locks Ltd is now in administration, what rights does the administrator have over the assets covered by Fail Safe Ltd's floating charge and the goods supplied under the reservation of title clause if he is now negotiating to sell Goldie Locks Ltd as a going concern?

 Commentary

This question raises elements of three topics: floating charges, reservation of title clauses, and the powers of the administrators in respect of property belonging to the company in administration. You are required to consider the application of **IA 1986, s. 245** in fixing the partial validity of the floating charge created for a combination of past consideration and new consideration. You must also discuss the significance for Fail Safe Ltd of the reservation of title clause. And you are finally required to discuss the extensive powers of administrators over property belonging to companies in administration which is covered by a charge.

 Answer plan

- Partial validity of floating charges under **IA 1986, s. 245**
- Extent of claim of Fail Safe Ltd in respect of goods supplied subject to a reservation of title clause
- Rights of an administrator of a company to set aside charges over company assets

Suggested answer

The directors of Goldie Locks Ltd have created a floating charge for £500,000 over the company's assets in favour of Fail Safe Ltd to cover past debts of £300,000 and future supplies. Within less than three months of creating this charge, the directors have placed Goldie Locks Ltd in administration. Directors can place a company in administration under **IA 1986, Schedule B1, para. 22**. The appointment of an administrator constitutes the onset of insolvency for the purposes of **IA 1986, s. 245** which relates to the avoidance of floating charges created within a relevant time prior to the onset of insolvency.

Fail Safe Ltd is an outsider in respect of Goldie Locks Ltd, the relevant period for an outsider being twelve months prior to the onset of insolvency: **s. 245(3)(b)**. In order for the period of time to be relevant for the purposes of the section, the company creating the charge must have been unable to pay its debts within the meaning of **IA 1986, s. 123** at the time of the creation of the charge, or have become unable to pay its debts in consequence of the transaction under which the charge is created: **s. 245(4)**. In this case, since the company has gone into administration within three months of the creation of the charge, the likelihood is that the company was unable to pay its debts when the charge was created. If this is the case the charge is invalid in respect of the existing debt of £300,000 for which it was created and is only valid to the aggregate of the value of so much of the consideration for the creation of the charge as consists of money paid, or goods or services supplied, to the company at the same time as, or after, the creation of the charge: **s. 245(2)(a)**. In this case, the question relates to the supply of goods to Goldie Locks Ltd. This is subject to a further proviso in that the value of the goods supplied is the amount of money which could reasonably be expected to be obtained for supplying the goods in the ordinary course of business: **s. 245(6)**. This means that the court can assess whether Fail Safe Ltd has charged an excessive amount for the goods supplied. If so, then the security will not cover the amount in excess of a reasonable amount.

In respect of supplies in reliance on the floating charge, Fail Safe Ltd made deliveries of goods on two occasions: 21 January and 30 April. The floating charge, although agreed between the parties on 10 January was not actually executed until 31 January. Since the charge is only valid in respect of goods supplied at the same time as, or after, the creation of the charge, the value of the goods supplied on 21 January does not fall within the provision of **s. 245(2)(b)**. This was established by the decision in *Power v Sharp Investments Ltd* **[1994] 1 BCLC 111**. As a result, the floating charge is valid only in respect of the supply of goods made on 30 April 2008; a total value of £25,000. As a result, Fail Safe Ltd is an unsecured creditor in respect of the £300,000 past debts and the goods to the value of £50,000 supplied on 21 January 2008.

There may be some protection for Fail Safe Ltd, however, in so far as both of these deliveries were made under the terms of a reservation of title clause in respect of payment under the contract in respect of which they were supplied. Ideally, Fail Safe Ltd would be able to reclaim from Goldie Locks Ltd any unsold items supplied under the contracts of 21 January and 30 April as long as they have required Goldie Locks Ltd to store the goods separately from other similar items and to clearly mark them as the property of Fail Safe Ltd. There is a problem, however, in that Fail Safe Ltd would be required to identify the goods supplied under each contract. Since it is likely that the goods supplied are of a similar nature, the danger is that they could have become mixed. The problem then is that the court could reject the validity of the clause because of the impossibility of establishing under which contract they were supplied since the reservation of title clause is not an all monies clause. This was the problem in *Re Andrabell* **[1984] 3 All ER 407** where the court refused to recognize a reservation of title clause over supplies of travel bags delivered under a number of contracts, since the passing of the property in the bags was only postponed until full payment was made for a particular consignment, rather than Andrabell's total indebtedness.

Goldie Locks Ltd is now in administration and administrators have a statutory power to dispose of or take action relating to property subject to a floating charge as if it were uncharged. Where the property is disposed of, the holder of the floating charge has the same priority in respect of the acquired property as in respect of the property disposed of. Acquired property refers to any property that directly or indirectly represents the property disposed of: **para. 70**. The administrator has this power without the need to request the leave of the court.

In respect of non-floating charges and hire-purchase property, the administrator can also dispose of the charged property as if it were not charged but only after having obtained a court order to that effect. An order may be made only where the court thinks the disposal would be likely to promote the purpose of the administration and is subject to the condition that the net proceeds of disposal of the property, and any additional money required to be added to the net proceeds so as to produce the amount determined by the court as the net amount which would be realized on a sale of the property at market value, should be applied towards discharging the sums secured by the security: **para. 71** and **para. 72**. For the purposes of the Act, hire-purchase property includes property subject to a reservation of title clause.

Thus, in conclusion, the floating charge held by Fail Safe Ltd will only be valid up to the total of £25,000 being the value of goods supplied after the creation of the charge. It may be that the reservation of title clause is also ineffective since it is not drafted as an 'all monies' clause. In any event, the administrator can dispose of the property covered by floating charge as if it were uncharged but Fail Safe Ltd's claim would transfer to the proceeds of the disposal. The same right of disposal is available to the administrator in respect of the property covered by a reservation of title clause, but only with court approval and with protection of the rights of Fail Safe Ltd.

Question 4

Junk Bonds plc sought to acquire control of City Limits plc, a property company listed on the Alternative Investment Market (AIM). Junk Bonds Ltd borrowed £8m from Merchant Bank plc secured by charges over its assets and acquired a 51 per cent stake in City Limits plc.

Junk Bonds plc nominated its employees, Horace, Morris, and Doris to the board of City Limits plc. Following instructions from Junk Bonds plc, the board of City Limits plc, dominated by Junk Bonds plc's nominees, disposed of a large part of the property portfolio of City Limits plc. The contract for the sale of the properties identified City Limits plc as the seller and was signed by two of its authorised signatories. One of the purchasers subsequently refused to complete the purchase on the ground that the contract did not contain words expressly stating that the signatures were 'by or on behalf of' City Limits plc.

With the proceeds of the sale of the properties, the board of City Limits plc then proposed a reduction of capital by reducing the nominal value of the shares from £1 to 50p per share to be financed out of the company's reserves. The special resolution was carried by the shares held by Junk Bonds plc, the shares held by the trust fund for employees and proxy votes.

The large dividend and the funds from the capital reduction enabled Junk Bonds plc to repay the debt from Merchant Bank plc.

Advise the minority shareholders of City Limits concerning the legality of these transactions and any action available to them.

 Commentary

This is a complex problem requiring you to discuss a number of topics including the proper execution of company contracts, financial assistance, the general duties of directors with particular emphasis on nominee directors, and the statutory derivative claim. As with most mixed topic questions, there is not the time to deal with every aspect in minute detail, the important thing is to recognize the issues and deal with them broadly.

Answer plan

- General duties of directors with particular regard to nominee directors
- The proper execution of company documents
- Financial assistance and unconditional exceptions: **s. 681**
- Legal basis for a derivative claim by the minority shareholders of City Limits plc

Suggested answer

Directors of a company owe general duties to that company as set out in **CA 2006, ss. 170–178**. Of these duties, the most relevant to this situation is the duty to promote the success of the company which requires directors to act in the way they consider would be most likely to promote the success of the company for the benefit of its members as a whole: **s. 172**. Matters that directors are called upon to have regard to in this respect include the likely consequences of any decision in the long term and the need to act fairly as between members of the company: **s. 172(1)(a) and (f)**.

In analysing the acts of Horace, Morris, and Doris as directors of City Limits plc, it seems clear that they have been acting solely in the interests of Junk Bonds plc which nominated them to the board to carry out its own schemes. The position of nominee directors is very clearly set out in UK law in the decision in *Scottish Co-operative Wholesale Society Ltd v Meyer* **[1959] AC 324**. In this case the Society formed a subsidiary company in 1946 to engage in the manufacture of rayon at a time when a government licence was required. Meyer and Lucas held such a licence and they were minority shareholders in the company and joint managing directors. The Society appointed three of its own directors to the board and held the majority of the shares. After licensing ceased in 1952, the Society transferred the company's business to another branch of its organization and cut off supplies of raw materials. The subsidiary company was forced to suspend its manufacturing activity, no profits were generated, and the value of its shares fell. Meyer and Lucas petitioned on the grounds of oppression under the **Companies Act 1948, s. 210**. With regard to the position of the nominee directors, Lord Denning pointed out that for as long as the interests of the Society and the subsidiary coincided, there was no problem and the nominee directors could do their duty by both companies without embarrassment. Once there was a conflict between the interests of the two companies, however, the nominee directors put their duty to the Society above their duty to the subsidiary company. He held that in thinking that their first duty was to the Society, the nominees were wrong and granted Meyer and Lucas the relief that they sought: the purchase of their shares at their value prior to the running down of the business.

The decision establishes that nominee directors of a company must act in the interests of the company on whose board they are nominees and not the interests of the person nominating them, a position endorsed in recent decisions *Re Southern Countries Fresh Foods Ltd* **[2008] EWHC 2810 (Ch)** and *Hawkes v Cuddy* **[2009] EWCA Civ 291**. It has been argued that some relaxation should be made in respect of the nominees reporting back to the party nominating them without fear of being in breach of their duty of confidentiality.

In respect of the failure to use the formula 'for and on behalf of' in relation to the signatures of the authorized signatories, the Court of Appeal in *Roger Williams & Ors v Redcard Ltd & Ors* **[2011] EWCA Civ 466** held that **s. 44(4) CA 2006** did not require the use of the formula and that it was sufficient that City Limits plc was described as 'seller' and that the signatures appeared at the end of the instrument under the words 'SIGNED ... SELLER'.

In respect of the distribution of money to Junk Bonds plc enabling Junk Bonds plc to repay its loan to Merchant Bank plc, it is clear that Horace, Morris, and Doris are not acting in the best interests of City Limits plc. Their actions do not, however, constitute the offence of financial assistance as long as the excessive dividend payment was made in accordance with the law in **CA 2006, Part 23**. Thus the payment must be made out of 'accumulated, realized profits, so far as not previously utilized by distribution or capitalization, less its accumulated, realized losses, so far as not previously written off in a reduction or reorganization of capital duly made': **s. 830(2)**. In addition, since City Limits plc is a public company, the distribution must only be made if the amount of the net assets is not less than the aggregate of its called-up share capital and undistributable reserves, and if, and to the extent that, the distribution does not reduce the amount of those assets to less than that aggregate: **s. 831(1)**.

Similarly, the reduction of capital made by City Limits plc does not constitute financial assistance as long as the reduction of capital is made in compliance with the law stated in **CA 2006, Chapter 10, Part 17**.

Both transactions are excepted from constituting financial assistance by virtue of being classified as unconditional exceptions: **s. 681**.

In so far as the nominee directors have clearly acted contrary to their general duty to promote the success of City Limits plc, this would give the minority shareholders the right to bring a statutory derivative claim on behalf of City Limits plc under **CA 2006, Chapter 1, Part 11**. Derivative claims may be brought by members of a company in respect of a cause of action arising from an actual or proposed act or omission involving negligence, default, breach of duty or breach of trust by a director of the company: **s. 260(3)**. The minority shareholders will need to apply for permission to continue the derivative claim (**s. 261**) and the court will, in refusing or granting permission, consider the matters that are required to be considered: **s. 263**. This would seem to be a clear case of breach of duty or breach of trust for which the derivative claim is designed.

Question 5

Julian is a minority shareholder with 40 per cent of the issued share capital of Bona Beach Ltd, a company running a seaside leisure complex. The remaining 60 per cent is held by Sandy.

Under an agreement between Julian and Sandy, Julian has the right to nominate a director of the company for as long as he holds 40 per cent of the issued shares.

The articles provide that a member wishing to sell his shares shall offer them to the other members who shall buy them at a value to be fixed by the company's auditors.

Julian nominated Ken as director, but Sandy rejected the appointment on the grounds that Julian had entered into an agreement with Hugh to hold 20 per cent of the shares as trustee for Hugh and to vote according to his wishes.

At a board meeting, Sandy recommended that no dividend should be paid for the current financial year despite the company making large profits. Sandy's remuneration as a director was, however, increased by 30 per cent.

Advise Julian who now no longer wants to be a shareholder in the company.

Commentary

This question raises issues concerning shareholder agreements, the prohibition on the entry of trusts on the register of members and the right to petition for unfair prejudice under **s. 994**. You are required to recognize these separate issues within this question and to give advice to Julian on his legal position.

Answer plan

- Enforcement of rights under a shareholder agreement
- Position of the company in respect of declaration by Julian of his position as trustee of 20 per cent of his shareholding
- Right of Julian to petition for unfair prejudice
- Possible remedies available to Julian

Suggested answer

As a shareholder holding merely 40 per cent of the issued shares in Bona Beach Ltd, Julian has no right to appoint a director of the company. The power to appoint directors rests solely with Sandy since he holds a 60 per cent stake in the company. The power to appoint directors to the board of a company is held by the person or persons who hold 50 per cent plus one shares in the company in question.

It is, however, possible to supplement the articles of the company by a shareholders' agreement and where there is such an agreement it is binding on the shareholders who are parties to it and it can be enforced by a minority shareholder. Thus, if Julian has been given a right to appoint a director to the board under an agreement, this can be enforced by action. In *Re A & BC Chewing Gum Ltd* [1975] **1 WLR 579** there was a shareholders' agreement which provided that the petitioner in an action for the just and equitable winding up of the company, an outside corporate investor which had put up one-third of the share capital of the company, should enjoy a 50–50 say in management in spite of its minority shareholding. The petitioner succeeded in the petition to wind up the company but it was argued that the petitioner should have been able to enforce the agreement as a shareholder agreement by way of an injunction. Thus the refusal by Sandy to accept Julian's nomination of Ken as a director is in breach of a shareholder agreement and can be enforced by Julian.

The ground on which Sandy has refused the nomination of Ken is that Julian is no longer a holder of 40 per cent of the issued capital of the company and is therefore in breach of the terms of the shareholders' agreement. In this respect it is important to recognize the significance of the statutory prohibition in UK law against the notice of any trust, expressed, implied, or constructive, being entered on the register of members of a company registered in England and Wales or Northern Ireland being receivable by the Registrar of Companies: **CA 2006, s. 126.**

The effect of this is that, although Julian has declared that he now holds 20 per cent of his stake in the company on trust for Hugh and that he will vote according to Hugh's instructions as a beneficial holder, this is not a fact of which the company can take notice. Julian remains the registered holder of the shares and as such is legally entitled to exercise the voting rights in respect of them. In *Pender v Lushington* (1877) **6 Ch D 70** the articles of a company provided that a member should not be entitled to more than 100 votes and should be entitled to vote only if he had possessed his shares for at least three months prior to the meeting. At a meeting, the chairman ruled out 649 votes on a poll. The grounds were that the votes were in respect of shares transferred to nominees by some large shareholders with the object of increasing the vote of the transferors. Pender, on his behalf and that of the other transferors brought an action to prevent the ruling out of the votes. It was held that since the shareholders were registered members who had held their shares for three months before the meeting, they were entitled to vote. It was immaterial that some were trustees for other persons. The register of shareholders, on which there could be no notice of a trust, was the only means of ascertaining the right of members to vote at the meeting.

It is not possible, therefore, for Sandy to claim that Julian no longer has the requisite shareholding to enforce his rights under the shareholders' agreement.

The recommendation by Sandy that no dividend should be paid would seem to indicate that there are no distributable profits. This is rather contradicted by the fact that his remuneration as director has been increased by 30 per cent. It is perfectly possible for Julian to construct out of this situation grounds to maintain a petition for unfair prejudice. In *Re Sam Weller & Sons Ltd* [1990] **Ch 682** the court upheld a petition of unfair prejudice where the company had not increased its dividends in 37 years, despite recent prosperity. The petitioner was unfairly prejudiced even though all shareholders enjoyed the same dividend rights, since the other shareholders received an additional income as directors.

Julian would presumably seek an order that his shares should be bought by the company or the other shareholder at a valuation to be fixed by the court: s. 996(2)(e). The court will not generally impose a valuation where the articles provide a fair valuation procedure. Julian would need to establish that the prescribed valuation method is arbitrary or that the auditor charged with the valuation cannot be relied on to act fairly. If the court does impose a valuation, the court will fix the date on which the valuation is to be made and there will generally be no escape clause in the order where those ordered to purchase the shares claim that they are financially unable to do so *Re Cumana Ltd* [1986] BCLC 430 and *Sethi v Patel* [2010] EWHC 1830 (Ch).

If he cannot succeed under **ss. 994–996**, there is a hope that he might be able to succeed in respect of a petition for the winding up of the company on just and equitable grounds: **s. 122(1)(g)**. In this respect he would argue that the infringement of his shareholders' agreement justifies an order for the winding up of the company on the basis that it guarantees his right to participate in the management of the company which has now been denied. Since this is an equitable remedy and discretionary, it could be argued, that his declaration that he holds 20 per cent of his holding as a trustee for Hugh is a barrier to his claim.

Index